Tattvabodha V

Tattvabodha

Essays from the Lecture Series of
the National Mission for Manuscripts

Volume V

General Editor
V. Srinivas
Joint Secretary, Ministry of Culture, and
Officiating Director, National Mission for Manuscripts

राष्ट्रीय पाण्डुलिपि मिशन
॥ विज्ञानमुपास्व ॥
National Mission for Manuscripts

NATIONAL MISSION FOR MANUSCRIPTS

and

DK
PRINTWORLD
Publishers of Indian Traditions

Cataloguing in Publication Data — DK
[Courtesy: D.K. Agencies (P) Ltd. <docinfo@dkagencies.com>]

Tattvabodha : essays from the lecture series of the National Mission for Manuscripts / general editor: V. Srinivas.
v. 5 cm.
English and Hindi.
Includes bibliographical references.
ISBN 9789380829326

1. Manuscripts, Indic – History. 2. Oral tradition – India. I. Srinivas, V. II. National Mission for Manuscripts (India).

DDC 091 23

ISBN 13: 978-93-80829-32-6 (vol. V)
ISBN 13: 978-81-904029-4-1 (series)
First published in India in 2015

Published by:
National Mission for Manuscripts
11, Mansingh Road
New Delhi - 110 001
Phone: (011) 2338 3894; *Fax:* 2307 3340
E-mail: director.namami@nic.in
Website: www.namami.nic.in

Co-published by:
D.K. Printworld (P) Ltd
Regd. Office: Vedaśrī, F-395, Sudarshan Park
(Metro Station: Ramesh Nagar), New Delhi-110 015
Phones: (011) 2545 3975; 2546 6019; *Fax*: (011) 2546 5926
E-mail: indology@dkprintworld.com
Website: www.dkprintworld.com

Printed by: D.K. Printworld (P) Ltd., New Delhi.

Foreword

THE journey of the National Mission for Manuscripts started in 2003 when it was established by the Ministry of Culture, Government of India. The Mission's objectives are to explore, encompass and understand the wealth of information contained in the manuscripts.

In its attempt to disseminate the traditional knowledge contained in the manuscripts, the Mission organizes the Tattvabodha — awareness of the Ultimate Reality — lecture series all around the country in collaboration with various academic institutions. This lecture series provides insights into different areas of knowledge delivered by eminent scholars who are specialists in their respective fields. The Tattvabodha lectures create a forum for intellectual engagement and subsequently tries to re-contextualize the approach to this traditional knowledge to make it relevant to the present and future generations.

The present collection is the fifth volume of Tattvabodha series comprising eleven papers presented by well-known scholars in different Tattvabodha lectures organized by the Mission. The lectures are presented in English, Hindi and Sanskrit and cover variety of areas of Indian knowledge system.

The Greek scholar Prof. Nicholas Kazanas, in his lecture, has taken us through a linguistic journey to conclude the closeness of the Vedic language of *Ṛgveda* to the Proto-Indo-

European language. In his paper, Prof. Karunasindhu Das, based on study of the manuscript collection of Jorasanko Tagore House, Kolkata, has described the prevalence of different branches of learning in medieval Bengal. Prof. Manabendu Banerjee, on the other hand, has identified certain unique manuscripts in the library of Asiatic Society, Calcutta, which may be further explored in-depth by interested students and scholars. Dr. Ranjit Sen, in his lecture, has portrayed an interesting picture of eighteenth-century Calcutta based on information gathered from British Official Records.

Prof. Lokesh Chandra has established that Sanskrit was the mind of the Silk Route. It was the language of refinement and thought, of religion and philosophy, of poetry and prose of the people who spoke several tongues.

Formation of the Kashmiri language is an interesting topic to ponder over. Dr. Shashi Shekhar Toshkhani has meticulously tried to sort out the misconceptions about the formation of the language. The scholar has mentioned of some early Kashmiri works in support of the actual process that led to its surfacing as the regional voice of Kashmir. Dr. Indra Nath Choudhuri has presented a comparative study of *Kṛttivāsa Rāmāyaṇa* (Bengali), *Tulsīdāsa Rāmāyaṇa* (Hindi) and *Ezhuthachan Rāmāyaṇa* (Malayalam). Dr. N.A.M. Abdul Kader informs us about the Arabic manuscripts and Arabi-Malayalam literature in Kerala during sixteenth to nineteenth century CE. Dr. Devendra has focused on Bhakti literature of Rajasthan. Dr. Shyam Singh Rajpurohit has compiled the manuscripts on Ayurveda and Dr. Gangadhar Panda has presented an informative paper in Sanskrit on published and unpublished commentaries of *Bhāgavata Purāṇa.*

I hope these papers covering diverse topics will be useful to the readers in general. My thanks goes to the scholars who have presented these papers and also to M/s D.K. Printworld for bringing out this volume. It would not be out of place to mention that the opinions expressed by the individual scholars in their respective papers are their own and the Mission does not take responsibility of expression of their viewpoints.

Dr. Sanghamitra Basu
Co-ordinator, Research & Publication
National Mission for Manuscripts

Contents

Foreword v

Scheme of Transliteration xi

1. The Collapse of the Aryan Invasion/Immigration Theory and the Prevalence of Indigenism 1
   – *N. Kazanas*

2. On Oriental Learning in Medieval Bengal and Collection of Manuscripts at Jorasanko Tagore House, Kolkata 53
   – *Karunasindhu Das*

3. The Anti-Colonial Approach in Arabic Manuscripts and Arabi-Malayalam Literature in Kerala 70
   – *N.A.M. Abdul Kader*

4. The Eighteenth-century Calcutta in the British Manuscript Records 104
   – *Ranjit Sen*

5. A Comparative Study of Bengali, Hindi and Malayalam Rāmāyaṇa 129
   – *Indra Nath Choudhuri*

6. श्रीमद्भागवतमहापुराण की टीकाओं की प्रकाशित एवं अप्रकाशित पाण्डुलिपियाँ 144
   – गङ्गाधर पण्डा

7. पाण्डुलिपियों में आयुर्वेद 161
– श्याम सिंह राजपुरोहित

8. पाण्डुलिपियों में निहित भक्ति साहित्य राजस्थान के विशेष सन्दर्भ में 184
– डॉ. देवेन्द्र

9. Formation of the Kashmiri Language and Some Early Kashmiri Works 194
– Shashi Shekhar Toshkhani

10. Sanskrit on the Silk Route 216
– Lokesh Chandra

11. Fascinating Sanskrit Manuscripts in the Asiatic Society, Calcutta 240
– Manabendu Banerjee

Scheme of Transliteration

Vowels

अ (a)	आ (ā)	इ (i)	ई (ī)	उ (u)	ऊ (ū)	
ऋ (ṛ)	ॠ (ṝ)	ऌ (ḷ)	ए (e)	ऐ (ai)	ओ (o)	औ (au)

Consonants

क (ka)	ख (kha)	ग (ga)	घ (gha)	ङ (ṅa)
च (ca)	छ (cha)	ज (ja)	झ (jha)	ञ (ña)
ट (ṭa)	ठ (ṭha)	ड (ḍa)	ढ (ḍha)	ण (ṇa)
त (ta)	थ (tha)	द (da)	ध (dha)	न (na)
प (pa)	फ (pha)	ब (ba)	भ (bha)	म (ma)

Semi Vowels

य (ya)	र (ra)	ल (la)	व (va)	ळ (ḷa)

Sibilants

श (śa)	ष (ṣa)	स (sa)

Aspirate

ह (ha)

Anusvāra and Visarga

ं (ṁ/ṃ)	: (ḥ)

Ānunāsika

ँ (~)	e.g.	अँ (ã)	आँ (ā̃)

1

The Collapse of the Aryan Invasion/ Immigration Theory and the Prevalence of Indigenism

Archaeological, Genetic, Linguistic and Literary Evidences

N. Kazanas

If only small numbers entered peacefully —
How was Saptasindhu Sanskritized?

1. Introduction

HERE we see the IE (Indo-European) languages or cultures in their historical habitats.

The better known ones are presented on this map (which is a modification of one in Ramat and Ramat 2006). And I stress that I don't mean races but languages and cultures. The

Iranian culture, for example, was shared by diverse peoples while the Greek culture also comprised several peoples and dialects. There are in the East the Indic culture with its Vedic and then Sanskrit; the old Persian or Iranian with its Avestan; then Anatolian with many tongues, some related to Hittite and others to Greek; Greek round the shores of the Aegean; Italic mainly with its Latin tongue and Roman civilization; Slavic with its many branches of Bulgarian, Russian, Polish and some others; the Celtic culture both in Gaul (Old France) and Britain (Wales and Ireland); then, in the North-West, Germanic with its Gothic (first, in the Balkans), Old High German and Old Norse; Baltic with its Lettish (or Latvian) and Lithuanian. There is also Albanian or Illyrian and Armenian and Tocharian.

The dotted line represents the alleged journey of the IAs (Indo-Aryans).

The AIT (Aryan Invasion/Immigration Theory) briefly states that the original homeland was somewhere in Europe: some favour the Germanic plains, others the south Russian or Pontic steppes, others the north-east Anatolian or South Caucasus region and so on. From that location spread groups of people in different directions to settle in the present habitats of the people speaking the various IE languages. One of them, the Indo-Iranians, came into what is Persia today. Some stayed there becoming the Iranians (Persians) while others moved south-eastwards into Saptasindhu, the Land of the Seven Rivers in north-west India and today's Pakistan. The older version says that these IAs conquered those valleys *c.* 1500 BCE driving the natives south and Aryanized the area. The newer version says that they entered in small waves *c.* 1700-1500 BCE and gradually their superior culture spread in the whole area. Now, some non-indigenists are generous enough to accept an earlier date of entry *c.* 2000 BCE!

2. Archaeology and Linguistics

But how was the Aryanization of such a large area possible? Why should the natives abandon their own language(s) and adopt the very difficult language of the Aryans. Vedic is an extremely complex language with singular, dual and plural for nouns and verbs; with eight cases in each number for the nouns and many classes of nouns, masc, fem and neuters. The verbs have present, past and future tenses, subjunctives and optatives and the past tense (aorist) alone is of six or seven kinds! If there was no conquest and coercion why would the natives adopt such a difficult language? There were no schools, no mass media, no central government with a Ministry of Education. How do we resolve this paradox?

Then, we know the native Haṛappans had literacy as is shown by their seals but no literature! But the incoming Aryans had no writing as evidenced by *R̥gveda*. Thus we have a strange paradox. On the one hand a culture with literacy but no literature, other than the still undeciphered seals. And an oral culture without literacy but an enormous literature — the Vedas. Both in the selfsame region and at about the selfsame period. How do we resolve this second paradox?

Moreover, archaeologists, expert in this area (Allchins, J.M. Kenoyer, G.L. Possehl, J.G. Shaffer and many others), emphasize the unbroken continuity of the native culture from *c.* 7000 to the last centuries BCE. There is no archaeological evidence of any entry before 600 BCE! American specialist on the ISC (Indus–Sarasvatī Culture) Kenoyer (1998: 174) wrote:

> (T)here is no archaeological or biological evidence for invasions or mass migrations into the Indus Valley between the end of the Haṛappan phase, about 1900 BCE and the beginning of the Early Historical Period around 600 BCE.

Even Agrawal (2005), an avowed non-ingidenist admits there is no evidence of an entry and calls the IAs "elusive".

All archaeologists, Western and Indian, agree that there is no evidence of any immigration.

Lord C. Renfrew (1989: 182) wrote of the AIT

> this comes rather from a *historical assumption* about the "coming" of the Indo-Europeans (my emphasis).

Then Edmund Leach (1990: 238) wrote:

> Because of their commitment to a unilateral segmented history of language development that needed to be mapped onto the ground, the philologists took it for granted that proto-Indo-Iranian was a language that has originated outside India or Iran. . . . From this we derived the myth of the "Aryan invasion".

These are the two legs of clay upon which stands the AIT and its variants.

Nevertheless the AIT persists.

ARGUMENTS SUPPORTING AIT

1. Linguistic:

(a) Iranian (Avestan) is older; therefore IAs moved from Iran into Saptasindhu.

(b) Palatalization: Latin *que,* Greek και/τε, Vedic *ca;* therefore Vedic is later.

(c) Vedic is a mixture of Muṇḍa and Draviḍian with Indo-Aryan.

(d) Isoglosses (palatalization; V *mā* = Gk *mē,* etc.) supposedly show that Vedic speakers entered Saptasindhu via southern Iran.

2. Horses and chariots:

(a) Not enough horse-remains at Haṛappan sites.

(b) Chariots in Andronovo *c.* 1800, Egypt *c.* 1300; therefore *Ṛgveda* must be later, since Haṛappans had no chariots of the Andronovo or Egyptian type.

However, we should note well that the AIT was not conceived initially in linguistic terms. Very far from it. It started as a theoretical explanation of a sociological puzzle, namely the existence of the caste system in India. This sociological hypothesis preceded all linguistic considerations.

Before 1750, Frenchman father Catrou (and several others) proposed that brāhmaṇas originated in Egypt, which had a strong priestly class. The Egyptian warriors conquered the people of Saptasindhu and became the kṣatriyas; the Egyptian priests became the brāhmaṇas and so on.

Between 1800-20 various English and French writers made similar suppositions. The "Hindu conquest" was postulated as the cause of the caste-system. Invaders became superior castes; the aboriginal natives became śūdras and Pariahs. Some writers favoured an Egyptian, others a Mesopotamian conquest (Wilks 1810; Campbell 1816; Ellis 1816; Langlès 1821; Rémusat 1822). The discussion of this hypothesis continued in the next twenty years (Burnouf 1833; Stevenson 1841; Elphinstone 1841; etc.).

Some wrote against the AIT (Langlois 1833; also Elphinstone 1841). But then Max Müller supported the AIT and this turned the balance in favour of the AIT.

However, although the initial Invasion Theory was formed to explain the caste system, with Müller and others after him it acquired linguistic characteristics due to the researches into Indo-European philology.

3. Not a Single Linguistic Argument Lends the Slightest Support to the AIT

Linguistic arguments and data do not provide dates of themselves. Dates come from archaeological or other historical evidences. Consequently they are of no help. But I say briefly this: Avestan, the old Iranian language is NOT older than Vedic, as we shall see further down. Palatalization is a subject that needs fresh study in depth. The usual mainstream view may be utterly wrong. That Vedic had loans from other languages is very probable since all languages do this everywhere at all times. I showed back in 2002 that Saptasindhu fits best as the homeland from which all these isoglosses spread and developed. But I understand that a recent study by Talageri (2008) may show this more clearly. (Soon Kazanas will be publishing a long paper on "Isoglosses" showing that the larger Saptasindhu alone can be the place of dispersal of isoglosses.) These aspects would need a whole lecture to themselves. So I leave them, repeating that linguistic data and arguments do not furnish absolute dates. I shall return further down.

4. Horses and Chariots

Yes, the remains of domesticated horse at Haṛappan sites in the third millennium are meagre, *c.* 2600–2400. But the *Ṛgveda* evidence shows only a small presence of horses: Evidence for horse-remains at various ISC sites is found at Malvan (Allchin and Joshi 1995: 95); at Kuntasi (Dhavalikar 1995: 116-17); at Shikarpur (Thomas et al. 1995; Kochhar 2000: 186, 192); also, of course, terracotta figurines as in Rākhīgharhī (Lal 2002: 73ff). Anyway, if the AIT is right and the IAs came *c.* 1700–1500, then the horse-evidence should increase enormously after this date. So where we had evidence of, say, ten, now we should find 500 or 1000. This is not so at all. The horse remains continue to be just as meagre until the late centuries BCE. So this argument is a bit of a red herring, totally worthless.

The same is true of chariots. The word *rá-tha* does not denote a war-chariot like those of Andronovo, Egypt, Greece and Rome. The word is from √*r̥* (go) giving primary *rá-tha* (a goer, car, vehicle). See similar formations with the suffix *-tha*: *ártha* (goal), *ukthá* (saying), *gā́thā* (song), etc. The R̥gvedic chariot did not come from abroad as some fanatic invesionists claim.

Chariots are said in *R̥gveda* to be made of native timber: from the trees *khadirá* and *siṁśápā* (III.53.19) and *kiṁsuká* and *śālmalí* (X.85.20). The last reference is the late 10th Maṇḍala but the first one is in an early Family Book, that of the Viśvāmitras. So right from the start, even according to the AIT scenario, even as the Aryans (allegedly) arrived, they fashioned cars from the wood of native trees; they did not bring chariots from abroad!

Then unlike the narrow contraption of the, say, Egyptian chariot, the R̥gvedic *ratha* is described as *pr̥thu* (broad) (I.123.1); *br̥hat* (tall, big) (VI.61.13); *variṣṭha* (widest) (VI.47.9). This is quite a difference. Thus it has space not for one only or two (i.e. the driver and the warrior with his spear and bow) but for three: it is said to be *trivandhurá* (I.41.2; VII.71.4) and then to carry eight *aṣṭāvandhurá* (X.53.7)!

Evidences of actual cart-remains come from after 300 BCE (Bryant 2009: 20, with references); otherwise, we find toys from ISC sites or depictions on rock art with vehicles drawn by antelopes, oxen and rarely, horses (Lorblanchet 1992). So the chariot-argument too is something of a red herring.

And here we see the evidence for spoked wheels from a seal (analysis by Parpola 1969) and terracotta ones with spokes painted on. Similar ones with painted spokes have been found in the Carpathian region; so the practice seems to have been quite widespread.

In fact, there is not one scrap of actual evidence, other than mechanical repetition of the theory, to support AIT. Let us now look at the evidence for indigenism, i.e. the IAs were in India in the fourth millennium at the very latest.

5. Mainstream Chronologies Founded on Fictions

First, the composition date of *Ṛgveda*. The usual date given under the AIT is 1200–1000 according to Max Müller's scheme:

MAX MÜLLER'S CHRONOLOGY

- *Chandas* (*ṚV*) 1200-1000; *mantras* (*Atharva*, *Yajus*) 1000-800;
- Brāhmaṇas 800-600; Sūtras, etc. down to 200 BCE.
- Identification of Kātyāyana (*c.* 400 BCE) from a ghost story in *Kathāsaritsāgara* (*c.* CE 1100!).

Müller's *History of Ancient Sanskrit Literature* (1859: 214-17) gives the chronological scheme that is repeated almost verbatim

Spoked Wheel

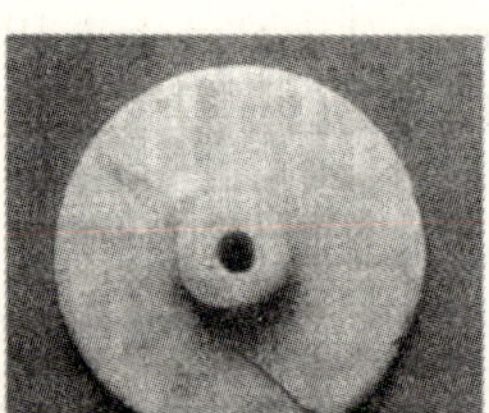

Rākhīgaṛhī: Terracotta wheel with painted spokes

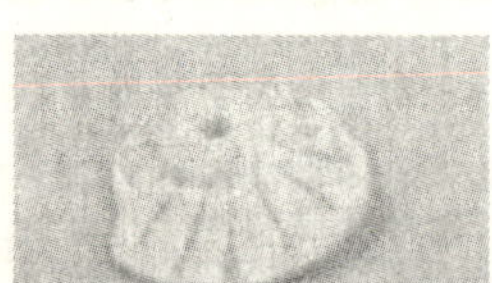

Kālībaṅgan: Terracotta wheel with painted spokes

in all modern textbooks (e.g. Burrow 1973: 43). This was based on a ghost-story in *Kathāsaritsāgara* (*c.* CE 1100) which mentions Kātyāyana, identified with Sūtra-writer Kātyāyana! It is shaped also according to Bishop Ussher's chronology, based on Old Testament: the creation of the world occurred at 4004 BCE! So all pre-Christian events had to fit in that span of time.

This, then, is the basis for the mainstream chronology of ancient Sanskrit literature. It is not based on linguistic evidence, as is generally and vaguely claimed, but on a ghost story composed 2,500 years after the alleged Aryan invasion and on a Christian myth — in other words, on two pieces of fiction! The linguistic and all other details connected with this subject were worked out gradually in the course of years to be in harmony with this chronological skeleton, suggested by the ghost story! What is more, the whole IE linguistic superstructure with its "laws" of phonetic changes and its reconstructions was built upon these fictions!

Of course, this chronology came under criticism at the time (by Goldstucker, Whitney and others) and even Müller admitted thirty years later that nobody could really determine the dates of the Vedic hymns which could be 1500, 2000 or even 5000 BCE. But his earlier dates stuck and are being taught in the universities today. And so M.B. Emeneau wrote in mid-twentieth century:

> At some time in the second millennium BCE . . . a band or bands of speakers of an Indo-European language, later to be called Sanskrit, entered India over the north-west passes. This is our *linguistic doctrine* which has been held now for more than a century and a half. There seems to be no reason to distrust *the arguments* for it, in spite of the traditional Hindu ignorance of any such invasion.
>
> — Emeneau 1954: 282 (emphasis added)

This linguistic arrogance was belied by archaeology.

Only twelve years after Emeneau's statement G. Dales showed that there had been no invasion, no fighting, no destruction (1966: 92-99) and therefore Emeneau's arrogant assurance was sheer ignorance. But like Emeneau, most mainstream Indologists ignored (and continue to ignore) data, luminous and clear like springtime mornings, that showed a very different situation. So they persisted in their theory of invasion. T. Burrow wrote in 1975, nine whole years after Dales:

> The Aryan invasion of India is recorded in no written document and it cannot yet be traced archaeologically but it is nevertheless established as a historical fact on the basis of comparative philology. — 1975: 21

Several scholars continued to write of the "invasion" and only then the "invasion" became "immigration" then "peaceful immigration in small waves".

However, for thirty years now archaeologists continue to stress the unbroken continuity of the material culture in Saptasindhu down to *c.* 600 BCE.

6a. Twelve Harappan Common Features Absent in Ṛgveda

The *Ṛgveda* itself provides ample evidence that the hymns were composed before the Harappan urbanized culture starting *c.* 3000.

HAṚAPPAN FEATURES ABSENT IN ṚGVEDA

(1) *Iṣṭakā* (bricks): Haṛappan building material;

(2) significant urbanization;

(3) fixed altars or hearths;

(4) ruins of abandoned towns (*ṚV* I.133: *armaka*);

(5) *karpāsa* (cotton);

(6) *rajata* (silver);

(7) *vrīhi* (rice);

(8) *godhūma* (earth's exhalation) = wheat;

(9) literacy (*lekha(-na)*, *lipi* — not before Sūtra-texts);

(10) perforated jars;

(11) Iconography (statuary, relief, painting); and

(12) seals.

All of these are present in post-R̥gvedic texts (Brāhmaṇas, Sūtras, etc.).

The Haṛappan or ISC has certain characteristics which help to define its uniqueness. A number of these features are absent from *R̥gveda* and this absence indicates that *R̥gveda* is pre-Haṛappan. Arguments *e silentio* are not decisive since absence of evidence is not always evidence of real absence. But in this case the features are far too many. (Some of these were noted by Sethna 1992.) The probability increases as the member of absent items increases and when this number becomes 8, 9, 10 then we must acknowledge certainty.

(1) *Iṣṭakā* 'brick'. *R̥gveda* mentions as building materials metal, stone, mud and wood but not "brick", which was the basic material in Haṛappan constructions. This is found in post-R̥gvedic texts: the word *iṣṭakā* is not in *R̥gveda*. Archaeologists write of the early Haṛappan or Rāvī phase (i.e. 3300–2800): "These early settlers built huts made of wood with wattle-and-daub" (Kenoyer and Meadow 2007: 125). This is the common habitation in the whole of *R̥gveda*. Brick-walls came later, as Kenoyer pointed out much earlier: these appear after this early phase, i.e. after 2800 (Kenoyer 1997/2000: 56). The dates 3300–2800 BCE are different from those given by S.P. Gupta (2007: 223) who places

this early phase *c.* 3700 and before and calls it Hakrā-Rāvī.

(2) Urbanization is wholly absent in *Ṛgveda*. There certainly was "nomad pastoralism" as mainstreamers emphasize repeatedly but there were also agricultural settlements (a fact which mainstreamers underplay or do not mention). The hymn to *kṣetrapati* (Lord of the Field/Soil) (IV.57) alone should suffice but also the girl Apālā refers to her father's *urvarā* (fertile field) (VIII.91.5); then there are many cultivation implements *khanitra* (shovel), *lāṅgala/sīra* (plough), *sṛṇī* (sickle), etc. Moreover, there is weaving with loom, shuttle, warp and woof (*ṚV* I.134.4; I.3.6; etc.) and metallurgy with smithies of sorts (IV.2.17; V.9.5; etc.). Such activities imply settlement.

Some scholars thought the Ṛgvedic and Haṛappan cultures converge (Gupta 2005; Bisht 1999; Lal 1998; Singh 1995). As evidence is cited the word *pur-* which denotes "city, citadel, fort, town" since its Greek and Baltic cognates *polis* and *pil(i)s* do. This is a very general misconception. In *Ṛgveda pur* never means anything other than an occult, magical, esoteric defence or stronghold which is not created nor ever destroyed by humans. The ISC cities had regular blocks, large buildings, also domestic and urban water supply (McIntosh 2001: 100-101; Gupta 2007: 235): *Ṛgveda* knows nothing of all these. There are references to *oka, gṛha, dama, dhāma,* etc. all of which can denote any type of "home/house" (made of wood and mud), or the thousand-pillared mansion of kings Mitra and Varuṇa in the sky (II.41.5; V.62.6: probably suggested by sunrays streaming down through clouds; for not even ISC cities had such mansions!). These most certainly do not indicate any urbanization: neither brick walls nor stonewalls are mentioned nor other features found in the ISC towns.

Such R̥gvedic settlements are pre-urban as known in the mature Haṛappan.

> These are found spreading from Taxila in the north-west through the eastern foothills of Baluchistan through Rajasthan and Haryana via Punjab, Sindh and Kachch. All this presupposes the existence of a very strong internal network which was fully operational by 3000 BCE. — Gupta 2007: 214

The words for "council" *sabhā* and *samiti* are also cited by some scholars but, surely, any community can have a council of elders without urbanization. Allusions in *R̥gveda* to chiefs/kings (*rājā*) and overlords/emperors (*samrāṭ*) also do not show urbanization since such offices can just as easily exist in rural communities. (The Red Indians in North America, nomadic and rural tribes, had local chiefs and overlords.) Pathways and/or roads (*path-*) also have been mentioned as crossing or branching out, but these too can be just as easily seen in a rural context. (For all these claims see Singh 1995; Bisht 1999; Lal 2002, 2005.)

(3) Fixed altars or hearths are unknown in *R̥gveda* but common in the ISC cities. The R̥gvedic altar is a shallow bed dug in the ground and covered with grass (e.g. *R̥V* V.11.2, VII.43.2-3; Parpola 1988: 225). Fixed brick-altars are very common in post-R̥gvedic texts.

(4) Many cities were abandoned and fell to ruination after 1900 BCE when the Haṛappans began to move eastward because of the drying up of Sarasvatī and of the more general desiccation due to tectonic disturbances and

climatic changes. *R̥gveda* knows nothing of such ruins even though, according to AIT, the IAs moved through these regions *c.* 1700–1500 (in small waves, settled there, in the midst of deserts, and wrote the hymns which praise the mighty Sarasvatī!). Some attempts have been made to read hymn I.133 with its *arma-ka* (of unknown meaning, perhaps "vortex") as a description of a ruined city (e.g. Burrow 1963; Rao 1991: 32) but, in fact, the hymn mentions no ruined buildings, no fallen walls and no materials such as wood, stone or bricks! It is a ghostly scene of frightful desolation, peopled only with unfriendly she-fiends and demons (*yātumatī, piśācī* and *rākṣasa*). In sharp contrast the Old English poem *The Ruin* contains such persuasive details of the ancient remains (from Roman times?) that some scholars think it refers to the town of Bath (Mitchell and Robinson 1996: 252-55).

(5) No cotton (*karpāsa*) appears in *R̥gveda* although this plant was extensively cultivated in the ISC and the fabric was exported as far as Egypt in the middle of the third millennium while the Mesopotamians adopted the name as *kapazum* (? from Prākr̥ta *kapāsa*). *R̥gveda* has "skin" (*eta*) (I.166.10; *ajina* in *AV* V.21.7, etc.), "wool" (*avi*) (*R̥V* IX.78.1) and *śāmulya* (X.85.29) and numerous terms for clothing and weaving but no mention of cotton. Be it noted that *karpāsa* is the only word for cotton in Sanskrit. It is found first in the Sūtra texts, in Gautama's (I.18) and in Baudhāyana's (XVI.13.10) *Dharmasūtra*. Now, although cotton seeds were found at Mehrgaṛh period II, *c.* 5000, none were found in subsequent periods. Cotton cultivation appears only in the Mature ISC, after 2500. Thus the Sūtra texts can be placed at this period at the earliest, i.e. *c.* 2600.

(6) Silver (*rajata*) also makes no appearance in *Ṛgveda* though gold and copper are well attested and silver is plentiful in the ISC. The word *rajata* occurs in *ṚV* VIII.25.22 and it denotes a steed or a chariot "shining white". Only in later texts is it used singly (*AV* V.28.1) or with *hiraṇya* to denote "silver" or "white gold" = "silver" (see *Vedic Index* 2: 196-97 and Lubotsky 1997, 2: 1169).

(7) Rice (*vrīhi*) too is absent from *Ṛgveda* although it appears in various sites of the ISC from at least 2300 (and in the Ganges Valley from the sixth millennium).[1] *Ṛgveda* knows only *yava* (barley). Rice becomes important in post-Ṛgvedic ritual and the more general diet. Some writers argue that *Ṛgveda* has food-preparations of rice like *apūpa*, *puroḷāś* and *odana* (Talageri 2000: 126-27). This is possible, of course. All three are in post-Ṛgvedic tradition said to be rice-preparations (though *apūpa* is given as flour-cake in most texts and "wheat" in Lexica). But *odana* is primarily a water or fluid preparation (*ud-*) and *odatī* (refreshing, dewy) is an epithet of Uṣas, (Dawn-goddess). The words *odana* and *odatī* appear only in the books of late *Ṛgveda*. Since *vrīhi* (rice) does not appear in *Ṛgveda* (but does appear in *Atharvaveda*) and Ṛgvedic *yava* is from the earliest tradition accepted as

---

1 Private communication from S.P. Gupta, Chairman of Indian Archaeological Society (June 2006). See also Sharma 1980 for rice in the Gaṅgā basin in the fifth millennium and R. Tewari et al. in *Purātattva* (2006), **36**: 68-75 for rice, again in the Gaṅgā basin, north-east, in the district Sant Kabir Nagar (Uttar Pradesh) in seventh millennium. These locations are too far from Vedic Saptasindhu but it seems likely that by 3000 the composers of *AV* had become acquainted with rice (*vrīhi*) and later this grain was cultivated in the ISC too.

"barley", I take it that the Ṛgvedic people had barley and not rice — nor wheat.

(8) Wheat was cultivated in the Saptasindhu (abundant wheat remains in Punjab) long before the alleged IA entry *c.* 1700. But the word *godhūma* (earth's exhalation) is not in *Ṛgveda*. Only *yava* (barley).

(9) Literacy is not known in *Ṛgveda*. Some scholars think it was known and cite *ṚV* X.71.4 or *AV* XIX.72 (Kak: 2003; Frawley 1991).

ṚV X.71.4a says:

> *utá tvaḥ páśyan ná dadarśa vācam, utá tvaḥ sṛṇván ná śṛṇoti-enām*
>
> Seeing indeed (*utá*) one sees not Vāk [and] hearing indeed one hears her not.

Vāk is the mighty goddess of Speech (or Language) through which all things excellent and pure were manifested (*níhitam-āviḥ*, stanza 1). What st. 4a-b says is that some people see and hear but, in fact, they don't know Vāk (a) and the goddess reveals herself to those [she chooses] as a well-dressed, loving wife to her husband (b). There is not a single hint in all eleven stanzas that there is writing. Here we have a poetic image: the personification of *vāc* as a wife; hence the visual aspect. In fact, st. 11 says that some sing (*gā-*) the psalms and prosper and some brāhmaṇas utter (*vad-*) knowledge and thus deal out (*vi-mā-*) the measures/regulations of sacrifice; there is no suggestion of writing: it is all oral. *Vāc* means "speech, utterance", never writing.

D. Frawley thought that a passage in *AV* XIX.72 may refer to writing: "From whichever receptacle *kośāt* we have taken the Veda, into that we put it down". Books in ancient India consisted in collections of palm-leaves or strips of birch-bark and were kept in boxes (Frawley 1991: 249). Whether this is enough to establish knowledge of writing is doubtful. The word *veda* is "knowledge" generally and not necessarily one of the three Vedas which in any case were transmitted orally. The word *kośa* could refer to some (metaphorical) non-material storing-place, e.g. memory, lower mind (*manas*), higher mind (*cetas, bodha,* both in *Atharvaveda*), etc. In any case, there is no other passage even remotely hinting at writing.

Words like *likh-, lekha(-na)* and mainly *lipi* (Pāṇini 3.2.21) denoting "writing" are not in use before the Sūtra texts. The vast corpus of Brāhmaṇa, Araṇyaka and Upaniṣad texts has not a single hint about writing and so creates an enormous gap between the *Atharvaveda* and the Sūtra period. Someone would have made a reference to writing somewhere in all these texts! So, writing was known in the ISC and the Sūtras but not in *Ṛgveda*.

True, *Aitareya Āraṇyka* 5.3.3 has both *ul-likhya* and *ava-likhya* and at first sight one might think these are references to writing particularly as they occur in a context about study (Deshpande 1966). But this very context, in fact, disallows the meaning "writing". For the text says "the student should not study/learn (*adhīyīta*) . . . after 'writing' (*ul-likhya*)"; if the student does not learn in conjunction with writing, then when would he do so? Moreover, the wider context stresses memorizing from the *guru*'s utterances; again, if there was writing, it would have been mentioned and memorization would not have been stressed. So here the verbs mean "scratch". The student should not scratch himself! (See Falk 1992 with full references.) So, in fact, there are no allusions (*likh-*, *lip-*) with the meaning "writing" before the Sūtra texts.

(10) No mention of iconography, relief, statues, paintings. *R̥gveda* has no allusions to artistic iconography — paintings, relief representations, statue(-tte)s, all so common in the ISC. (*R̥gveda* IV.24.10 asks "who will buy this my Indra" and this is thought by some to refer to a statuette, but this could be a transfer of favour and it is the only reference in the whole *R̥gveda* without the use of any word for statue or icon.)

(11) We must also take into account that many iconographic motifs, Haṛappan artefacts, decorations or seals, show affinity with elements found in post-R̥gvedic texts. Thus P.K. Agrawala (2005) draws attention to round-bottomed perforated pots from Haṛappan sites and a vessel (*kuṁbha*) with nine holes (*navavitr̥ṇṇa*) or 100 holes (*śatavitr̥ṇṇa*) mentioned in *Śatapatha Brāhmaṇa* 5.5.4.27 and *śatatr̥ṇṇā kumbhī* (a pitcher with 100 perforations) in 12.7.2.13. These and other similar descriptions echo the *White Yajurveda* (*Vājasaneyī Saṁhitā*) verse 19: 87 "a pitcher with 100 streams". Such vessels were used for ritual sprinkling. A second parallel is furnished by the two-horned bovine-like animal, duplicated and facing itself, on a Moheṅjo-Daṛo seal with long necks and the *pīpal* tree growing out of their juncture. This corresponds (writes Agrawala) to the two-headed cattle *dvāyā* in *AV* 5.19.7. Agrawala mentions other parallels of a two-headed tiger and a two-headed bird (2005: 10-13). Thus it is indeed the later Vedic texts that have parallels with the Haṛappan arts and crafts, not *R̥gveda.*

(12) Finally, there is not the slightest indication in *R̥gveda* of the presence of seals, so common in the ISC. We started with bricks and finish with seals, two of the commonest features of the ISC, both absent from *R̥gveda.*

Thus *R̥gveda* must be pre-Haṛappan!

6b. All These Features Present in post-R̥gvedic Texts

Now all the fore-mentioned features are found in post-R̥gvedic texts — Saṁhitās, Brāhmaṇas and fully in Sūtra literature. For

Iconography; *dvāya* in *Atharvaveda* 5.19.7?

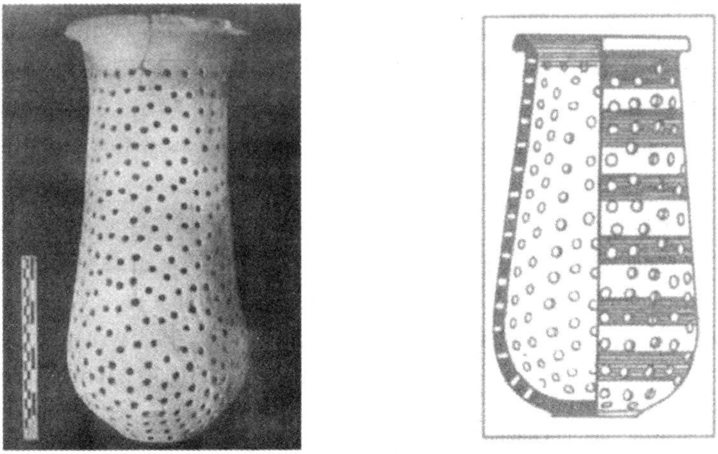

Pot with 100 perforations: *Śatapatha Brāhmaṇa* 12.7.2.13

instance, brick altars are mentioned in *Śatapatha Brāhmaṇa* 7.1.1.37, or 10.2.3.1, etc. Rice (*vrīhi*) is found in *AV* VI.140.2; VII.1.20; etc. Cotton (*karpāsa*) appears first in Gautama's (I.18) and in Baudhāyana's (XIV.13.10) *Dharmasūtra*s. The fact of the convergence of the post-Ṛgvedic texts and the Haṛappan culture was noted long ago by archaeologists. B. and R. Allchin stated unequivocally that these features are of the kind "described in detail in the later Vedic literature" (1982: 203).

If we had a case of two or three items we could bypass them saying indeed that absence of evidence is no evidence of absence; but the items are many and the absence of the building material *iṣṭakā* in *Ṛgveda* (against the presence of wood, stone, mud and metal) seems to me quite decisive. It is like writing a large volume of poems or a novel in the years, say, 2000-13 and not mentioning mobile phones, TV, the effects of the 2008 economic crisis, pollution, terrorism, the European Union, tourism, jets, ferry-boats and digital technology.

So *Ṛgveda* must belong to a period before the Mature Haṛappan, *c*. 3000–2800.

7. Some Brāhmaṇas Comment on or Give Explanations of Incidents in the Ṛgvedic Hymns

For example, *Aitareya Brāhmaṇa* 7.13.33 narrates extensively the story of Śunaḥśepa, alluded to briefly in *ṚV* I.24.12-13 and V.2.7, while *Śatapatha Brāhmaṇa* 11.5.1 comments on the the Pururavas and Urvaśī love story given elliptically in dialogue form in *ṚV* X.95. Another point to note. Some legends in *Ṛgveda* remain unexplained. For instance, who was Bhujyu whom the Aśvins saved from a tempest (I.116.3-4; etc.) and how did he find himself in that predicament? The later texts say nothing more. Or, take the birth of Indra; was he an unwelcome child to Aditi and did he commit parricide (IV.18.1ff; etc.)? Again, the Brāhmaṇas tell us nothing. Obviously such exegetical texts would not have been composed until the understanding regarding the older texts had lapsed: this implies many centuries.

What is the date of Brāhmaṇas? Well, S. Kak ascribes the *Śatapatha* to the early third millennium (1997, 1994) saying that the Pleiades/Kṛttikās not swerving from the east, as is stated in this Brāhmaṇa (2.1.2.3), could only occur *c.* 2950 BCE. Narahari Achar (Professor Astrophysics, Memphis, USA) using computer and planetarium apparatus arrived at a date *c.* 3000 pointing out that S.B. Dikshit had arrived at similar conclusions 100 years earlier but was ignored by Western scholars (1999): these scholars really had no knowledge of astronomy. B.B. Lal too thought that "astronomical calculations (re. *Aitareya Brāhmaṇa*) would place *Ṛgveda* in the fourth millennium" but did not then adopt such a date only because he could not judge the evidence (1998: 286).

So we could again place *Ṛgveda* easily before 3000 BCE

8. Consider now Some Facts Concerning Bṛhadāraṇyaka Upaniṣad

Traditional Upaniṣadic teaching:

aupaniṣadaṁ puruṣaṁ pṛcchāmi
I ask about that Upaniṣhadic Person — 3.9.26

Lists of 60 teachers	(× 15 years	= 900).
Upaniṣad's date in AIT		*c.* 550 +
		= 1450 BCE

Ṛgveda date 1200; *Atharvaveda* date 1000 (in AIT).

ātman-Brahman doctrine unknown in *Ṛgveda*!

Names of early teachers unknown in *Ṛgveda* and *Atharvaveda*!

Bṛhadāraṇyaka Upaniṣad has three *vaṁśas*, i.e. list of teachers, each comprising sixty-five to seventy names. The first four or five are names of gods in the normal Indic way which ascribes the beginning of every human activity to some deity. Let us take the mainstream date of early sixth century for this text (say 550) according to the AIT premises and let us take sixty teachers giving to each one an average of fifteen years, though twenty and thirty would be more realistic. This exercise has now been tilted very heavily in favour of AIT and mainstream views because, in truth, in this text we read "I ask about that Upaniṣadic person (*aupaniṣadaṁ puruṣaṁ pṛcchāmi* III.9.26)" which indicates that there was a traditional Upaniṣadic teaching about *Puruṣa* as a spiritual being (Self) and this aspect we meet in *Atharvaveda*. However, let us bypass this point. These calculations (60 × 15 = 900 plus 550) give us a date *c.* 1450 for the inception of the doctrines in this Upaniṣad. The chief doctrine is that the self of man (*ātman*) is the same in all beings and the same as the Self of the universe (*Brahman* "Mystic Spirit" or "Absolute"). We should also bear in mind that the teachers' names are quite different from those of the seers of *Ṛgveda* hymns as given by the native tradition. Following others, M. Witzel thinks these lists "rest on typically weak foundations" (2001: §19) but this is a typically weak subterfuge because the results of calculating the number of years prove how unrealistic the AIT chronologies are! Let us see, then.

The Upaniṣadic doctrine of the identity of the individual self and the universal self, in the formulations *ayam ātmā brahma* and *ahaṁ brahmāsmi* "the Self is the Absolute" and "I am the Absolute", should be known, then, *c.* 1500 or 1300 or 1200, when, according to AIT, *Ṛgveda* was composed. Yet, quite surprisingly, this doctrine is totally unknown in *Ṛgveda* in these terms (although enunciated differently) and begins hesitantly to appear in *Atharvaveda* (e.g. X.2.32-33, XI.4.23, etc.).

Consequently, *Atharvaveda* should be placed at least *c.* 1600 and the *Ṛgveda c.* 1800, always following the AIT assumptions. But *Ṛgveda* is composed, even according to Witzel (2005: 90), in Saptasindhu, yet the IAs do not appear in this area before, at the very earliest, 1700, and *Ṛgveda* gets composed after several centuries!

This is one of the comical paradoxes that the mainstream chronology refuses obdurately to resolve. Yet, on the grounds given in §§ 6, 7 above, we saw that *Ṛgveda* should be assigned to the fourth millennium. Now subtracting 200 years for the *Atharvaveda* hymns and the start of the Upaniṣadic doctrine and a further 900 or 1,000 years (for the teachers) we should place the early Upaniṣads at the start of the period of the Mature Haṛappan, i.e. 2500 (with the *ātma-Brahman* doctrine having come down orally) and the Sūtra texts immediately after. These dates satisfy yet another requirement. The word for cotton (*karpāsa*) is first used in the Sūtra texts as we saw in § 6a(5) above and the cultivation of the plant (although seeds of it were found in much earlier periods) gets well established *c.* 2500. All these dates are, of course, approximate.

PALAEOASTRONOMY

- S. Raghavan (1969) calculated that many astronomical references in *Mahābhārata* converge in year 3067.
- This date 3067 was confirmed with computer and planetarium by astrophysicist Narahari Achar (2003 and 2012).
- *Mahābhārata* completed just before CE. But inception of epic songs at 3067. *Ṛgveda* is *linguistically* very much older.
- However this early date is disputed by another scientist, R. Iyengar (2005), who prefers a date *c.* 1700 BCE.

9. Palaeoastronomical Research

Astrophysicist Achar pursued his "palaeoastronomical research" into *Mahābhārata* epic also examining astronomical references in books 3, 5 and 18. His sky map showed that all these converge in the year 3067. (Achar 2003, 2012). Achar acknowledged that, in 1969, S. Raghavan had arrived at the same date. Now, it is obvious that *Mahābhārata* had acquired many accretions over many centuries and that it was streamlined stylistically perhaps first in the second millennium and finally at about the start of the Common Era. It is obvious that it contains much late material like 2.28.48-9, which mentions Rome and Antiochia (*romā* and *antakhī*): this could not be earlier than 300 BCE since Antioch was founded in 301. On the other hand, the frequent use of the bow and, moreso, the use by Bhīma of a (tree trunk as a) club show much more primitive conditions.

Thus the war evidently took place in 3067 and the core of *Mahābhārata* in poems and songs was laid down in that year. This and the native traditional view that the Kali Yuga came at 3102 are both correct, according to Achar. He pointed out that the Kali Yuga had no full force until the death of Kr̥ṣṇa which occurred thirty-five years after 3067, at 3032 (private communication June 2006); but immorality had set in already, as is shown by the unjust behaviour of the Kauravas and some reprehensible acts during the war itself. Surely no bards (compilers or redactors) in the third century CE or the third century BCE could possibly know the star and planet positions relative to the *nakṣatra*s (zodiac signs) of the year 3067. The astronomical references examined by Achar (and Raghavan) are so numerous that chance coincidence has to be discarded (Achar 2003). However, that the war took place in 3137 and bards began to sing of these events two generations later should not be precluded. Personally, I still tend towards the traditional view of the war taking place in 3137. The Megasthenes report (from *c.* 300 BCE) of the ancient kings from 6000+, surviving in Arrian and other classical writers, supports these long periods of the past (paper One in Kazanas 2009). Then, deterioration in behaviour would have started in the *sandhyā* transitional period before the onset of the Kali Yuga — when also the kṣatriyas passed away. Here a question remains: how did the astronomers (and Āryabhaṭa especially) determine the date for Kali Yuga as 3102? Is there an answer?

10. River Sarasvatī

- *R̥V* II.41.16 *nadītamā, ambitamā, devitamā (*best river, best mother, best goddess).
- VI.52.6 *pínvamānā síndhubhiḥ (*swollen by three or more rivers).
- VII.95.2. It ows clear *giríbhyaḥ ā́ samudrā́t* (from the mountains to the ocean).
- (Here *samudrá* not confluence, terminal lake, gathering place of water on the Himalayas.)
- VII.96.2. The Pūrus inhabit its two bushy banks.
- X.64.9 calls Sarasvatī and Sarayū and Indus "great and nourishing".
- X.177 hymn prays to Sarasvatī for continuation of sustenance and good fortune.

a. SARASVATĪ'S COURSE

Sharma et al. in *Purātattva* 2006 present photographs of the Sarasvatī(-Hakrā) down to the sea. Francfort (1992), Possehl (1998), Lal (2002) give 3600 and before! Also Danino 2010. Note that the Nadīstuti-Sūkta of *R̥gveda* (X.75) places Sarasvatī between the Yamunā and Sutlej (Śatadru), just as the satellite photos do.

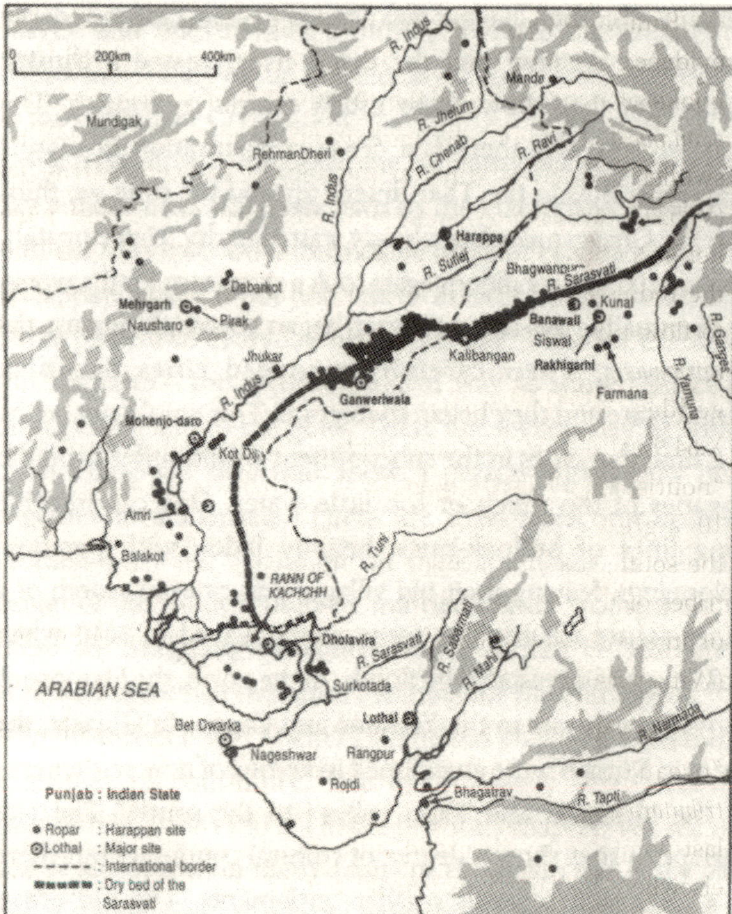

The course of Sarasvatī as photographed by satellite, from Sanyal 2012.

b. ETYMOLOGY:

Sáras-vatī (she who has swirls/ponds, currents). This comes from *dhātu* √*sṛ gatau*: moving, leaping, rushing (cf. L. *sal*, Gk *hial-*, Toch. *sal* (leap)): > *sará, sáras, sara-ṇyū, sarít, sāra,* etc.

- Avestan *Hara^{x}vaiti* a river in south-east Iran.
- *hara^x*- only occurrence: isolated.
- *vairi*- "lake" in Avestan.

Sarasvatī River furnishes useful literary and archaeological evidence for dating *Ṛgveda.* It is a mighty river extolled in all books of *Ṛgveda* except the fourth. It is *nadītamā, ambitamā, devitamā* (best river, best mother, best goddess) (II.41.16); it is swollen and fed by three or more rivers *pinvamānā sindhubhiḥ* (VI.52.6); it is endless, swift moving, roaring, most dear among her sister rivers; together with her divine aspect, it nourishes the Indo-Aryan tribes (VI.61.8-13). In VII.95.2 the river is said to flow pure in her course "from the mountains to the ocean" (*giribhyaḥ ā samudrāt*). Then VII.96.2 and X.177 pray to the river goddess for continued sustenance and good fortune while X.64.9 calls upon her (and Sarayū and Indus) as "great" and "nourishing". Clearly then, we have here, even in the late Bk 10, a great river flowing from the Himalayas to the ocean in the south, fed and swollen by other rivers and sustaining the tribes of the IAs on its banks — not a river known in the past or in some other region, or a river now considerably shrunk (Witzel 2001).[2]

Some scholars claim that here *samudra* does not mean "ocean" but confluence and especially the place where a *tributary owed into the Indus* (e.g. Klaus 1989; Witzel 2001). The last point can be discarded since there is not the slightest hint elsewhere that the Sarasvatī flowed into the Indus — in which case the Indus and not Sarasvatī would have been lauded as "the best river" (II.41.16). We can also aver with full certitude (as the *Vedic Index* does under *Samudra*) that the Ṛgvedic people

2 The mainstream view — Witzel's really — that the Vedic river is merely a memory of the Iranian Hara^{x} vaiti which belongs to the common Indo-Iranian period, when the Iranoaryans lived together in Iran before the IAs moved further southeast (according to AIT), is no more than modern myth-making. Mainstreamers often invoke Occam's razor (i.e. that the simpler solution is more probable) but here they forget it and prefer their own complex scenario.

knew the ocean (see paper Five, Kazanas 2009; also Prabhakar 1994). The meaning "terminal lake(s)" adopted by Witzel is entirely fanciful. In his *Dictionary* M. Mayrhofer gives for *samudra* only "confluence" and "ocean/sea" (1996 *EWA*). And the Vedic poet would certainly have used (not *ā samudrāt* but) *ā sarobhyaḥ* (to the terminal lakes) maintaining his – ⏑– – cadence. This phrase would then have indicated clearly the alleged fanciful etymological connection of the name *Saras-vatī* "she who has (terminal) lakes". The name means rather "she who has swirls and currents", since the primary sense of √*sr̥* (>*saras*) is "movement" (*gatau*) or "moving, leaping, rushing".

Please, consider also that the Vedic -s- is inherited from PIE, according to all IEnists, whereas Avestan -h- is a devolved, not PIE, sound. Vedic √*sr̥* has many primary and secondary cognates like *sara* and *sarit*. Now Avestan has no cognates for √*sr̥* and its products, and the Avestan noun for lake is *vairi-*, while *vār* - is "rain(-water)" = S *vāri* (?). The stem *hara-* (cognate with Vedic *saras*) occurs only in the river name *Hara*^{x}*vaiti*. Consequently, it is the Iranians that moved away from the Indo-Aryans as, indeed, is shown by their memory of having lived in a location they called *Haptahəndu* = Saptasindhu. The root *sr̥* has cognates in other IE branches, Gk *hial-*, L. *sal-*, Toch. *sal-*, etc. as is shown by Rix (1998). Now, it would be ludicrous to claim that the IAs left the common Indo-Iranian habitat, as per AIT, moved into Saptasindhu and turning the *Hara*^{x}*vaiti* name into *Sarasvatī* gave it to a river there to remember their past while they proceeded to generate the root *sr̥* and its derivatives to accord with other IE languages. Occam's razor, which here is conveniently ignored by AIT adherents, commands the opposite: that the Iranians moved away, lost the root *sr̥* and the name Sarasvatī in its devolved form *Hara*^{x}*vaiti* was given to a river in their new habitat. This should be enough to question, if not refute, various IEnists' claims that Avestan retains older forms of nouns and verbs and that therefore the Indo-Aryans were with the Iranians in Iran in the common Indo-Iranian period — before moving to Saptasindhu. One should also note that these linguists rely entirely on linguistic facts amenable to a reverse interpretation and ignore other aspects — literary, mythological, archaeological and genetic.

The River Sarasvatī in Saptasindhu is thought to have dried up almost completely by 1900 (Allchins 1997: 117; Rao 1991: 77-79). In previous years it had lost tributaries to the Indus in the west and the Ganges in the east. Is there any evidence that it flowed down to the Indian (or Arabian) ocean at any earlier period?

G. Possehl examined (1998) all the palaeoenvironmental and geological data relevant to the Sarasvatī River and concluded that the river could have owed down to the ocean only before 3200 at the very latest and, more probably, before 3800! He re-stated his finds in his study (2002: 8-9). Bridget Allchin has been quite certain of a date 3600–3800 in her survey of 1999. So is B.B. Lal (2002). Then there are the satellite photos mentioned above in § 10a and below.

All this helps us place the passages ascribing the grandeur of River Sarasvatī at a date before 3200 at least. (For more recent scientific investigations through satellite showing the course of the old Sarasvatī reaching the ocean see Sharma J.R. et al. 2006.)

11. More Linguistics

(a) *Vedic is older than Avestan* (see Kazanas 2012).
In Avestan *-a>* *ə/e/i/o* (*nar-əm* against V *nar-am*);
voiced aspirates like *dh* > *d* (*dā* against V *dhā*);
original **s* > h (*haoma* against *soma* and *ahura* against *asura* "lord")

r̥ > *ar/ər* (as in *ar̆sti* - *against r̥ṣṭi* "spear");
Periphrastic perfect: acc. fem. ptcpl + *ah-* (to be)
V acc. fem. + *kr̥*, (*AV*); then in Brāhmaṇas *as-* and *bhū-*.

(b) Isoglosses are better accommodated by Out of India Movements. Palatalization is one that groups Vedic, Avestan, Slavic and Baltic and separates them from other IE branches. The augmented Aorist separates Vedic (*a-*) and Greek (-e) from the others.

Celtic, Germanic, Slavic, etc. have only anaugmented aorist. Vedic has both — and *ádhāt* and *dhā́t*!
(Greek has generally augmented and certain unaugmented forms of the aorist).
(Arm has generally augmented aorist.)

Then Vedic has negative, prohibitory *mā* (e.g. *mā pibet* "one should not drink"), as Greek has *mē*, Armenian *mi* and Tocharian *ma*; but all others have *na/ni/no* (which Vedic has also as in *na pibati* "one does not drink").

One of the most baffling isoglosses is one shared by Tocharian in the east, Hittite and Phrygian (in Anatolia, i.e. modern Turkey) in the centre, Italic in the south and Celtic in the west. This is the marker *-r-* found in the medio-passive

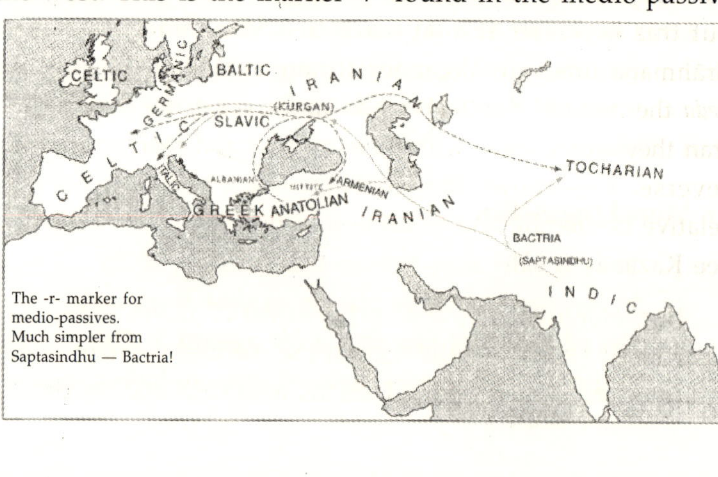

The -r- marker for medio-passives. Much simpler from Saptasindhu — Bactria!

aspects of verbs in these branches (and to a minor extent in Sanskrit — e.g. *dadhi-ré/dadh-ré* "they have placed").

It would have been impossible for the speakers of Tocharian, Hittite, Phrygian (near Greek, Albanian and Anatolian), Italic and Celtic to have coexisted in close contiguity and apart from the others at the centre which was the Kurgan culture so as to have developed this *-r-* isogloss. South is the Black Sea. East is the Caspian and, in any case, then the Italic and Celtic speakers would have to move westwards again! Similarly if the location was west, the Tocharians would have to double back across the central Kurgan region. If the place was north, then the Hittites and Phrygians would have to double back southward across the central region.

But if they all moved north-west from Saptasindhu, then the Tocharians would move north and the others westward. No problem.

These above linguistic facts show that Vedic is anterior; more so, if we consider that Vedic has a much more obvious system of *dhātus* (like √*sṛ*, *bhū* and *dhā*) giving verbs and nouns, primary and secondary derivatives. But the periphrastic perfect is conclusive. Avestan has only the acc. fem. with perfect auxiliary of *ah-*. Sanskrit has this auxiliary *as-* in the perfect but this is a later format (as is also the common *bhū-*) of Brāhmaṇa times. In Vedic texts there is first in the *Atharva-veda* the perfect of *kṛ* (*cakāra*) as auxiliary. If the IAs had left Iran they would have with them *as-* first and then *kṛ-*, not the reverse. This shows that Avestan left when *kṛ-* passed in relative desuetude and *as* came into use. (For further details, see Kazanas 2012.)

But, moreover, the Italian Iranianist G. Gnoli showed in clear terms (1980) that the data in the old and younger *Avesta* indicate a movement of the Iranians westward and northward

— not southeasterly. And, of course the Indo-Aryans have no memory at all of a movement towards and into Saptasindhu.

12. Vedic and Mesopotamian Religions

In a 2003 publication S. Levitt (of New York), who is by no means an indigenist, examined the development of the "early Indic tradition" and the development of religion in ancient Mesopotamia.

After comparing several elements in the Vedic and Mesopotamian religions, Levitt concluded:

> We can date the early Indic tradition on the basis of comparable points in ancient Mesopotamia. By this, the *Ṛgveda* would date back to the beginning of the third millennium BCE, with some of the earliest hymns perhaps even dating to the end of the fourth millennium BCE.
>
> — 2003: 356

However, unaware of Levitt's paper, I myself made at about that time a very detailed comparative study of Vedic and Mesopotamian religious (mythological) motifs, published in *Migration and Diffusion*, vol. 24, 2005.[3] In this I showed that since more than twenty motifs in the Vedic texts had close parallels in other IE branches (e.g. the horse mythology, the skyboat of the Sungod, the flood, the elixir from heaven, the creation of cosmic parts from the dismemberment of a divine being, etc.) and were therefore of Proto-Indo-European provenance, they could not have been borrowed by the Vedics from the Mesopotamians as is usually alleged (McEvilley 2002; Dalley 1998) but must be inherited and therefore older than the Mesopotamian (Sumerian, Babylonian, etc.) parallels. Since

---

[3] This was badly printed and the Sanskrit transliterations are unreadable! A revised version was published in *Adyar Library Bulletin* 2007. This is now paper Seven in Kazanas (2009).

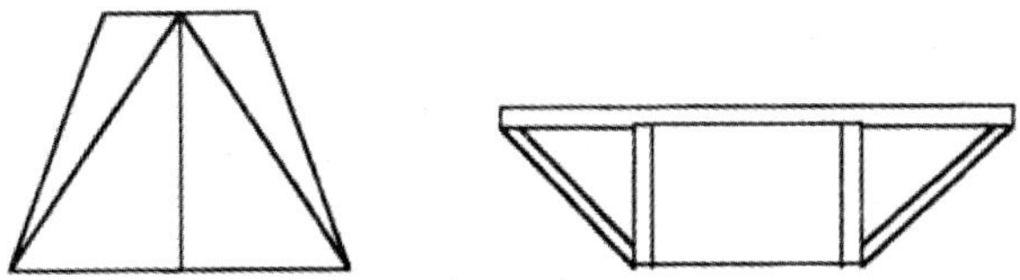

Trapezoid figures found in the Śulbas and in Egypt and Mesopotamia
(Frawley and Rajaram 1997: 162)

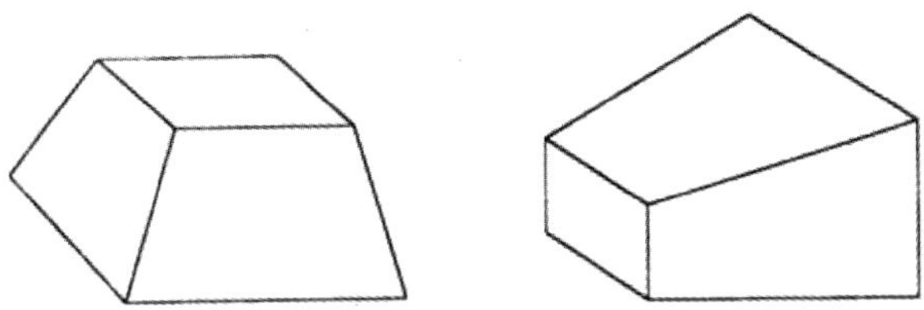

The Egyptian *mastaba* (left) and the Vedic *śmaśāna-cit* altar
(Frawley and Rajaram 1997: 162)

the Mesopotamian culture (starting with old Sumerian) surfaces *c*. 3000, the Vedic motifs must be earlier. Most of these have no parallels in Ugarite, Hebrew and other intermediate Near-Eastern cultures.

Thus again we arrive at a date before 3000 for the bulk of *Ṛgveda*.

13. Mathematics and Genetics

A. One modern authority, A. Seidenberg, American mathematician and historian of science, has written:

> It is very difficult to derive "the Vedic ritual application of the theorem [of Pythagoras] from Babylonia. (The reverse process is easy.) . . . The application involves geometric algebra and there is no evidence of geometric algebra from Babylonia. And the geometry of Babylonia is already secondary whereas in India it is primary. Hence we do not hesitate to place the Vedic altar rituals, or, more exactly, rituals exactly like them, far back of 1700 BCE. . . . The elements of ancient geometry found in Egypt and Babylonia stem from a ritual system of the kind observed in the Sulvasutras."
>
> — 1962: 515

Seidenberg reiterated his finds in another paper in 1978.

Note that the Mesopotamian ziggurats (= temples with steps) and the Egyptian *mastamba*-tombs and the step-pyramid of Djoser, all in the third millennium BCE, are based on trapezoid figures which are found in the Śulbasūtras and those figures are at the basis of Vedic altar brick-constructions like the *śmaśana-cit* (Frawley and Rajaram 1997: 162).

· Thus latest date for Śulbasūtras must be *c.* 2600 BCE.

B. (i) *Anthropological studies* show a possible break of continuity in the craniosceletal features of the ISC inhabitants at *c.* 6000–4500 (Kazanas 2009: 16). See also Kennedy (1995: 101ff).

The data undermine "any theory of a 'male invasion' of India" (Oppenheimer 2003: 152); they "argue against any major influx from regions north and west of India" (Sahoo et al.

(ii) Genetic Studies:

Cavalli-Sforza et al. (2003); Oppenheimer (2003); Sahoo et al. (2006); Danino M. (2006b); Sharma et al. (2009); Underhill et al. (2010).	All agree now that there was no significant inflow of genes into India after 10000 BCE!

2006: 843). Again Underhill et al.:

> the virtual absence of M458 Chromosomes outside Europe speaks against substantial patrilinear gene flow . . . to India, at least since the mid-Holocene. — 2010: 479

14. More Genetics

Since, according to the preceding discussion we must now assign (bulk of) *Ṛgveda* to *c.* 3200 at the latest and since *Ṛgveda* by general consent was composed around the Sarasvatī, then it follows that the IAs were ensconced in Saptasindhu by 3200 and that the ISC was a material manifestation of the early oral Vedic tradition expressed in *Ṛgveda*. This issue was treated by me extensively in preceding papers and no more need be said now. I should only add that, in fact, more and more scholars in the West have re-examined the issue and rejected wholly or in part the mainstream view advocating instead a movement Out of India into Europe: Schildmann 1998; Klostermaier 1998, 2000; Friedrich 2004; Hasenpflug 2006.

To all this I should add the increasing evidence from genetics which declares that no substantial flow of genes occurred from Europe or the north-western adjacent areas into India before 600 BCE. On the contrary, recent genetic studies show an outflow from India into countries west and north and Europe (Sahoo et al. 2006; Oppenheimer 2003). M. Danino has made a useful overview of the evidence produced by studies over the last ten years in his paper "Genetics and the Aryan Debate", published in *Purātattva* (2006b). All this is confirmed by Underhill et al. (2010). Thus the Indo-Aryans are now shown to be indigenous to Saptasindhu and there is nothing to undermine my contention that *Ṛgveda* in its bulk is pre-Haṛappan. What I am arguing for primarily and most emphatically is the proposition that, since the only biological change is in the skeletal record of the area and occurs *c.* 6000–4500 (Kazanas 2009: 16 with references), if the Indo-Aryans made an entry it would have happened at that period; but by 1700 BCE they certainly were indigenous. Genetic evidence, however, suggests strongly now an Out-of-India scenario.

Cavalli-Sforza et al. (2003) state that

> Indian tribal and caste populations derive largely from the same genetic heritage of Pleistocene [= 10000 to 3 mya] southern and western Asians and *have received limited gene flow from external regions since the Holocene* [= *c.* 10000 to

> present]. The phylogeography [= neighbouring branches] of the primal mtDNA and Y-chromosome founders suggest that these southern Asian Pleistocene coastal settlers from Africa would have provided the inocula for the subsequent differentiation of the distinctive eastern and western Eurasian gene pools (emphasis and square brackets added).

Another geneticist, S. Oppenheimer, offers independent confirmation (2003: 152) that there was no Aryan entry, either male or female; he focuses on the M17, or so-called "Caucasoid" (= Aryan!), genetic marker:

> South Asia is logically the ultimate origin of M17 and his ancestors; and sure enough we find highest rates and greatest diversity of the M17 line in Pakistan, India and eastern Iran, and low rates in the Caucasus. M17 is not only more diverse in South Asia than in Central Asia but diversity *characterizes* its presence in isolated tribal groups in the south, thus **undermining any theory of M17 as a marker of a 'male Aryan invasion' of India** (emphasis mine).

He adds that this M17 marker travelled from India or Pakistan (= our Saptasindhu) through Kashmir, Central Asia, Russia and then Europe after 40000 BP (p. 154). Thus migration is from east-westward.

Another study (Sahoo et al. 2006: 843) concludes:

> The Y-chromosomal data consistently suggest a largely South Asian origin of Indian caste communities and therefore argue against any major influx, from regions north and west of India.

Then again:

> It is not necessary, based on the current evidence, to look beyond South Asia for the origins of the paternal heritage of the majority of Indians at the time of the onset of settled

> agriculture . . . our findings do support a local origin of haplogroups F* and H. —p. 847

Yet another later study by Sharma et al. (2009) establishes again the Indo-Aryan indigenism:

> The Indian origin of paternal haplogroup R1a1 substantiates the autochthonous origin of brāhmaṇas and the caste system.

This is confirmed by P. Underhill's study in 2010 (see below § 16(v)). The indications now are that there will be no reversal. If there was a migration, this was most probably out of Saptasindhu and the adjacent region. It is significant that non-indigenists no longer refer to genetic studies!

15. Archaeological and Literary Evidences

Sir E. Leach (1990), Provost of King's College (Cambridge, UK):

> Because of their commitment to a unilateral segmented history of language development that needed to be mapped onto the ground, the philologists took it for granted that proto-Indo-Iranian was a language that has originated outside India or Iran. . . . From this we derived the myth of the "Aryan invasion".

After the discovery of the ISC:

> Indo-European scholars should have scrapped all their historical reconstructions and started again from scratch. But this is not what happened. Vested interests and academic posts were involved.

This is still true. But the new genetic evidence will soon perhaps force linguists to reconsider their theories.

And we must not forget that there may well have been an IE continuum from the Steppe to Saptasindhu and the IAs did not move from their location. It is worth noting that S. Zimmer (2002) admitted that (although himself a mainstream non-indigenist) he could not be certain of the exact location of the PIE homeland since the facts are so obscure in those far-off times. More recently, H.-P Francfort, the eminent excavator of Shortughai, expert on Central Asia Oxus area (or BMAC) and north-west India, critiqued V. Sarianidi, E. Kuzmina and J. Mallory and their theories about [proto-]Indo-Iranian movements through the Oxus region (2005: 262-68); further on (pp. 283ff) he pointed out that the pantheon in the Oxus iconography has a dominant goddess and so does not tally with Iranian and Indo-Aryan religions: on the whole he is most reluctant to accept Indo-Iranians (or Aryans) passing through that area *c.* 1800–1400 BCE. So even some mainstreamers have now serious doubts about the alleged Aryan immigration/invasion.

Indian (proto-)history must be restored and revalued in a correct time-frame. It is sad, indeed, as Frawley wrote (2002, *The Hindu*, 18 June), "to note how intellectuals in India are quick to denigrate the extent and antiquity of their history".

The new picture may well come to be as follows:

In one of the older hymns of *R̥gveda*, addressed to the goddess and the River Sarasvatī, it is said:

> She, the holy follower of Universal Order, [Sarasvatī,] has spread us all [the five tribes of the Vedic people (stanza 12)] beyond enmities, beyond the other [seven] sister-rivers, as the sun spreads out the days. — VI.61.9:[4]

---

4 The river Sarasvatī was in those ancient times regarded supreme and the "seven sisters" (sometimes, daughters or young ones) are the other rivers, which are in fact more than seven; but seven is an auspicious mystical number.

sā́ no víśvā áti dvíṣaḥ svásr̥ anyā́ r̥tā́varī ।
átann áheva sū́ryaḥ ॥

R̥V IV.1.13, VIII.4.2.16 Aṅgirases VII.76.4 Vasiṣṭhas	Our ancestors have always made sacrifices "here", i.e. in Saptasindhu.

R̥V V.10.6 *asmā́kasaś ca sūráyo víśvā ā́sās tarīṣáṇi* (Let our sages pervade all regions).

VII.6.3 Agni turned the unholy *dasyus* from the east to the west *pū́raś-cakāra áparam*!

VII.18.6 ". . . spread far over the earth."

X.65.11 Spread far the Aryan laws.

Then, Baudhāyana's *Śrautasūtra* 18.44:

> eastern migration Āyava; Western one Āmavasa, i.e. Gāndhāris, Parśus (= Persians) and Arātttas (Ararat/ Urartu?).

A post-R̥gvedic text, *Baudhāyana Śrauta-Sūtra* 18.44 mentions explicitly two movements from the central region of Saptasindhu:

> *prāṅ āyuḥ pravavrāja; tasyaite kurupañcālāḥ kāśi-videhā ity etad āyavaṁ pravrājam; pratyaṅ amāvasus, tasyaite gāndhārayas parśavo 'rāttā ityetad āmāvasavam.*
>
> Āyu migrated eastward; his [descendants] are the Kuru-Pāñcālas and the Kāśī-Videhas: this is the Āyava migration. Amāvasu [migrated] westward; his [descendants] are the Gāndhārīs, the Parśus and the Arāṭṭas: this is the Āmāvasa migration.

The Kuru-Pāñcālas and Kāśī-Videhas are people (and regions) east of Sarasvatī in the basins of Yamunā and Gaṅgā. The Gāndhārīs are obviously west of the Indus, and the Parśus

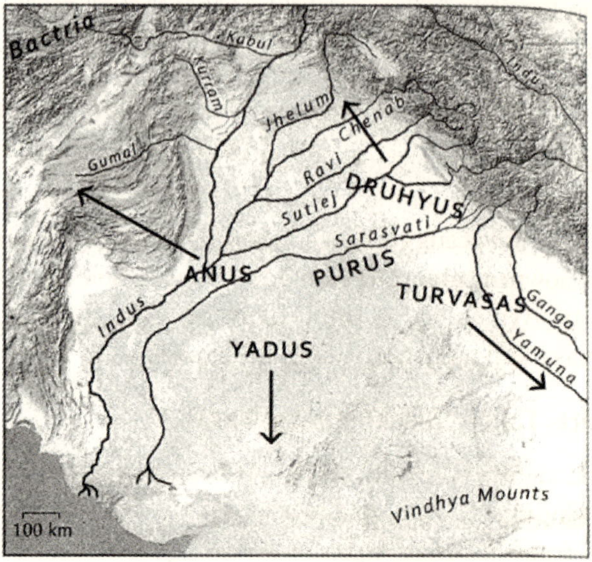

Map (S24) shows the new situaton

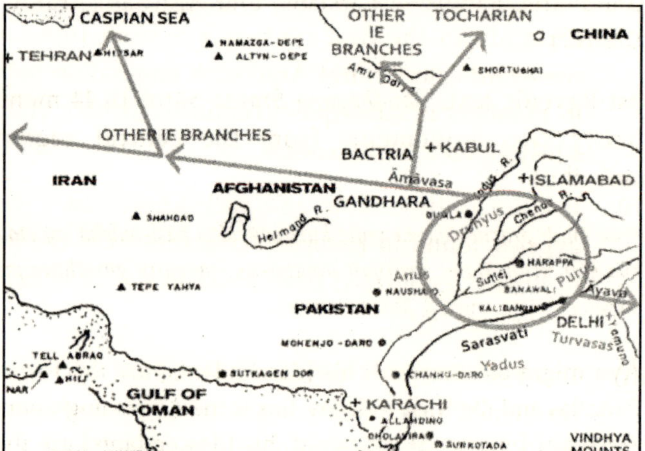

Map showing distant sites with Haṛappan artefacts (after Lal 2009: 77); the "seven rivers" and Sarasvatī; larger Saptasindhu and five Vedic tribes with Purus, etc. expansion by Āyu eastward and by Amāvasu west and north (to Tocharian speakers) from Bactria. Isoglosses accommodated also.

are the Persians (= Iranians) while the Arāṭṭas must be even further west. Now, the Mesopotamian text *Emmerkar and the Lord of Araṭṭa* (Kramer 1952) refers to Araṭṭa as north-west of Uruk. So Araṭṭa here cannot be the region in Punjab as Frawley thought (2001: 224, 226) and as I concurred (Kazanas 2009: 234). On the basis of the Mesopotamian text and Baudhāyana's text, B.B. Lal's suggestion of mount Ararāṭ (Lal 2009: 134) seems now probable; but I would add the region Urartu, south-west of Armenia. So Anatolians probably belong to the Āmavasa emigration of the Indo-Aryans.

16. Facts Taken from Historical Times

All this may well sound fanciful or even prejudiced, fabricated by an Indiophile with an agenda. So let us consider some facts taken from historical times.

(i) Indian Buddhists (with Sanskrit) began to emigrate certainly in the first century BCE from India north-westward into Central Asia; such emigration increased in numbers in subsequent centuries (Bryant 2001: 139; Klostermeier 2002, passim).

(ii) It is an indisputable and well-known fact that the gypsies, found in European countries from the Balkans to Britain, emigrated from India in the early centuries CE (Fraser 1995).

(iii) In at least two studies, Heinrich Hock, a world-renowned linguistic comparativist, points out that, apart from other emigrations, speakers of the dialect Niya Prakrit moved in early medieval times north-ward into Khoṭan and further east; then the dialect of Dumakī moved out of north-west India into south Central Asia; also the Parya moved via Afghanistan into what is now Uzbekistan (Hock 1993, 1996).

(iv) The Yezidis are a tiny religious group of about 150,000 adherents among the Kurds of northern Iraq, eastern Turkey and Armenia. Their religion seems to have a pagan basis with overlays of Zoroastrian, Christian and Islamic elements. They have a tradition that they came to the Middle East from India about 4,000 years ago! Their language Kurdī (= Kurdish), like many others of the Middle East and central Asia, derive from ancient Iranian (= Avestan) which had close affinities with Vedic. Like Hindus, the Yezidis believe in *avatāra*s and in reincarnation, they pray facing the sun at dawn and dusk and have endogamous castes. Their temples have conical spires like Hindu ones. A central figure in their religion is the "Peacock Angel" (Tawuse Melek); but the peacock is not found naturally in the Yezidi areas while it is native to India (see Reshid 2005).

(v) A study by P. Underhill, one of the foremost geneticists, shows that the gene R1a1a is common in north India and among Europeans like the Czechs, Poles and Lithuanians. The oldest strain of this gene mutation was concentrated in Gujarat, Sindh and West Rajasthan. This together with the M458 mutation is estimated to have travelled north-westward out of India at the latest 8000 years ago (see Underhill et al. 2010).

Thus it is quite acceptable that Vedic tribes moved away from Sapta-Sindhu to Bactria and thence to other areas where IE languages have been found.

17. Vedic Itself is a Derivative Language in the Process of Undergoing Changes

Here I should emphasize that Vedic as we have it in *Ṛgveda* and other early Vedic texts cannot be regarded as the Proto-

Indo-European language from which sprung the other IE branches. It is abundantly obvious that Vedic itself is a derivative language in the process of undergoing changes. A few examples should suffice.

(a) The masculine nominative dual has both, e.g. *áśvinā* and *áśvinau* two *Aśvins* (= horse-deities) but only the second remains in the later language.

The masc. nom. plural has both, e.g. *devā́sas* and *devā́s* (gods) but only the second remains in the later language. (Also for the feminine nom. pl.)

(b) For the neuter nom. plural we find more commonly *priyā́* than *priyā́ṇi* but the former disappears from post-Vedic.

(c) The feminine instrumental singular, say, *śúcyā* has variants *śúcī* and much commoner *śúci* both of which disappear in post-Vedic.

(d) In *Ṛgveda*, compounds with *nṛ-* are common and only one with *nára-*. Later *nṛ-* compounds cease while *nara-* ones increase.

(e) The verbal forms also show changes. E.g. for the 2nd or middle person singular *ihí* and *itā́t* (go thou) but only *ihi* remained. Similarly in the plural of the two forms *itá* and *itána* only *ita* remained.

(f) The accent, indicated above for the *udātta*, ceases in post-Vedic.

The Vedic language must have undergone many changes prior to the formation of *Ṛgveda* but, of course, we have no means of tracing such changes. Vedic must be much nearer to the proto-Indo-European mother tongue than any other branch, but it must be treated as a daughter like the others, yet eldest and closest.

As T. Burrow, whose *The Sanskrit Language* is still the authority in its field, puts it: Vedic is a "language which in most respects is more archaic and less altered from original Indo-Euroepan than any other member of the family" (1973: 34).

18. The Idea of a Primal Unity

Ṛgveda, finally, preserves for us, from that so ancient period, the idea of a Primal Unity that is the First Cause of the universe and all its phenomena: not only in the Nāsadīya-Sūkta and the Puruṣa-Sūkta (X.129 and 90) but also in I.164.6; III.55 refrain; VI.75.19; VIII.58; X.114.5 and less obviously in others. This concept is absent from all other IE traditions (Hittite, Greek, Roman, etc.) and may well have been an essential constituent of PIE culture lost in the other branches. Thus the Ṛgvedic IA culture (and perhaps PIE) consisted not so much of material artefacts but of inner knowledge and spiritual strength — *bráhma várma mamā̃ntaram* (the holy-power is my inner defence) *ṚV* VI.75.19.

Let us hope that the noxious AIT and all notions rooted in it will sooner rather than later end up in the only place they should be — the dustbin of history. Let us also hope that *Ṛgveda* will be re-examined not only for its historical information but its cultural ideas that will illuminate many other studies and disciplines in ancient history, anthropology, civilization, linguistics, religion, sociology, etc.

References

Achar, B.N.N., 1999, "On Exploring the Vedic Sky . . .", *Electronic Journal of Vedic Studies*, **5**(2): 3-9.

———, 2001, "Planetarium Software and the Date of the Mahābhārata War", paper read in Montreal, sent to N. Kazanas privately.

———, 2003, "Date of the Mahābhārata War. . .", in *Quarterly Journal of the Mythic Society*, **XCIV** (1-2).

———, 2012, "Chronology of Vedic Ṛṣis", *Vedic Venues*, **1**: 28-75.

Agrawal, A. (ed.), 2005, *In Search of Vedic Haṛappan Relationship*, New Delhi: Aryan Books International.

Agrawala, P.K., 2005, "Two Haṛappan Motifs & Their Vedic Affinity", in A. Agrawal (ed.), *In Search of Vedic Haṛappan Relationship*, pp. 10-13.

Allchin, B. and R. Allchin, 1982, *The Rise of Civilization in India & Pakistan*, Cambridge: Cambridge University Press.

———, 1997, *Origins of Civilization*, Delhi: Viking Penguins.

Allchin, F. and J. Joshi (eds.), 1995, *Excavations at Malvan*, Delhi: Archaeological Survey of India (Memoir No. 92).

Bisht, R.S., 1999, "Haṛappan and *Ṛgveda*: Points of Convergence", in G. C. Pande (ed.), *The Dawn of Indian Civilization* (up to *c*. 600 BC) pp. 393-442.

Bryant, E., 2009, in A. Marcantonio (ed.), *The Indo-European Language Family: Questions about Its Status*, chap. 4, Journal of IE Studies Monograph Series 55, Washington DC: Institute for the Study of Man.

———, 2002, "Somewhere in Asia and No More", *JIES*, **30**: 136-48.

———, 2001, *The Quest of the Origins of Vedic Culture*, Oxford: Oxford University Press.

Burnouf, E., 1833, "Discours sur la Langue et la Littérature Sanscrite, Prononcé au Collège de France", *Journal Asiatique*, **63**(2): pp. 251-72.

Burrow, T., 1963, "On the Significance of the Terms arma-, armaka-", *Journal of Indian History*, **41**: 159-68.

———, 1973, *The Sanskrit Language* (1955 rev. edn.), London: Faber.

———, 1975, "The Early Aryans" in A. Basham (ed.) *A Cultural History of India*, Oxford: Oxford University Press.

Campbell, A.D., 1816, *A Grammar of the Teloogoo Language, Commonly Termed the Gentoo, Peculiar to the Hindoos Inhabiting the North Eastern Provinces of the Indian Peninsula*, Madras: College Press.

Cardona, G., H. Hoeningswald and A. Senn, 1970, *Indoeuropean and Indoeuropeans*, Philadelphia: University of Pennsylvania Press.

Catrou, F., 1708, *Histoire Générale de l'Empire du Mogol depuis sa Fondation*, La Haye.

Cavalli-Sforza et al., 2003, "The Genetic Heritage of the Earliest Settlers . . .", *American Journal of Human Genetics,* **72**: 313-32.

Chakrabarti, D.K., 1999, *India: An Archaeological History,* Cambridge: Cambridge University Press.

Dales, G., 1966, "The Decline of the Haṛappans", *Scientific American,* **241:** 92-99.

Dalley, S. (ed.), 1998, *The Legacy of Mesopotamia,* Oxford: Oxford University Press.

Danino, M., 2006a, *L'Inde et l'invasion de nulle part,* . . . Paris: Les Belles Lettres.

———, 2006b, "Genetics and the Aryan Debate", *Purātattva,* **36**.

———, 2010, *The Lost River: On the Trail of the Sarasvatī,* New Delhi: Penguins.

Day, J.V., 1994, "The Concept of the Aryan Race in the 19th-century Scholarship", *Orpheus,* **4**: 15-48.

———, 2001, *Indo-European Origins,* Washington: Institute for the Study of Man.

Deshpande, M., 1966, "Evidence of Writing in Vedic Age", *Nagpur University Journal,* **16**(2).

Dhavalikar, M.K., 1995, *Cultural Imperialism* . . ., Delhi: Books & Books.

Ellis, F.W., 1816, "Note to the Introduction", in Alexander D. Campbell (ed.), *A Grammar of the Teloogoo Language,* Madras, pp. 1-31.

Elphinstone, M., 1841, *The History of India,* vol. 1, London: John Murray.

Elst, K., 1999, *Update on the Aryan Invasion Debate,* Delhi: Aditya Prakashan.

Emeneau, M., 1954, "Linguistic Prehistory of India", *Proceedings of the American Philological Society,* **98**: 282-92.

Erdosy, G. (ed.), 1995, *The Indo-Aryans of Ancient South Asia,* Berlin/New York: Guyter.

———, 1994, "The Meaning of Ṛgvedic pur . . .", in J.M. Kenoyer (ed.) *From Sumer to Melucha,* Wisconsin: University of Wisconsin Press.

EWA, see Mayrhofer 1996.

Falk, H., 1981, "Vedische arma", *Zeitschrift der deutschen morgenländischen Gesellschaft,* **131**: 160-71.

———, 1992, "Nollikhya Nāvalikhya", *Indo-Iranian Journal,* **35**(1): 1-17.

Francfort, H.-P., 1992, "Evidence for Haṛappan Irrigation System", *Eastern Anthropologist*, **45**: 87-103.

———, 2005, "La Civilisation de l'Oxus et les Indo-Iraniens et Indo-Aryens en Asie Centrale", in Fussman et al.

Fraser, A., 1995, *The Gypsies*, Oxford: Blackwell.

Frawley, D., 1991, *Gods, Sages & Kings*, Salt Lake City: Passage Press.

———, 2001, *The Rigveda and the History of India*, Delhi: Aditya.

———, 2002, "Witzel's Vanishing Ocean . . .", http://voiceofdharma.com/indology/ReplytoWitzel.html

Frawley, D. and N. Rajaram, 1997, *Vedic Aryans & Origins of Civilization*, Delhi: Voice of India.

Friedrich, H., 2004, "A Diffusionist's View on the Concept of 'Language Families'", *Migration & Diffusion*, **5**(19): (July–September): 6-14.

———, 2003, "Hebrew Ethnogenesis and Diffusion", *Migration & Diffusion* **4**: 16 (October–December).

Fussman, G., J. Kellens, H.-P Francfort and X. Tremblay, 2005, *Aryas, Aryens et Iraniens en Asie Centrale*, Paris: College de France, Publications de l'Institut de Civilisation Indienne.

Gnoli, G., 1980, *Zoroaster's Time and Homeland*, Naples: Instituto Universitario Orientale (Series & Minores VII).

Gupta, S.P., 2005, "The Saraswatī and the Homeland of Early Rigvedic Rishis", in A. Agrawal (ed.) *In Search of Vedic Harappan Relationship* pp. 55-73.

———, 2007, "City in Protohistoric India", in G. C. Pande (ed.) *Golden Chain of Civilizations . . .*, PHISPC, vol. 1, pt. 4, pp. 209-355, Delhi: Centre for Studies in Civilization.

Hasenpflug, R., 2006, *The Inscriptions of the Indus Civilization*, Ciando: Books on Demand.

Hock, H.H., 1993, "Subversion or Convergence? . . . ", *Studies in Lingquistic Sciences*, **23**(2): 73-115.

———, 1999, "Out of India? The Linguistic Evidence" in J. Bronkhorst and M. Deshpande (eds.) *Aryan and Non-Aryan in South Asia*, Cambridge, M. HOS, pp. 1-18.

———, 1996, "Pre-R̥gvedic Convergence . . ." in Jan E.M. Houben (ed.), *Ideology and Status of Sanskrit*, pp. 17-58, Leiden: Brill.

Iyengar, R.N., 2005, "Historicity of Celestial Observations of Mahābhārata", in S. Kamath (ed.), *The Date of the Mahābhārata War Based on Astronomical Data,* Bangalore: Mythic Society, pp. 150-86.

Kak, S., 1994, *The Astronomical Code of the Rigveda* (revised edn. 2000), Delhi: Manohar.

———, 1997, "Archaeoastronomy and Literature", *Current Science* **73** (7): 624-27.

———, 2003, *How Old Is Indian Writing?*< http://subhash-kak.sulekha.com/blog/post/2003/12/how-old-is-indian-writing.htm>

Kazanas, N., 1999, "The Ṛgveda and Indoeuropeans", *ABORI,* **80**: 15-42.

———, 2002, "Indigenous Indoaryans & the Ṛgveda", *Journal of IE Studies,* **30**: 275-334.

———, 2003, "Final Reply", *Journal of IE Studies,* **31**(1 2): 187-240.

———, 2007a, "Vedic, Mesopotamian and Egyptian Religiophilosophical Thought", in *Golden Chain of Civilizations,* Delhi & Shimla: PHISPC.

———, 2007b, "Coherence & Preservation in Sanskrit", *Research Bulletin of the Vishveshvarand Vedic Research Institute,* vol. 5.

———, 2009, *Indo-Aryan Origins and Other Vedic Issues,* Delhi: Aditya Prakashan.

———, 2012, "Vedic and Avestan", in *Vedic Venues* vol. 1, pp. 183-229.

———, 2014 (in press), "Isoglosses: What They (Don't) Show Us", in *Vedic Venues,* vol. 2, R.N. Jha et al. (eds.).

Kennedy, K., 1995, "Have Aryans Been Identified . . ." in G. Eadosy (ed.) *The Indo-Aryans of Ancient South Asia,* Berlin: de Gruyter pp. 99-107.

Kenoyer, J.M., 1997/2000, "The Ravi Phase: A New Cultural Manifestation at Harappa", *South Asian Archaeology,* pp. 55-76, Rome.

———, 1998, *Ancient Cities of the Indus Valley Civilization,* Karachi: Oxford University Press.

Kenoyer, J.M. and R.H. Meadow, 2007, "The Early Indus Script at Harappa", in E. Olijdam and R.H. Spoor (eds.) *Intercultural Relations between South & Southwest Asia,* BAR International Series.

Klaus, K., 1989, "Samudrá im Vedá": Deutscher Orientalistentag 1985, Würzburg, XIII, E von Schuler (ed.) *Ausgewählte Vorträge,* Wiesbaden, pp. 364-71.

Klostermaier, K., 1998, "Questioning the Aryan Invasion Theory . . .", *Iskcon Communications Journal,* **6**(1): 5-16. Republished in *International Quarterly of Indian Philosophy,* June 2001, pp. 63-78.

———, 2000, *Hinduism,* Oxford: Oneworld Books.

———, 2002, *Buddhism,* Oxford: Oneworld Publications.

Kramer, S.N., 1952, *Enmerkar & the Lord of Aratta,* Philadelphia: University of Pennsylvania.

Kochhar, R., 2000, *The Vedic People,* (1997) Hyderabad: Orient Lougman.

Lal, B.B., 1998, *India 1947-1997: New Light on the Indus Civilization,* Delhi: Aryan Books International.

———, 2002, *The Sarasvatī Flows On,* Delhi: Aryan Books International.

———, 2005, *The Homeland of the Aryans,* Delhi: Aryan Books International.

———, 2009, *How Deep Are the Roots of Indian Civilisation,* Delhi: Aryan Books International.

Lal, B.B. and S.P. Gupta (eds.), 1984, *Frontiers of the Indus Civilization,* Delhi: Indian Archaeological Society.

Langlès, L.M., 1821, *Monuments Anciens et Modernes de l'Hindoustan, Décrits Sous le Double Rapport Archaeologique et Pittoresque, et Précédés d' une Notice Géographique, d' une Notice Historique,* 2 vols., Paris.

Langlois, A., 1833, "Manava Dharmasastra", *Journal Asiatique,* **69**: 142-55.

Leach, E., 1990, "Aryan Invasions over Four Millennia", in E. Ohnuki-Tierney (ed.) *Culture Through Time,* Stanford: Stanford University Press, pp. 227-45.

Levitt, S.H., 2003, "The Dating of the Indian Tradition", *Anthropos,* **98**: 341-59.

Lorblanchet, M., 1992/2001, *Rock Art in the Old World,* Delhi: Indira Gandhi National Centre for the Arts and Aryan Books International.

Lubotsky, A., 1997, *A R̥gvedic Word Concordance,* New Haven: American Oriental Society.

Mayrhofer, M., 1956, *KEWA* (*Kurtzgefasstes . . .*), Heidelberg: Carl Winter.

———, 1996, *Etymologisches Wörterbuches des Altindischen,* Heidelberg: Carl Winter.

McEvilley, Th., 2002, *The Shape of Ancient Thought,* New York: Allworth Press.

McIntosh, J.R., 2001, *A Peaceful Realm,* Boulder (Colorado): Westview.

Misra, S.S., 1992, *The Aryan Problem: A Linguistic Approach,* Delhi: Munshiram Manoharlal.

Mitchell, B. and F.C. Robinson, 1996, *A Guide to Old English,* Oxford: Blackwell.

Müller, M., 1859/1968, *The History of Ancient Sanskrit Literature,* Varanasi: Chowkamba Sanskrit Series.

Nichols, J., 1997-98, "The Epicentre of the IE Linguistic Spread" and "The Eurasian Spread Zone . . .", in R. Blench and M. Spriggs (eds.) *Archaeology & Language,* New York/London: Routledge, vol. 1, pp. 122-48 and vol. 2, pp. 220-66.

Oppenheimer, S., 2003, *The Real Eve: Modern Man's Journey Out of Africa,* New York: Carroll & Graf.

Parpola, A., 1969, *Decipherment of Proto-Dravidian Inscriptions,* Copenhagen: Scandinavian Institute of Asian Studies.

———, 1988, "The Coming of the Aryans to Iran and India and the Cultural and Ethnic Identity of the Dasas", *Studia Orientalia,* by: 195-302.

Piggott, S., 1992, *Wagon, Chariot and Carriage,* London: Thames & Hudson.

Possehl, G.L., 1998, "Did the Sarasvati Ever Flow to the Sea?", in G.S. Phillips et al. (eds.) *Arabia and Its Neighbours (in Honour of Beatrice de Cardi),* Turnhout: Brepols, pp. 339-54.

———, 2002/03, *The Indus Civilization Roman and Littlefield* (*Non-NBN*); New Delhi: Vistaar Publications.

Prabhakar, C.L., 1994, "The Ancients' Approach to the Ocean", *Quarterly Journal of the Mythic Society,* **85**(2): 30-45.

Raghavan, S., 1969, *The Date of the Mahabharata War,* Srinivasanagar: Srirangam Printers.

Ramat, A. and P. Ramat (eds.), 2006 (1998), *The Indo-European Languages,* New York/London: Routledge.

Rao, L.S., 2006, "The Haṛappan Spokedwheels . . .", *Purātattva,* **36**: 59-67.

Rao, S.R., 1991, *Dawn and Devolution of the Indus Civilization,* Delhi: Aditya Prakashan.

Rémusat, A., 1822, "Monuments Anciens et Modernes de l'Hindoustan; par L. Langlès", *Journal des Savans,* Avril, pp. 220-32.

Renfrew, C., 1989, *Archaeology and Language,* Hammondsworth: Penguins.

Reshid, T., 2005, "Yezidism: Historical Roots", *International Journal of Kurdish Studies,* cited in Sanyal (2012: 68), below.

Rix, H., 1998, *Lexikon der indogermanischen verben . . .,* Wiesbaden: Reichert.

Sahoo, S., A. Singh, T. Kivisild et al., 2006, "A Prehistory of Indian Y-chromosomes", *Proceedings of the National Academy of Sciences* (USA), **103**(4): 843-48.

Sanyal, S., 2012, *Land of the Seven Rivers: A Brief History of India's Geography,* Delhi: Penguin-Viking.

Schildmann, K., 1998, "Indus/Burrows Cave USA-Deciphering Bonn", *Studia Orientalia et Indo-Atlantica,* Fascicle 1.

Seidenberg, A., 1962, "The Ritual Origin of Geometry", *Archive for History of Exact Sciences,* **1**: 488-527.

———, 1978, "The Origin of Mathematics", *Archive for History of Exact Sciences,* **18**: 303-41.

Sethna, D.K., 1992, *The Problem of Aryan Origins,* 2nd edn., Delhi: Aditya Prakashan.

Shaffer, J.G. and D.A. Lichtenstein 1999, "Migration, Philology & South Asian Archaeology", in J. Bronkhorst & M. Deshpande (eds.) *Aryans and Non-Aryan in South Asia,* Cambridge, Mass: HOS.

Sharma, G.R., 1980, *History to Protohistory: Archaeology of the Vindhyas and the Ganga Valley,* Allahabad: University of Allahabad.

Sharma, J.R., A.K. Gupta and B.K. Bhadra, 2006, "Course of Vedic River Saraswatī. . .", *Purātattva,* **36**: 187-95.

Sharma, S. et al., 2009, "The Indian Origin of Paternal Halpogroup R1a1 . . .", *Journal of Human Genetics,* **54**: 47-55.

Singh, Bhagwan., 1995, *The Vedic Haṛappans,* Delhi: Aditya Prakashan.

Stevenson, J., 1841, "An Essay on the Language of the Aboriginal Hindus", *Journal of the Bombay Branch of the Royal Asiatic Society,* **1**: 103-26.

———, 1839, "On the Ante-Brahmanical Worship of the Hindus in the Dekhan", *Journal of the Royal Asiatic Society of Great Britain and Ireland,* **5**: 189-97.

Talageri, S., 2000, *The Rigveda,* New Delhi: Aditya Prakashan.

———, 2008, *The R̥gveda & the Avesta . . .,* Delhi: Aditya.

Tewari, R., R.K. Srivastava, K.K. Singh and K.S. Saraswat, 2006, "Further Excavations at Lahuradeva, District Sant Kabir Nagar . . .", *Purātattva*, **36**: 68-75.

Thomas, P. et al., 1995, "Haṛappan Subsistence Patterns . . .", *Man and Environment* (India), **20**(2): 33-41.

Underhill, P., N. Myers et al., 2010, "Separating the Post-Glacial Co-ancestry", *European Journal of Human Genetics*, **18**: 479-84.

Vedic Index, 1995 (1912), A. MacDonnell and A. Keith, Delhi: Motilal Banarsidass.

Wilks, M., 1810, *Historical Sketches of the South of India*, vol. 1, London.

Winternitz, M., 1981, *History of Indian Literature* (tr. V.S. Sarma), 3 vols., Delhi: Motilal Banarsidass.

Witzel, M., 2001, "Autochthonous Aryans", *Electronic Journal of Vedic Studies*, **7**(3): 1-93.

———, 2005, "Central Asian Roots and Acculturation in South Asia", in Osada Tosiki (ed.), *Linguistics, Archaeology and the Human Past*, Kyoto: Indus Project, Research Institute for Humanity and Nature.

Zimmer, S., 2002, "The Easy Way to Truth . . .", *JIES*, **30**: 192-201.

2

On Oriental Learning in Medieval Bengal and Collection of Manuscripts at Jorasanko Tagore House, Kolkata

Karunasindhu Das

MEDIAEVAL Bengal can rightly boast of extensive studies in different branches of learning, Sanskritic or otherwise, including systems of philosophy, viz. Nyāya-Vaiśeṣika, Prābhākara-Mīmāṁsā, Yogācāra Buddhism, Vedānta of both Śaṅkarite and Vaiṣṇavite varieties, Āyurveda, Tantra, Abhidhāna, and Vyākaraṇa of Pāṇinian and post-Pāṇinian systems, viz. *Kalāpa, Mugdabodha, Saṁkṣiptasāra, Sārasvata, Supadma, Harināmāmṛta* and *Prayogaratnamālā* to name a few.

Hundreds of texts, commentaries, sub-commentaries, scholia, appendices and disquisitions were authored and discussed in academic circles during those days. That during early medieval days the Buddhists of eastern India, for example, contributed much to Pāṇini's grammar can be substantiated from such works as *Tantrapradīpa* and *Dhātu-pradīpa* by Maitreya Rakṣita, *Bhāṣāvṛtti* and *Paribhāṣāvṛtti* by Puruṣottama, *Durghaṭavṛtti* by Śaraṇadeva, *Pāribhāṣāvṛtti* by Sīradeva and the like to be followed by succeeding generations of commentators. Against this Bengal School of Pāṇini, so to say, some non-Pāṇinian schools were patronized in certain quarters, religious or secular. Neo-logicians of Navadvīpa, for instance, followed *Kātantra*, otherwise called Kalāpa and developed a philosophy of language opposed to that of the Pāṇinian school. Śrīcaitanya-deva, the Vaiṣṇava savant to whom Gauḍīya Vaiṣṇavism owes its origin was in his pre-*saṁnyāsa* days a brilliant exponent[1] of Kalāpa and was honoured with the epithet, viz. Vidyāsāgara whose commentary on the system was widely acclaimed as an authentic book[2] for learners. To him, however, realization occurred gradually that every Śāstra is but a manifestation of Lord Kṛṣṇa's name and this led to the origin and development of *Harināmāmṛta* school of grammar widely accepted among the Gauḍīya[3] Vaiṣṇavas. Uplift of the old *rasa* theory of art to devotional plane of divine love is another achievement of this sect.

Besides, all the major commentaries on *Saṁkṣiptasāra* and *Mughabodha* were composed by Bengali grammarians during the past few centuries.

---

1 *vyākaraṇ paḍaha nimai paṇḍit tomār nām* ।
bālyaśāstre loke tomār kahe guṇagrām
vyākaraṇ-madhye jāni paḍāha kalāp.
— *Caitanyacaritāmṛta* 1.16.29-30

2 *āpani karen prabhu sūtrer ṭippanī*
— *Caitanyabhāgavata, ādikhaṇḍa,* Ch. VII

also,

āmrā sav tomār ṭippanī । *lai paḍi paḍāi śunaha guṇamaṇi*
— *Bhaktiratnākara, Taraṅga* XII

3 *āviṣṭa haiyā prabhu karen vyākhyān* ।
sūtra-vṛtti ṭīkāy sakal harināṁ ।
prabhu vale sarvakāle satya kṛṣṇanām ।
sarvaśāstre kṛṣṇa vai nā valaye ān ।
— *Caitanyabhāgavata* 2.1

Curricula prescribed for learners in oriental institutes those days naturally included some of the contemporary works along with classical ones. Śrīpati in Mukundaram's *Caṇḍīmaṅgala,*[4] for instance, is stated to have read for learning Sanskrit language a number of texts belonging to different schools.

As it appears, books were selected for linguistic training cutting across the boundaries of schools and systems of grammar. Scholars, therefore, had the scope of mastery in various alternative systems at a time. It is no wonder that Maitreya Rakṣita concluded his *Dhātupradīpa* by stating that he had consulted works belonging to the schools of Pāṇini, Candra, Kalāpa, Kṣapaṇaka, etc. for authoring his book.[5] Similarly, Rāmadāsa's *Kātantracandrikā* refers to Jayāditya, Jinendra-buddhi and Maitreyarakṣita of Pāṇinian school and Durga's commentary, Kulacandra's *Durgavākyaprabodha*, Puṇḍarīkākṣa's *Kātantrapradīpa* of the Kātantra school

---

4 गुरुवाक्ये दिआ कर्ण । चिनिल अनेक वर्ण ।
अष्टशब्दि सुवन्त पाणिन।

पड़े दत्त श्रीयपति । सन्धिमूल सन्धिवृत्ति
पड़िल व्याकर्णटीका । गणवृत्ति समासिका
अमर जुमर वर्ण नाना

जानिते सन्धिर तत्त्व पड़िल उज्जवल दत्त
पड़िल दुर्घटवृति । धीर सभाय चक्रवर्त्ती
निरन्तर करेन विचार

दिवानिशि यत्नवान । पड़े छय अभिघान ।
पुथि शोधे विविध प्रकार ।
नानाछन्दे पड़िल पिङ्गल ।

— Vaṇik-Kāṇḍa of *Caṇḍīmaṅgala* by Kavikankan Mukundaram

5 *ākṛṣya bhāṣyajaladher atha dhātunāma-pārāyaṇa-kṣapaṇa-pāṇini-śāstravedī ।kālāpa-cāndra-mata-tattva-vibhāgadakṣo dhātupradīpam akarojjagato hitāya ।*

— *Dhātupradīpa*, concluding verse

together.[6] The last named grammarian, too, was equally conversant with Pāṇini and *Kātantra*. He authored commentaries on *Bhaṭṭikāvya* (*Kalāpadīpikā* by name), *Kāvyādarśa, Kāvyaprakāśa, Kāvyālaṁkārasūtra,* all as per Kātantra rules with an eye to popularizing the system besides Pāṇini's one which was more widely accepted:

pāṇiniprakriyāyāṁ me prasiddhatvān na kautukam ।
kalāpa-prakriyā tasmād aprasiddhā ca kathyate ॥

For testifying to coexistence of different systems of Sanskrit grammar in Bengal during the days of Rāmacaraṇa Tarkavāgīśa authoring his commentary, viz. *Pramodajananī* on *Mugdhabodha* his following observation, too, is equally significant:

pare 'tra pāṇinīyajñāḥ, kecit kālāpakovidāḥ ।
eke vidyānivāsāḥ syu ranye sāṁkṣiptasārakāḥ ॥

True, academic debates also went on among scholars belonging to different schools subscribing to conflicting opinions on many a point. Sometimes sub-schools thriving under one umbrella engaged themselves in vexed debate. Conflict between followers of Durga and those of *Pariśiṣṭa* is a case in point in Bengal *Kātantra* school. But "give and take" was not unusual altogether. Patañjali's *Mahābhāṣya,* for instance, is found cited as an authority in non-Pāṇinian circles. Questions raised in opponent circles helped each one in developing existing formulations in course of responding thereto and led to betterment. *Darśana-Vyākaraṇa* interface, in fact, played catalysis in development of philosophy of language of the

---

[6] *durgaṭīkāṁ samālokya kulacandrādisaṁgrahān* ।
rakṣita-nyāsakārāṇāṁ jayādityañca saṅgatim ।

jinendra-rudradāsānāṁ sāgaraṣya ca saṁgrahān ।
ādāya dhīmatā samyak śrīrāmadāsaśarmaṇā ।

kātantra-pariśiṣṭasya nibandho'yaṁ kṛto mayā ॥

grammar schools. One may cite with pleasure in this respect deliberations noted in Vaṁśīvadana's *ṭippaṇī* of the *Saṁkṣipta-sāra* school on *kartṛ* where the commentator examined several definitions of agent case available in different quarters and accepted in fine the one propounded by Naiyāyikas as the most effective one. In his commentary on Jayakṛṣṇa's *Sāramañjarī*, a text of Navya-Nyāya following, on the other hand, Kālīpada Tarkācārya is found to have preferred *Kātantra* definition of *kāraka* to what his own school of Navya-Nyāya tradition had put forward earlier.

There had been search for a synthesis all the way in different quarters. But it is with Tārānātha Tarkavācaspati's *Āśubodha Vyākaraṇa* in mid-nineteenth-century Bengal that contending schools could find a common text of rules relating to morpho-syntactical studies in Sanskrit language.

Development of Gauḍīya Vaiṣṇavism at the backdrop of two very powerfully prevailing systems of philosophy, viz. Śaṅkarite Vedānta and Navya-Nyāya is no less important as an event of cultural upsurge in medieval Bengal. Interestingly, Madhusūdana Sarasvatī of *Advaitasiddhi* fame did not stick to dogmatic propagation of Śaṅkarite monism; and in his *Prasthānabheda* he rather opted for upholding coexistence of viewpoints on the plea that every system agrees ultimately to embracing the supreme soul (*bhagavatī tātparyam*). Advent of Śrī Caitanya was felt so intensively that Madhusūdana did not feel shy of composing a verse eulogizing Lord Kṛṣṇa and proposing total submission to Him.

Needless to say, this vast literature of philosophy, grammar and the like has been largely preserved in manuscript form till date in repositories either as personal collections or family libraries or at institutes of oriental learning. The city of Kolkata in its history of existence of 300 years can rightly claim a pride of place in housing some libraries of this type. The name of the Asiatic Society of Kolkata, established in CE 1784 figures prominently as one of the oldest and the biggest storehouses of manuscripts acquired either as inheritence from Tipu Sultan's library through Indian Museum or by collection through donation or purchase in subsequent days. Of the family libraries, that of the Jorasanko Tagore House deserves our special attention. Interestingly the oldest part of this Thakurbari too was built in CE 1784. Like many of the sociocultural movements of national importance resurgence of oriental learning including collection and preservation of manuscripts, too, owe much to these Tagores. Rabindranath Tagore and his nephew Kshitindranath played the pioneering role in this respect.

In an article entitled *"Pracin Puthi-Uddhar"* (1891) Rabindranath stressed upon retrieving ancient knowledge from manuscript sources. Ten years thereafter, he is found collecting manuscripts for Santiniketan. He donated more than 100 manuscripts to Bangiya Sahitya Parisad in 1911. Visva-Bharati established its manuscript section in 1923. Anantha-krishna Sastry of Baroda was invited as an expert in manuscriptology to help in the project. Tagore sent him to different parts of the land for collecting manuscripts. An open letter from Tagore's pen appeared in 1923 in *Behar Herald* featuring an appeal to all for helping in this collection drive. Sastryji's tour resulted in procurement of several thousands of manuscripts in Sanskrit, Bengali, Oriya, Tamil and Malayalam. Another south Indian pundit N. Aiyaswami Sastrigal who joined Visva-Bharati in 1924 as director of manuscripts library, prepared a descriptive catalogue of this vast and valuable collection.[7] Rabindranath's visit to South-

---

7 *Prācīn Puthi-Uddhār: Rabindra Udyog* by Bishwanath Roy, Pustak Bipani, referred to in Mrinmoy Chakraborty's article in *Kṛtirakṣaṇa*, vol. 6, nos. 1-2, 2010.

East Asia (1927) and Persia (1932) also bore fruits in terms of collection of manuscripts on *Mahābhārata* and Persian literary texts. He knew that many ancient Sanskrit works particularly related to Buddhism which were lost in original could be available in translation in Tibetan, Chinese, Mongolian, Japanese, etc. In 1902 a Japanese scholar of 27 years Sitoku Hory visited Santiniketan as the first ever foreign student and stayed there in close contact with Tagore's family for six months engaging himself in Sanskrit studies in general and he translated entire *Amarakoṣa* into Japanese within that period. As his diary notes (published in 1964) show, Tagore advised him a thorough search of Sanskrit manuscripts that had reached China and Japan from India and enquired about the way to receiving their copies.[8] Jagadish Chandra Basu, the famous scientist friend of Rabindranath, was equally fascinated with this idea. He suggested that a student expert in both Sanskrit and English, be trained up for six months at the Asiatic Society of Bengal in Tibetan and other languages and scripts on Buddhism and that he and Sitoku Hory would then visit monasteries in China and Japan for copying Buddhist manuscripts in Devanāgarī scripts.[9] "Recovering lost works in Sanskrit from Tibetan and Chinese sources" thus, became one

---

8 रवीन्द्रनाथ आमाके अनुरोध करेन ये आमि येन ताँके भारतवर्ष थेके चीन ओ जापाने प्रेरित संस्कृत पाण्डुलिपिसमूहेर सन्धान एवं उक्त पाण्डुलिपिगुलिर प्रतिलिपि भारते निये आसवार उपाय जानाइ ।

– प्रसङ्ग शितोकु होरि in जापान ओ रवीन्द्रनाथ: शतवर्षेर विनिमय by काजुओ आजुमा,
N.E. Publishers, Kolkata, 1st edn., 2004, p. 14.

9 एकटि संस्कृत ओ इंरेजीविद छात्र सन्धान करिया 6 मास Asiatic Society — ते बुद्धधर्म सम्बन्धे Tibet — एर Mss एवं अन्यान्य लिपि याहा आछे ताहा अभ्यस्त करिते हइवे । तारपर तोमार Mr. Hory — के सङ्गे करिया तिनि चीन देशेर ओ जापानेर नाना विहारे वाङ्ला ओ देवनागरी पुँथिर कपि करिवेन ।
– चिठिपत्र, षष्ठ खण्ड, परिशिष्ट, pp. 213.14

of the major goals of Visva-Bharati's research centre for all different cultures of the East.

Tagore was quite aware of the importance of manuscript library as a citadel of socio-cultural studies. He admitted that popular texts, viz. *Rāmāyaṇa, Mahābhārata* or *Kabikankan Caṇḍī* because of their wide popularity among the masses for centuries, are sure to have undergone certain textual variations at different regions in different ages. A nodal manuscripts library may arrange preserving old copies of such texts at its disposal for a scholarly and critical edition of the work(s) by an accomplished editor. Besides a peep into variations can surely lead us to[10] comprehending social reasons behind linguistic changes effected on a text in manuscripts.

The other Tagores who followed in the footsteps of Rabindranath were three of his nephews, viz. Gaganendranath and Abanindranath, the two artist sons of Gunendranath who was the poet's cousin and Kshitindranath (1869–1937), the son of Hemendranath, an elder brother of the poet. Gaganendranath donated to Bangiya Sahitya Parisad thirteen manuscripts including one on *Kṛṣṇamaṅgala* by Dvija Mādhava. He is reported to have eagerly tried to buy an autocopy of Mukundaram's poem from one of the descendants of the medieval poet at the cost of Rs. 300 only. Another Tagore of the Pathuriaghata branch, viz. Jatindramohan was ready to

---

[10] वांला भाषातत्त्व-सन्धानेर एकटि व्याघात, प्राचीन पुँथिर दुष्प्राप्यता । कविकङ्कनचण्डी, रामायण, महाभारत प्रभृति प्राचीन काव्यगुलि जनसाधारणेर समादृत हओयाते काले काले अल्पे अल्पे परिवर्तित ओ संशोधित हइया आसियाछे । प्राचीन आदर्श पुँथि कोनो एक पुस्तकालये यथासम्भव संगृहीत थाकिले अनुसन्धित्सुर पक्षे सुविधार विषय हय । साहित्य-परिषदेर अधिकारे एरूप एकटि पुस्तकालय स्थापित हइते पारिवे इहाइ आमरा आशा करि ।

– वङ्गभाषा in वांला शब्दतत्त्व
वैशाख, 1304 वङ्गाब्द

pay Rs. 500 for the same. Abanindranath handed over to Rabindranath for Visva Bharati fifty-one Islamic manuscripts he had collected from Battala. The master painter was fascinated by the style of writing therein from the right side to the left.

Kshitindranath served Ādi Brahma Samāja initially as assistant secretary and associate of his illustrious grand-father Maharshi Devendranath, as one of the then secretaries and finally as the secretary after Rabindranath laid down the post of the Samāja. Editing *Tattvabodhinī* was an essential part of secretarial responsibility of this religious movement and Kshitindranath played his role with commendable success by authoring and editing philosophical disquisitions of merit especially those delivered by the Maharshi. His other passion was collection of manuscripts from remote areas of our land. From village Vasudevpur in Ghatal sub-division of the undivided Midnapore district of Bengal he was able to collect a few hundred manuscripts which were later donated by late Smt. Menaka Tagore, wife of his son Kshemendranath, to Rabindra Bharati University Library and Museum. As on date the museum has been taking care of 417 manuscripts at its disposal (Mc) while the library transferred its manuscript assets numbering 472 to Kshitindranath Tagore (K.N. Tagore). Centre for Preservation and Studies in Manuscripts was established in 2009 at Jorasanko Tagore House. The library collection (Lc) was subsequently enriched and augmented with donation of manuscripts by Late Prof. Haripada Chakravarty, Subodh Ranjan Ray, Panchanan Chakravarty, Prof. Nirmal Das, Dr Minakshi Sinha and Gopal Biswas. Shri Biswas, an ex-student of Rabindra Bharati University, from Sonamukhi collected and donated a number of manuscripts including one of *Dharmamaṅgala*. The corpus of this Jorasanko treasure thus comprised about 900 manuscripts at initial count covering wide range of subjects in Sanskrit and Bengali, viz. Veda, Purāṇa, Tantra, Jyotiṣa, Smṛti, Āyurveda, Sāhitya, Darśana, Vyākaraṇa, etc. Of the Museum assets, we may cite the following:

Veda — *Sāṁkhyāyana Brāhmaṇa; Kenopaniṣad.*

Purāṇa — *Śiva-Puraṇa; Padma-Purāṇa; Kūrma-Purāṇa; Bṛhannāradīya-Purāṇa; Bhāgavata-Purāṇa.*

Tantra — *Kāmadhenutantra; Kulārṇavatantra; Nīlatantra; Nigamatantrasāra; Kālīvilāsatantra.*

Stotra — *Navagrahastotra; Śanistotra; Śītalāstotra; Mahimākhyāstuti-vyākhyā* by Madhusūdana Sarasvatī; *Jagaddhātrī-sahasranāma-stotra; Indrākṣīstotra.*

Smṛti and Kṛtya — *Manu-Saṁhitā; Tithitattva; Gotranirṇaya; Śuddhitattva; Ekādaśītattva; Dāyatattva; Tithikṛtya; Grahayāga; Śivasthāpanavidhi; Ghaṭasthāpanamantra; Kālikāpūjā; Rādhā-Kṛṣṇapūjā-paddhati; Vṛṣotsargapaddhati; Agastyapūjā; Annapūrṇāpūjā; Ṣaṣṭhīdhyāna; Sandhyāvidhi; Govadhaprāyaścitta; Sāvitrīvrata, Rāma-navamī-vrata; Śyāmā-saparyā-vidhi; Lakṣmīpūjā; Sarasvatīpūjāpaddhati; Viśālākṣīpūjāmāhātmya; Śūdravivāhapaddhati; Śūdratarpaṇavidhi; Varṇa-jātisaṅkaramālā; Dūrgāṣṭamīvrata; Aśauca-saṁkṣepa; Vṛkṣapratiṣṭhāvidhi; Yajurvedīya-vāstuyāga; Yajurvedīya-kuśaṇḍikā.*

Jyotiṣa — *Horāṣaṭpañcāśikā; Sāmudraka; Rāśiphalavyākhyā; Subhaśakuna.*

Aṣṭaka — *Gaṅgāṣṭaka; Jagannāthāṣṭaka; Gauracandracaritāṣṭaka, Caitanyacandrāṣṭaka; Gopijanavallabhāṣṭka; Manaḥśikṣāṣṭaka.*

Āyurveda — *Rogaviniścaya; Nidāna.*

Sāhitya — *Kumārasambhava; Ghaṭakarparakāvya; Gītagovinda; Caurapañcāśaka* by Sundararāja; *Cāṇakyaśloka; Kāvyacandrikā* by Śukadeva; *Haṁsadūta.*

Darśana — *Vidhivicāra; Mīmāṁsānyāyaprakāśa; Mahāvākyasiddhānta* and *Ātmānātmaviveka* by Śaṅkarācārya; *Bhaktirasāmṛtasindhu; Gītābhāṣya; Avadhūtagītā; Brahmagāthā.*

Besides, the collection also comprises manuscripts of such Bengali texts as *Rasikarasodaya* by Rāmeśvara Dvija, *Draupadīr Vastraharaṇ Pālā, Satyanārāyaṇ-vrata-kathā,* etc. Also, five palm-leaf manuscripts in Oriya script, viz. *Acyutānandamālikā, Brahmāṇḍabhūgola, Yumaracarita* (2) and *Amaracarita,* all by Acyutānanda Dāsa and one manuscript in Grantha script (comprising 17 folios) adorn this collection.

Let this be put on record in this connection that almost all manuscripts in Sanskrit deposited here are in Bengali script scribed mostly on handmade paper and in some cases on palm-leaf. Similar is the case with Lc which is much richer in variety of content. Against *Jagaddhātrī-sahasra-nāma-stotra, Indrākṣīstotra, Śītalāstotra, Śanistotra, Navagrahastotra* in Museum collection, Lc has, for examples, *Vāsudevastotra, Vaiṣṇavastotra, Puruṣottama-stotra, Āditya-hṛdayastotra, Sāvitrī-stotra, Gaṇeśastotra, Stotra-saṁgraha, Devīśatanāmastotra, Rucistotra,* etc. in addition to *Caṇḍīśataka, Harikathāmṛta, Dvijāṣṭaka, Jagannāthavandanā, Bhāratasāvitrī, Śatasahasranāma,* etc. Both collections, however, have one copy each of *Mahimākhyā-stuti-vyākhyā* by Madhusūdana Sarasvatī. On Jyotiṣa, Lc has got *Samayapradīpa, Hāyanaratna, Jyotiṣtattva, Muhūrtacintāmaṇi, Jyotiṣacakra;* on Āyurveda: *Jvaratimirabhāskara, Jvaraśānti* and *Nakṣatradoṣopaśānti;* on Vrata: *Kārtikeyavrata, Vratamālā, Paramavaiṣṇavāparājitā-dvādaśa-yāgopavāsa-vrata,* etc.; on Sāhitya; *Raghuvaṁśa,*

Meghadūta, Bhaṭṭikāvya, Śiśupālavadha, Naiṣadhīyacarita (along with a commentary), *Ānandalaharī, Prahlādacarita, Anargharāghava, Prabodhacandrodaya* (and *ṭīkā* thereon), *Ratimañjarīṭīkā, Cāṇakyaślokamālā*; on Purāṇa and Epic: *Viṣṇu-Purāṇa, Brahmavaivartta-Purāṇa, Liṅga-Purāṇa, Narasiṁha-Purāṇa, Śrīmadbhāgavatakathāsaṁgraha, Mahābhārata* (*Virāṭa*), *Adhyātma-Rāmāyaṇa, Caṇḍī*; on Vaiṣṇavism: *Gopāla-caritakathā, Bhāgavatāmṛta, Govindavijaya, Tulasīcandrikā, Bhakticintāmaṇi, Premabhakti-candrikā, Vaiṣṇavavandanā, Harikathāmṛta, Govindalīlāmṛta, Gaurāṅgastavavṛkṣakalpa, Śrīkṛṣṇārjunakathā, Ujjvalarasa, Rādhārasakārikā*; on Nyāya philosophy: *Tattacintāmaṇi* and *Bhāṣāratna* (by Kaṇāda Tarkavāgīśa) and so on.

Works on various domestic rites, however, strike the highest number — *Divyatattva, Kṛtyatattva, Mahādānanirṇaya, Karmavipāka, Smārtavyavasthānvaya, Śivaliṅgapūjāvidhi, Śāktābhiṣeka, Adhivāsavidhi, Kālikāpurāṇoktadurgotsavavidhi, Aśaucamālā, Aśauca-saṁkṣepa, Daśasaṁskārapaddhati, Puraścaraṇavidhi, Puraścarṇaprayoga, Ravi°, Śanaiścara°, Rāhugraha°, Āhnikācāratattva, Mahiṣavalidāna, Śālagrāmacakranirūpaṇa, Samagra-śrāddhavidhi, Āraṇyaṣaṣṭhīvratakathā, Jalāśayotsargatattva, Ṛgvedivṛkṣotsarga, Yajurvediśrāddhatattva, Yajurvidāmadhivāsatattva, Yajurvidāmmaṭhapratiṣṭhāprayoga, Yajurvidām-Jalāśayotsargaprayoga, Sāmavedoktavratapratiṣṭhā-prayoga, Maṇḍapavidhi, Yajurvedivivāhapaddhati*, being some of the important manuscripts.

In Bengali language and script we have here *Caitanyacaritāmṛta, Caitanyamaṅgala, Śrīkṛṣṇamaṅgala, Rāsalīlā, Kṛṣṇamaṅgala, Bhāgavatāmṛta, Nāmasaṁkīrtana, Kṛṣṇakarṇāmṛta, Govinda-vijaya, Dhruvacarita, Śyāmā-kalpalatā, Vidvanmodataraṅgiṇī, Rasamayasaṅgīta, Kalaṅka-bhañjana, Rasabhāṣākāhinī, Kavicandrer Pālā, Sītādevīr Kāhinī, Dakṣayajñabhaṅga, Rāmagītā, Hariścandrer Upākhyān, Sudāmācarita, Phakirnāmer Pāñcālī, Vaiṣṇavapadāvalī, Śāktānandataraṅgiṇī, Sāradācarita*, etc.

As it is evident, a part of this treasure preserved now at Jorasanko under two separate heads (Mc and Lc) was collected by Kshitindranath Tagore with the help of such people as Satīśacandra Rāya, father of Parivrājaka Pañcānana Rāya of Vasudevpur, Midnapore, a village and its locality still famous for its traditional interest in and faithful devotion to various disciplines of Sanskritic learning. The family of Rāya is traditionally devoted to Sanskrit. As regular collectors of manuscripts they have been able to set in their dwelling house at their native villlage a manuscript library named after Pañcānana. Incidentally, the repository[11] named after Pañcānana Rāya comprises about 1,500 manuscripts (Bengali and Sanskrit) of which the following are noteworthy:

On Saṁkṣiptasāra, *Jumaravṛttī* Section I-VII, *taddhita-pariśiṣṭa*, Vaṁśīvadana's *Kṛdanta-ṭippanī*, Vidyālaṁkāra Bhaṭṭācārya's *Samāsa-ṭippanī*, Narottama Vidyālaṁkāra Bhaṭṭācārya's *kārikā* on *taddhita* and *Dīpikā* (*Sandhipāda*) by Nyāyapañcānana; *Kavikalpadruma* by Vopadeva; *Harināmāmṛta-vyākaraṇa*, *Viṣṇusargasandhi*; *Sārasvatacandrikā*; *Gītāsāra* (*Kṛṣṇārjuna-saṁvāda*); *Arthakaumudī* commentary on *Prabodhacandrodaya* by Gopālacakravartin; *Rudracaṇḍī* (*Rudrayāmala*, *Hara-Gaurī-saṁvāda*); *Āhnikatattva*, *Caṇḍīmaṅgala* by Akiñcanacakravartin; *Kālikā-Purāṇa*, *Śītalāmaṅgala*, *Jāhnavīmaṅgala*; Gopālacakravartin's *Bālabodhinī* commentary on *Adhyātmarāmāyaṇa*, Bhavadevabhaṭṭa's *Daśakarmapaddhati*; *Durgāṣṭamīvratakathā*, *Maṭhādipratiṣṭhāprayogatattva* by Maheśvara Nyāyālaṁkāra Bhaṭṭācārya.

---

11 (a) Pranab Roy, *Medinīpurer Itihās* (in Bengali), Kolkata, Sades 1st edn., 2009, pp. 544-82.

(b) "Panchanan Roy Manuscript Collection" in *Aspects of Manuscriptology*, Kolkata: The Asiatic Society Kolkata, 1st edn., 2005, repr. 2009, pp. 154-65.

Commentary on *Sāhityadarpaṇa* by Gopālacakravartin; *Mahāvākyaviveka-vyākhyā* by Rāmakṛṣṇa, Kaṇāda's *Bhāṣāratna; Koṣṭhīpradīpa Vṛṣotsargapramāṇa, Karmavipāka*, etc.

Needless to say, copy of some of the aforesaid works is available at Jorasanko Tagore House collections too and for obvious reasons one may be tempted to consider all these collections complementary to each other.

It is not clear whether Kshitindranath was selective during manuscript collection or he gathered at random whatever reached him on the way. This much we can say that even though a devout Brāhma leading his Samāja which was opposed to almost every traditional Hindu rite, Kshitindranath sincerely preserved a sizeable number of manuscripts offering prescription for performance of such socio-religious Hindu rites as propitiation of planets, placement of a holy pitcher, daily rites, planting of a tree, offering an ox in memory of the deceased, offering a buffalo in sacrifice, purification of a waterbody, expiation for killing a cow, worship of deities, viz. Kālikā/Śyāmā, Durgā, Lakṣmī, Annapūrṇā, Rādhā-Kṛṣna, Sarasvatī, Viśālākṣī, Agastya, Kārttikeya, etc. *vratas* relating to Sāvitrī, Janmāṣṭamī, Rādhāṣṭamī, Rohiṇyāṣṭamī, Rāmanavamī, Akṣaya, Kārttikeya, Ekādasī, etc. along with eulogy of devotees and deities including the folk deities, viz. Śītalā, etc. Texts on ascertaining a lineage (*gotra*), or, for that matter, occasional rites for śūdras, viz. in marriage, *tarpaṇa*, etc. and list of mixed castes also find pride of place herein.

Notably, works on distinctive rites for followers of *Ṛgveda, Sāmaveda* and *Yajurveda* were not left aside either. Purāṇic and epic tales and their Bengali adaptation also share space with *Satyapīrer Pāñcālī, Phakirnamer Pāñcalī* and *Kavicandrer Pālā* — all based on Bengali folklore. Same is the case with manuscripts of works, Sanskrit and Bengali, belonging to different sects including the Vaiṣṇavas. On literary criticism in Sanskrit of traditional variety, *Sāhityadarpaṇa* alone finds a place. With *Bhaktirasāmṛtasindhu* and *Ujjvalarasa* of the Gauḍīya Vaiṣṇavas the collection surely attained greater importance.

The other area of learning that deserves special mention here is Vyākaraṇa and, what strikes most, is a noticeable number of manuscripts on some non-Pāṇinian Sanskrit grammars and lexicon. Mc and Lc have got at their disposal more than 110 manuscripts belonging to this group. In the former we have fourteen belonging to *Saṁkṣiptasāra*, six on *Mugdhabodha*, one on *Sārasvata*, four on *Amarakoṣa* and one on *Ekākṣarakoṣa*, the most important grammatical works being *Lukcihnārthaprakaraṇa* (three copies), *Dhātucandrikā* by Rāmacaraṇa, *Nakārapradīpa* (with commentary), *Vakārapradīpa* (73 folios) by Pañcānanaśarman, *Varṇalopa*, *Ākhyātaprakriyā*, *Dhātumañjarī* (by Rāmaśaraṇa) and *Daśabhāṣā*. In Lc, too, the highest number of manuscripts on Vyākaraṇa goes to *Saṁkṣiptasāra* with each of the seven *pāda*s in multiple copies and *Kṛdantaṭippanī*, *Vṛttivivaraṇīṭīkā*, etc. though *Mugdhabodha* and *Kavikalpadruma*, *Liṅgaprakaraṇa*, *Dhāturūpaprakaraṇa*, *Śabdarūpaprakaraṇa*, *Kṛtpratyayaprakaraṇa*, *Durgasiṁhavṛtti* of the Kātantra school, *Lukcihnārthaprakaraṇa* (incomplete and brittle), *Sandhikaḍcā*, *Subantakaḍcā*, *Adhikaraṇakaumudī*, etc. also adorn the repository. It is not easy everywhere to identify the particular school to which a certain work belongs. Very often, more than one school might have been consulted for authoring a text. What is certain in that case is that different schools were thriving in a region in mutual cooperation. In Midnapore and adjoining districts of Bengal, *Saṁkṣiptasāra*, *Mugdhabodha* and *Sārasvata* schools had been predominantly nurtured while Kātantra had its home in eastern part of Bengal and on both sides of the Ganges. Interestingly, Abhirāma's *Kārakaṭippanī* of the *Saṁkṣiptasāra* school of which one manuscript collected from Vasudevapur is lying with the K.N. Tagore Centre indicates at one place that the commentator was prone to supporting the Mīmāṁsā viewpoint (*mīmāṁsā-pakṣapātitvāt*) whereas another *ṭippanī* by Vaṁsīvadana adopted Nyāya viewpoint in upholding the desired definition of agent case. A *darśana–vyākaraṇa* interaction of this type is indeed an interesting event in Bengal's intellectual traditions. An atmosphere of pluralism reigned almost everywhere in composition, deliberation and collection along with conservation of manuscripts.

It is quite natural that many of the titles occurring in Jorasanko and Vasudevpur collections are available in Varendra Research Museum (VRM), Rajshahi, Bangladesh[12] as the common cultural heritage, particularly in respect of religious and domestic rites while some others are not. A few important manuscripts in VRM may be cited here:

Ṛgvedīya-daśakarmapaddhati, Ṛgvedīya-pārvaṇa-śrāddha-prayoga, Ṛgvedīya-kuśaṇḍikā; Sāmagānāṁ-ghaṭasthāpana, Sāmavedapārvaṇa-śrāddha-prayoga; Chandogānāṁ-vṛṣotsarga-prayoga, Sāmavedīya-kuśaṇḍikāvidhi; Jagadīśvarīpūjā, Gajāśvādivadha-prāyaścitta, Kūpapratiṣṭhā, Kūpotsargavidhi, Amāvasyāvratakathā, Anantavrata-vidhi, Tālanavamīvrata (*Kūrmapurāṇokta*), *Vanadurgāpūjāvidhi, Tīrthayātrāvidhi, Viṣaharipūjāvidhi, Sarvadevapratiṣṭhenduśekhara, Sahagamanavidhi, Harināmasaṁgrahakavaca, Sāktānandataraṅgiṇī; Vidvanmodataraṅginī* by Cīrañjīva Bhaṭṭācārya, *Bhaṭṭiṭīkā* by Puṇḍarīkākṣa, *Ghaṭakarparaṭīkā* by Rājīvaśarman, *Rāmagītāṭīkā, Kāvyaprakāśaṭīkā* by Nyāyavāgīśa, *Rucistava* (from *Mārkaṇḍeya-Purāṇa*), *Satyanārāyaṇavratakathā, Satyanārāyaṇa-pūjāvidhi, Nakṣatraśānti, Kāvyacandrikā* by Rāmacandra; *Ratimañjarī, Janmāṣṭamīvrata*, etc.

---

12 *A Descriptive Catalogue of Sanskrit Manuscripts in the Varendra Research Museum*, vol. II, University of Rajshahi, Bangladesh, first printed in January 2007.

The most interesting part of this collection, however, relates to philosophical systems with special reference to Navya-Nyāya (numbering more than 150), Vaiśeṣika, Mīmāṁsā and Vedānta, *Tantravārttika, Padārthadharmasaṁgraha, Tantraratna, Pañcakoṣavivekavyākhyā, Yogaprakaraṇa* and *Yogyānupalabdhivāda* to name a few manuscripts. It transpires from the above that while Navya-Nyāya and Navya-Smṛti were widely studied, Mīmāṁsā was not left uncared for. Bengal's love of Prābhākara school of Mīmāṁsā was ridiculed in *Prabodhacandrodaya*. Whether subsequent centuries could keep up this interest in same vein or not is another question.

It is gratifying to note that National Mission for Manuscript extended its hand of cooperation though CUMRC and CUMCC towards preservation and conservation of the manuscripts lying with Rabindra Bharati University Museum and K.N. Tagore Centre[13] both housed at Jorasanko Thakurbari, Kolkata. Intensive counting and identification of stray folios are going on revealing that actual number of manuscripts at their disposal shall be much higher than that arrived at initially. A descriptive catalogue of these manuscripts is a desideratum. Some of them are unique in content and very few have been attended to till date. I would like to extend an open invitation to scholars for exploring this treasure house for their academic needs. Institutions, viz. Visva-Bharati, Rabindra Bharati and the like may join hands in organizing workshop, symposia, research and publication of critical edition from manuscript sources with the help of NMM. We look forward to launching such joint ventures in near future.

---

13 The author is thankful to curator, R.B.U. Museun and Director, K.N. Tagore Centre for placing tabular catalogue and handlist of MSS at his disposal for consultation and academic use.

3

The Anti-Colonial Approach in Arabic Manuscripts and Arabi–Malayalam Literature in Kerala

With Special Reference to Sixteenth–Nineteenth Centuries

N.A.M. Abdul Kader

It is a well-known historical fact that the Arabs had commercial relations with Kerala coast from very ancient time onwards and even before the advent of Islam. The Arab merchants had close familiarities and contacts with the Malabar region and the linguists and philologists attribute that the term Malabar had derived from such contacts of the Arabs. There are differences of opinion as to whether Islamic propagations started in these regions during the lifetime of Prophet or later. Anyhow, it has been established beyond doubt that Muslims had become a distinct community in Kerala by ninth century CE; and as a result, Arabic language has struck deep roots in the region at least in the first millennium.

The conversion of a Kerala king to Islam and his meeting with the prophet and his consent for propagation of Islam in the region are popular legends spread far and wide. It is known that Malik Dinar and his followers visited some of the harbour towns in Kerala and built the first mosque at Kodungallur and later built other mosques at Madayi and

Kasargod. The descendants of these first immigrants were known as Mappilas who extended their settlements to several harbour towns of the Malabar coast. The local rulers never prohibited conversion to Islam.

When Calicut became a prominent maritime trade centre by the end of fourteenth century, the Mappilas and the Arabs became a potential merchant class in the town with substantial economic resources. They enjoyed the major share of maritime trade in Calicut. In the village markets and trade centres they were able to achieve a prominent place with the active support of local rulers and landlords. Along with this progress in different localities they established their own *mahals*, mosques and *dars*, and strengthened their social organization.

Advent of the Portuguese

During the sixteenth century Muslims were compelled to fight against the Portuguese who struggled to establish their political and economic authority in Malabar. The advent of Portuguese on the western coast of Malabar had introduced new maritime regulations with regard to free trade. From the time of Vasco-da-Gama's arrival, the Portuguese sought monopoly in the lucrative spice trade from India. During his second visit in 1502 Vasco-da-Gama introduced a system of passes called Cartaz system wherein every ship plying Indian waters for trade had to carry cartaz issued by the Portuguese. They as a naval power established their authority over Asiatic waters and found that the vessels crossing the sea without their permission were pirates. This situation brought in a new political and economic condition in a fairly prosperous free trade harbour of Calicut.[1]

---

1 Captain G. Prakash, "Strategy and Technology in Maritime Warfare in Sixteenth Century: The Portuguese vs Forces on the Malabar Coast" Seminar paper, pp. 8-9.

The ruler of Calicut, King Zamorin, honouring his traditions of free trade initially allowed the Portuguese to buy spices despite his low opinion about them both for their conduct and quality of goods brought as gifts and for sales. But, the local Muslims since the very outset saw a danger and a clear threat to their traditional monopoly of trade about to be diluted. The Portuguese soon showed extreme cruelty by committing mass murder, mutilation and other depravation of the kind the locals were never used to. This was in fact willful employment of terror and might be an instrument of polity to facilitate their strategy of subduing a numerously superior opposition.

Naturally the economic ambitions, political designs and hidden religious motives of Portuguese were counteracted by the Muslims in different parts of Malabar. Anyhow, these conflicts and constant efforts for resisting the Portuguese domination gradually resulted in diminishing Muslims authority and prosperity in the region. The international trade in which the Arabs and the Mappilas jointly participated came to gradual decline due to the Portuguese intervention. The continuous encounters which had taken place between the Arabs and the Portuguese over a century for control of the Arabian Sea resulted in the withdrawal of the Arabs from Malabar. Later, when Malabar was exposed to colonial expansion by other European powers and their repeated conflicts and struggles for resources restricted the growth of the Mappilas also as a trading community.

This does not mean that Muslim community of Malabar has been reduced into total infirmity as a result of this setback. On the other hand, its members had shown sufficient dynamism and devotion that worked a common brotherhood even during the period that ensued. The emergence of the house of Kunjhali Marakkar as a house of naval commandants and their heroic struggles against Portuguese that lasted for more than a century remained a landmark in the history of resistance to colonialism in the Kerala regions. They were first rate admirals of the century who under the leadership of Zamorin led several encounters against the Portuguese for keeping up the independence of Arabian Sea. The last commandant from this house, Kunjhali Marakkar IV was executed in CE 1600 by the Portuguese in Goa. The leadership of the house had played considerable role in resisting the Portuguese advent in Gulf countries which were also included in their offensive and defensive strategies, and finally resulted in the independence of Red Sea countries.[2]

The encounters of the Mappilas against the Portuguese colonial forces gave birth to famous writings in Arabic, which may be the first forms of anti-colonial literature originated in the region. The most significant one was Sheikh Zainuddin Makhdum II's *Tuhfatul Mujāhideen* (CE 1538). He was the first historian of Kerala to write a historical account in Arabic. He has narrated the caste-oriented communities of Kerala and the beginning of the settlements of the Mappilas. The encounters against the Portuguese including the necessity of a holy war (*jihād*) against the Portuguese and the sufferings of the Mappilas were recorded in this work. His work propagated an anti-imperialist ideology in Malabar and all over the Arabic-speaking world.

Sheikh Zainuddin Makhdums II's grandfather Sheikh Zainuddin bin Ali, popularly known as Zainuddin Makhdum senior was also an ideologue against the Portuguese conquest. He even suggested a *Jihād* against them in his famous poem *Tahriḏ Ahlil Īmān 'Ala Jihādi 'Abadati S̱ulbān*. When the Zamorin

---

2 K.K.N. Kurup, *The Legacy of Islam* Kannur, Kerala: Samayam Publications, 2006, pp. 11-13.

and the Mappilas took steps to capture the fortress of Chaliyam, Qadi Muhammed bin Abdul Aziz wrote another poem named *al-Fath ul Mubeen* to inspire the military action. This poet inspired the Mappilas for a *jihād* against Portuguese. The *khutba* (Friday sermon) named *Al Khutbatul Jihādiyya* prepared by Qadi Muhammed to be delivered to those assembled before Chaliyam Fortress is another anti-colonial text. This text together with a poem named *Al Qaseedatul Jihadiyya* by the same author is a rare manuscript found out by this researcher quite recently after a hard labour. It may be specially remarked that the *jihād* initiated through these three texts was not to convert Darul Harb into Darul Islam, but contained a message to strengthen the authority of a Hindu ruler or the Zamorin. Such practices give a new meaning to *jihād* contrary to what was understood by many theologians during the British occupation.

The British occupation of Malabar did not contribute to the commercial, agricultural and social growth of the Mappila community. The rural poverty was made intensive and extensive during this period. The colonial administration introduced unhealthy changes in the *Kānam Janmam* system and other agrarian relations in Malabar. The tenants lost their fixity of tenure and were frequently evicted from their holdings. These developments made the Mappilas to turn against the landlords and the British administration. However the British land policy and revenue system made possible of land sales for revenue arrears. Those commercial and trading groups who had liquid capital could purchase lands and become landlords. Some of the Mappilas deposited their capital in land and became lords. However the ordinary people lost their houses and holdings.

These frustrations of the community turned to outbreaks in nineteenth century. The Khilafat movement in Malabar initiated by the Congress gave political leadership to the mobilization of the Mappilas. This development had finally turned to the Rebellion of 1921. When it was briefly suppressed several Muslim members were transported to Andaman Island. Many of them were killed in action and hundreds were hanged to death under the martial law. Leaders like Ali Musliyar spread an anti-imperialist ideology in Malabar particularly among the Mappilas.

Prior to 1921 and after several heroic Mappila songs were composed and propagated to rejuvenate the Mappila enthusiasm. These songs in Arabi–Malayalam, recollecting the heroic deeds of Shahids and also the anti-colonial ideology, inspired the Mappilas and activized them for any political programme. The major battles fought at the time of the Prophet like Badr, Uhd, Hunain and Khandaq as well as a number of local struggles including that of Malappuram, Cheroor and Puthanangadi were celebrated in this manner. These songs popularly known as *Padappāttu* (war songs) numbering above fifty remained a constant source of inspiration to the warriors and provided spiritual solace to the Mappila womenfolk who were mostly kept in loneliness and perpetual anxiety over the fate of their men in struggle. Such corpus of songs and many other contemporary compositions provide us with an invaluable branch of literature exclusively contributed by the Mappila community.[3]

During the period, the Mappilas as a separate religious community was exposed to puritan religious reforms by their scholars and the community as a whole was in search of its identity. The question of identity was more intensified in the colonial context as there were efforts on parts of the Christian missionaries to convert the lower segments of native society.

---

[3] Kurup, op. cit., pp. 15-17.

Therefore an ideological conflict was even taking place in the social order against the dominant sections in authority. The question of land, religion and identity came before the Mappila with all their intensity than any other time before. The great intellectual scholars like Sayyid Alavi Thangal, his son Sayyid Fadl Pookoya Thangal of Mamburam and Umar Qadi of Veliyankode, who lived in nineteenth century had an exceptional puritan approach to the religious and social affairs of the Mappilas. Umar Qadi had even issued *fatwā* criticizing the British and their revenue system. Sayyid Alavi Thangal had also taken a strong stand against the British rule and his tract *al Saiful Battār* advised a fight against the enemies of God till the end. He always stressed the unity of Islamic community and endorsed a revitalization among its members. His son Pookoya Thangal led the community more rigorously to the direction in which his father moved, and compiled several works exhorting the believers to defy and resist the colonial force.

Tahrid̠ Ahl il Īmān

Tharid̠ Ahl il Īmān 'Ala Jihādi 'Abadat al S̠ulbān is a poem of 135 lines composed by Sheikh Zainddin bin Ali al Ma'bari who was born in Cochin in CE 1467 and died in Ponnani in CE 1521. He was also known as Zainuddin Makhdum I, who having educated in Mecca and Madina for a long time later became the supreme Qadi of Ponnani who built the grand mosque of Ponnani and laid foundation to the Dars system of Islamic higher learning there.

The title itself means "Rousing the people of faith to struggle against the Portuguese". It was written at a time when the power of King Zamorin had considerably declined as a result of the continuous encounters against the Portuguese and that reduced the Muslims into a helpless situation. Sheikh Zainuddin depicts the barbarous nature of the Portuguese and narrates the atrocities committed by them against Muslims. He tries to sensitize the believers of the true situation with a view to awaken their spirit. He says:

فإنا كربنا بارتكاب شـــداند   بإفرنج عبّاد الصـــليب وصورة
طـــغوا في بلاد الله من كل ممكن   وقد اكثروا فيها الفســـاد بشهرة
بغوا في مليبار بأصـــناف بغيهم   وأنواع شـــدات وأجـــناس فتنة
من الأسر والنهبي وإحراق مسجد   وخرق كتاب ثم هـــتك لحرمة
وتحريق اموال وتخنيق مســـلم   وتعويق أسفار وتعطيل عيشـــة
تخريب بلدان وتعـــبيد مؤمن   وتزيين نسوان لتفتن نســـوة [4]

It means that the Muslims are in great grief due to the atrocities of the Portuguese, who worship the cross and image.

They transgressed beyond all bounds in the lands of God and resorted to all sorts of mischief openly.
They practised various sorts of violence in Malabar and caused many hardships and disorders,
by means of captivations, loot, burning the mosques, tearing Holy Book and violation of honour.
Burning the properties, fighting the Muslims, blocking the travel and stripping of livelihood.
Devastating the lands, enslaving the faithful
Fielding their women in charming attire for tempting Muslim women.

جهادهم فرض على كل مســـلم   قوي بنفـــس ثم زاد وعـــدة
حتى على عبد بلا اذن ســـيد   وولد بلا اذن وزوج قـــوية [5]
جزى الله من يغزوا جزاء موفرا   وأنقذهم من كل شـــر ومحـــنة
فيا أهل إســـلام وأمة احمد   هلموا الى هذه الجـــهاد بهمة
ففيه رضى الخلاق والخلق اسهم   وجن ووحش والطـــيور ودابة
ولا تجـــعلوا افرنج يا قوم اوليا   وان خفتم هلكا وفوت تجـــارة [6]
فان تهمـــلوا هذا الجهاد خسرتم   غنا دار دنيا ثم اخرى بحســـرة [7]

---

4 Sheikh Zainuddin bin Ali Al Ma'bari, *Tahrid ahlil Īman 'ala Jihadi 'abadat Sulbān,* lines 7-2.

5 Ibid., lines 26-27.

6 Ibid., lines 81-84.

7 Ibid., line 86.

He goes on describing their cruelties and oppression and finally calls the believers to get up and fall in line for *jihad* against those tormentors.

He found that it was the duty of all Muslims who have physical strength, provision and equipment to wage holy war against the Portuguese. As for slaves, they need not get permission of their masters, so also for children without requiring permissions, and for strong wife. May God give those who fight ample rewards and save them from any hardship and misery. O people of Islam, people of Prophet Ahmed, come on to this holy war with zeal and fervour. Therein lies the pleasure of the creator and creation including mankind, *jinn*, animals and birds. O people, you should never take the Portuguese as your friends or masters, even though you fear ruin and loss of trade. If you neglect this holy war, you will lose the riches of this world as well as of hereafter.

In this manner he roused the fighting spirit of the oppressed believers by citing the pleasures of heaven and warning those who desist from the battle and those who hesitate to spend their wealth for its sake, of hell fire and its horrors. Thousands of copies of this revolutionary poem were produced in writing and were sent to *mahal*s in various parts of Malabar, as a result of which several outbreaks have occurred. It may be under the influence of this poem that the house of Kunjhali Marakkars proceeded to Calicut and assumed leadership of the maritime warfare of Zamorin against the Portuguese.

Tuhfat ul Mujāhideen

Tuhfat ul Mujāhideen is a pioneering historical work written in sixteenth century CE. It is the first authentic work on the history of Kerala which was widely circulated among learned circles within Malabar as well as in the various parts of the world for more than three centuries. It was first printed in Lisbon in the year 1898 and the copy of which is still available in the library of the world famous Al-Azhar University of Egypt.

Sheikh Zainuddin Makhdum, the author, also known as Sheikh Zainuddin Makhdum II, was born at Chombal, near Mahe, North Malabar, in the sixteenth century. He was the grandson of Sheikh Zainuddin Makhdum I, the author of *Tahriḏ ahl al Īman* and many other works. The full title of the work is *Tuhfat al Mujāhideen fi ba'd Akhbar al Burthughāliyyin* (Tribute to the holy warriors in respect of a brief account of the Portuguese). The work consists of an introduction and four sections. The introduction sets forth the reasons which led the author to compile this narrative, mainly to stir up the Muslims into activity against the unbelievers who had invaded the territories of the Muslims and oppressed them. The first section deals with the merits of *jihād*, citing the verses of the Koran and the sayings of the Prophet that relate to the rewards for those who engage themselves in holy war against unbelievers. The second section gives an account of the first appearance of Islam in Malabar and the growth of various prosperous sea ports on the west coast. In the third section, the author enumerates the strange usages and customs of the Hindu inhabitants of Malabar and the treatment accorded to the Muslim subjects by the Hindu rulers. The fourth section is entirely historical, giving an account of the Portuguese from the time of their first arrival in Malabar in CE 1498 right up to CE 1583.

In this work the author describes the Portuguese atrocities in Malabar, particularly stressing on their animosity towards Muslims. The author narrates the condition of peace and prosperity that Muslims enjoyed in Malabar before the advent of Portuguese and compares it with the pathetic situation that ensued.

ان جمعا من المسلمين دخلوا في بنادر مليبار وتوطنوا فيها، ودخل أهلها في دين الله يوما فيوما، وظهر فيها الإسلام ظهورا بالغا حتى كثر المسلمون فيها وعمر بهم بلدانها مع قلة ظلم رعاتها الكفرة، وعدم تعديهم عن رسومهم القديمة، وأتاهم الله نعمة وسيعة، فغبروا على ذلك زمانا، ثم بدلوا نعمة الله كفرانا، اذنبوا وخالفوا فسلط الله عليهم اهل برتكال من الإفرنج خذلهم الله تعالى، فظلموهم، وأفسدوهم، واعتدوا عليهم بما لا يحصى من أصناف الظلم والفساد الظاهرة بين اهل البلاد، ومضوا على ذلك برهة من الأزمنة تنيف على ثمانين سنة، حتى آلت احوال المسلمين الى شر مآل من الضعف والفقر والذل، وصاروا لا يستطيعون حيلة، ولا يهتدون سبيلا، ولم يعتن بدفع ما حل بهم من البلاء والفتنة سلاطين المسلمين وأمراؤهم اعز الله انصارهم مع كثرة عساكرهم وأموالهم، بالجهاد وإنفاق الأموال في سبيل الله، لقلة اعتنائهم بأمور دينهم، وإيثارهم الدنيا الفانية على آخرتهم، فجمعت هذا المجموع ترغيبا لأهل الإيمان في جهاد عبدة الصلبان، فإن جهادهم فرض عين لدخولهم بلاد المسلمين، وأيضا أسروا منهم من لا يحصى كثرة وقتلوا منهم كثيرين، وردوا جملة منهم الى النصرانية، وأسروا المسلمات المأسورات، حتى خرج لهم منهن اولاد نصارى، يقاتلون المسلمين ويؤذونهم. 8

A party of foreign Muslims entered some of the seaports of Malabar and settled there. In course of time, the inhabitants of these towns began to embrace Islam day by day. Before long, Islam spread all over the region at great pace and Muslim population began to grow and soon in the cities of Malabar heralded the settlement of Muslims in big numbers. In those days, they did not face any kind of opposition or oppression from the non-Muslim rulers who were then in power. As for these rulers, they continued to live adhering fully to their own ancient religion and its rites and practices.

Thus Muslims continued to live in peace and prosperity by the boundless grace and blessings of Allah. But this condition did not last long. The Muslims began to deviate into sinful living, forgetting the blessings of Allah and disobeying Him, and then Allah sent the cruel and wicked Portuguese Europeans to dominate over them.

The Portuguese invaded the Muslim abodes and subjected them to all kinds of oppressions. The abominable atrocities and cruelties the Portuguese openly unleashed on Muslims were countless. This Portuguese reign lasted for more than eighty years. By that time, the condition of the Muslims had become extremely pathetic. They had become impoverished,

---

8 Sheikh Zainuddin bin Ali Al-Ma'bari, *Tuhfat at Mujāhideen*, ed. Hamza Chelakodan, Calicut, 1996, p. 14.

> weak and powerless. They could not find a way to get out of this wretched hole. And the militarily and economically powerful Muslim sultāns and *amīrs* reigning elsewhere did not come forward to rescue the Malabar Muslims from the calamity that had befallen on them. The reason was that these sultāns and *amīrs*, having little interests in religion and who loved this transient world more than the next, would not struggle (*jihād*) in the path of Allah and spend their wealth in His cause.
>
> I have undertaken the composition of this book in these circumstances. I have composed this with the intention of giving inspiration of the believers to wage war (*jihād*) against the cross-worshipping Portuguese. The occasion for this effort is the fact that waging a holy war has become an obligation of all individual Muslims as the Portuguese had invaded and occupied the Muslim abodes. They killed innumerable Muslims. Those who were caught, bound and confined were countless in number. Many were forcefully converted to Christianity. Kidnapping Muslim woman and raping them in custody to produce Christian children was rampant. Their intention behind these deeds was to prepare these children to harass and fight the Muslims when they are grown up.[9]

The author has made it clear in unambiguous terms that the intention of the narration is nothing but rousing the believer to fight against the oppressive colonialists. He elucidates that it was only by the sincere support of Muslim-friendly Zamorin, the Muslims who lacked a powerful leader of themselves — could keep fighting the foreign enemies. He also accuses Muslim sultāns and *amīrs* for not taking any interest in the affairs of the Muslims of Malabar:

---

9 Sheikh Zainuddin, *Tuhfat al Mujāhideen*, tr. M.H. Hussain Nainar, Calicut, 2006, pp. 4-5.

ولا يخفى ان مسلمي مليبار ليس لهم أمير ذو شوكة يحكم عليهم ويراعي مصالحهم بل كلهم رعايا الكفرة ومع هذا كانوا جاهدوهم وصرفوا في جهادهم الأموال على قدر طاقتهم بمعونة محب المسلمين السامري وإنفاقه الأموال في أول مرة حتى ضعف المسلمون بتعطيل تجاراتهم وإهلاك نفوسهم وتخريب ديارهم وأموالهم، وهكذا مرارا حتى ازداد ضعفهم واشتد فقرهم وفاقتهم وعجزوا ولم يعتن بأحوالهم سلاطين المسلمين وأمراؤهم - أعز الله انصارهم - مع وجوب الجهاد عليهم [10]

The author appreciates and praises lavishly the Hindu rulers of Malabar for their tolerance and friendly relations with their Muslim subjects, after pointing out the fact that the places like Calicut, Veliyankode, Tirurangadi, Tanur, Ponnani, Parapanangadi, Paravanna, the localities surrounding Chaliyam port, Kakkad, Tikkodi, other localities surrounding Panthalayani, Kannur, Edakkad, Mahe, Chemmanad, the localities surrounding Dharmadam on its south Valapattanam and Nadapuram, on the south Kodunagallur, Kochi, Vypeen, Pallippuram and several other coastal areas became thickly populated and grew into towns with thriving trade and commerce, all because of Muslims.

لما دخلوا مليبار وعمروا المساجد في البنادر المذكورة وفشا فيها دين الإسلام دخل أهلها في الدين قليلا قليلا ووصل إليها التجار من أطراف كثيرة وعمرت بلاد غيرها مثل كاليكوت، وبلينكوت، وتروررنغادي، ثم تانور، ثم فنان، وبربورنغادي، ثم برونور من حوالي بندر شاليات ومثل كابكات وتركودي وغيرهما من حوالي فندرينة ومثل كننوز، وادكاد، وترونكاد، وميلي وجمنيا من حوالي درمفتن وفي جنوبيها بدفتن، ونادورم وفي جنوبي كدنغلور كشي، ويت، وبلبرم وكذا غيرها من البنادر وكثر فيها سكانها وعمرت بالمسلمين وتجاراتهم لقلة ظلم رعاتها مع كونهم وكون عساكرهم كفرة ومع رعايتهم عاداتهم المتقدمة وعدم مخالفتهم لها الا نادرا والمسلمون فيها رعايا وقليلون لا يبلغون عشر معاشيرهم. [11]

He asserts in the above lines:

> The Muslims and their trade prospered because of the great tolerance with which the rulers and their military, though they were Hindus, treated the Muslims. They were not Hindus only in name, but pious people who strictly observe their ancestral customs and rites in Practice. Seldom did

---

[10] Sheikh Zainuddin, *Tuhfat al Mujahideen*, ed. C. Hamza, Calicut, 1996, p. 18.

[11] Ibid., p. 24.

> they do anything amiss so far as their religious rites were concerned. The Muslims then were, in fact, their subjects and not even accounted one-tenth of the population. Yet, they did not treat the Muslims in any way hostile or unfriendly except on rare occasions.[12]

K.K.N. Kurup, the renowned historian of Malabar remarks:

> Thucidides had given a detailed account of the Peloppenacian wars. In the same way Zainuddin had become Thucidides of Kerala by writing this historical account of Kerala's resistance against the Portuguese. The great achievement of Zainuddin was his devotion to Islam and its philosophy. He was a pragmatist and tried his best to inspire the native elements in a total fight against the Portuguese in the sixteenth century. His notion of a *jihad* was not to convert the Darul Harb into Darul Islam but to safeguard the interest of the native ruler, the Zamorin. Such a broad mind in a theologian was not generally found in the middle ages. Thus his philosophy has relevance even in the present century in a total fight against the ideology of neo-colonialism which consolidates the resources all over the world.[13]

Al Fath ul Mubeen

Qadi Muhammed bin Abdul Aziz of Calicut who passed away in CE 1616 (AH 1025) was a renowned philosopher, poet and *sūfī*. He had composed more than twelve works and profusely contributed to the growth of Arabi–Malayalam literature. He was the Qadi of Calicut and the spiritual leader of Muslims belonging to Qadiri *sūfī* order founded by Sheikh Muhyiddin Abdul Qadir al Jeelani of Baghdad. His composition of

---

12 *Tuhfat al Mujahideen,* tr. M.H. Hussain Nainar, p. 45.

13 K.K.N. Kurup, *The Legacy of Islam*, p. 79.

Muhyiddeen māla a ballad in Arabi–Malayalam paying rich tribute to Sheikh Abdul Qadir al Jeelani was a landmark in the literary history of Malabar and a great contribution to Islamic devotional literature.

The most significant work of Qadi Muhammed is *al Fath ul Mubeen,* which is on a historic theme and it seems that he was an eyewitness to those events which determined the course of the Portuguese political power in the history of Kerala. This war poem was written in CE 1579. The text was a criticism of communal intolerance and atrocities committed by the Portuguese in Kerala. While narrating a historical event of 1571, the conquest of Chaliyam fortress constructed by Portuguese on the right bank of the river of Beypore at Chaliyam, the poet had also shown that only a united movement of Muslims and Nair warriors could resist the Portuguese intrigues and political designs. As he was the Qadi of Calicut, the poem also reflected his loyalty and patriotism in favour of the ruler, the Zamorin. His loyalty towards the ruler was deep. The main motivation of a poem like this, as expressed by the poet, was to obtain the blessings of God. For a Muslim, patriotism is a way to godly blessings.[14] Full title of poem is *Al Fath ul Mubeen li Samiriyyi Alladhi Yuhibbu al Muslimeen. Al Fath ul Mubeen* means the manifest victory and the rest denotes that it has been dedicated to Zamorin who loves Muslims. It may be found strange that such a great Islamic scholar and spiritual leader had celebrated a manifest victory gained for a Hindu ruler in 537 lines which was also dedicated to him.

He starts the narration qualifying Zamorin as Muslim-friendly:

---

[14] Kurup, op. cit., pp. 73-74.

فإن هذي قصـــــة عــــجيبة　　في شرح حرب شـانها غريبة
واقعـــــة في خطـــة المليبار　　ومثلها لم يجر في تلك الـــديار
بين محب المسلمين السامري　　وبين خصـــــمه الفرنج الكافر

Let me narrate a wonderful story of a strange war
broke out in Malabar province,
The like of which had never occurred in that province before.
This occurred between Zamorin, the lover of Muslims
and his antagonists the ungrateful Portuguese.

He goes on describing the virtues and noble qualities of Zamorin:

وعلها تســـير فـــي الأفاق　　لا ســـيما في الشام والعراق
ويعلموا لهمة الســـــلطان　　السامري المشهور في البلدان
وهو محب ديننا الإســــلام　　والمســـــلمين بين ذا الأنام
ناصر ديننا ومجرى شرعنا　　حتى بخطبة على ســـلطاننا
والمســـــلمون كلهم رعيته　　وإن يكن في أي أرض بلدته [15]

The world famous Zamorin's mental strength
Be known to the whole world,
Particularly in the foreign countries of Syria and Iraq.
He likes our religion, and loves
Muslims than all others.
He helps our religion and
Implements our religious laws
In Malabar, or wherever the Muslims live
They are his subjects.

The poet admires the commitment of Nair soldiers and praises the ruler again and again. This ruler will not attack any other country without a reason and he will not confiscate the property of anyone. He will not adopt dubious and treacherous methods in a war. He is also a man of vision, strategy, courage, patience and forgiveness:

---

15 *Al Fath ul Mubeen*, lines 14-19.

لا يأخذ المال بغير جرم   وليس يؤذي أحدا بظلم
لا يأخذ البلدان ممن دونه   وإن عصوا يعفوا بما يهدونه [16]
ويخبر الأعدا بوقت حربه   ليستعد خصمه بحربه
فخرا لدى الملوك بالشجاعة   اذ حرب غير السامري بالخدعة [17]
ذو الرأي والتدبير والشجاعة   والصبر والعفو لدى الشفاعة [18]

Then he prays for the Zamorin's welfare and proclaims that it is the duty of every Muslim to pray like that:

فواجب على جميع المسلمين   ان يدعوا بمثل ذا يا مسلمين [19]

While applauding the ruler's will to fight for his religion and religion of Muslims, he finds fault with other Muslim rulers for their inaction and compromise with enemies (lines 50-51):

لأنه مع كفره يحارب   والملك المسلم لا يحارب
لأجل دينهم ودين المسلمين   لكنهم قد صالحوا للكافرين [20]

He describes the ugly features, unruly behaviour and barbarous dealings of the Portuguese:

فاستمعوا قصة حرب السامري   يا أيها الناس بقلب حاضر
وذاك ان اخبث الخلائق   المقتدي لا نجس الطرائق
اعدى عدو الله والرسول   ودينه وأمة الرسول
وهو الفرنجي عابد الصلبان   وساجد الصورة والأوثان
كريهة الهيئة والأشكال   ازارق العينين كالأغوال
يبول كالكلب ومن يطهر   فخارج عن دينه فيزجز
ذو المكر والطغيان والخديعة   ابعد خلق الله عن طهارة

كذاك اجرى ما جرى من امره   ولا نطيق حصره بذكره
من حرق بلدان وهدم مسجد   وجعله للخلق مثل الأعبد
وقتلهم من غير ذنب صادر   وظلم كل وارد وصادر [21]

---

16 *Al Fath ul Mubeen*, lines 34-35.

17 Ibid., lines 41-42.

18 Ibid., line 44.

19 Ibid., line 49.

20 Ibid., lines 50-51.

21 Ibid., lines 52-58.

So, O people listen to the war tale of Zamorin in rapt attention.
The worst sort of human beings who follows the most impure way,
The staunchest enemy of Allah, His messenger,
His religion and the community of the messenger.
He is the Portuguese, the worshipper of cross
who prostates before idols and images;
Despicable in figure and appearance
feline eyed like devils.
He urinates like the dog and whoever cleans for it
outcasted by them and driven away.
Master of trickery, aggression, betrayal
most distant from cleanliness.
Thus they made several similar attacks
those beyond any reckoning.
They burnt countries, demolished mosques
kept the men as slaves.
They killed many innocent persons
harassed those who pass by.

The poet threw light on the violation of civil rights of the indigenous especially in lines 168-96. The Portuguese even compelled their enemies "to eat one's own flesh and to shoot arrows themselves into their bodies":

ونزلة يطعمه بلحمه   ودفعة يهدفه لسهمه [22]

In the early stages of the battle narrated here, there were several setbacks to the soldiers of the Zamorin. Then the Zamorin himself marched to a nearby hill and proclaimed that he will go on starvation till the fortress was captured by him. The Mappilas then declared a *jihād* against the Portuguese and initiated a life and death struggle with a single motivation

22 *Al Fath ul Mubeen*, line 188.

that their ruler should not go without food and prolong his vow of starvations.

Finally the Nairs and Mappilas succeeded in capturing the Portuguese fortress with great valour and heroism. Here *jihād* was declared to support a local ruler who was the follower of Hinduism. In fact, it was not to crown a Muslim ruler or for making a country of non-Muslims into a country of Muslims. Even the meaning of *jihād* is demanded re-interpretations in social and theological conceptualizations. The texts like *Al Fath ul Mubeen* and their ideologies be brought out to the masses for promoting communal harmony, spirit of nationalism and patriotism. Only such efforts would be able to resist the onslaught of neocolonialism in developing and multi-religious countries like India.[23]

Al- khutbat ul Jihadiyya

This another anti-colonial text by Qadi Muhammd of Calicut in the form of a *khutba* prepared by him and sent to Chaliyam fortress and neighbouring mosques during the war narrated in *al Fath ul Mubeen;* to be delivered there by the preacher most probably as a Friday sermon. This is a unique document remained unknown to the outside world and found out only recently in the course of the survey conducted by this researcher for National Mission for Manuscripts and procured by one of his students following a hard task.[24]

---

23 K.K.N. Kurup, *The Legacy of Islam*, p. 76.

24 It was kept hidden in a volume of several works bound together and among a number of other handwritten books at the house of Pangil Ahamed Kutty Musliar, a highly-renowned Islamic scholar of the last century. The student visited this repository several times in search of this work and could find it out only after a highly tiresome effort. The student is M.K. Abdu Rahman Kutty Faidi, a UGC Junior Research Fellow under my supervision in the Department of Arabic, University of Calicut.

It is a highly instigative speech in written form composed with a view to stimulate the faithful towards a hard battle against the Portuguese till the achievement of total victory. A number of Koranic verses and sayings of Prophet were cited to awaken the spirit of the Muslim warriors who had been assured of either reward and booty or honorable martyrdom and ensuing eternal bliss.

Following the abundant quotations from Holy Koran and due formalities of speech it enters into an open call for *jihād* against the hostile aliens, the Portuguese who entered Malabar and created all sorts of mischief there.

أيها الناس من أراد الجهاد فهذا أوانه، ومن ابتغى السعادة العظمى فهذا إبانه، فان النصارى عبدة الأصنام والأوثان، قد خطوا في اقليم مليبار في كل بلدان، وأكثروا فيه الصولة والفساد،واظهروا انواع التعدي والعناد،وهدموا مباني الإسلام، ومحوا شعائر الأحكام، وتسلطوا على المسلمن تسلط المالك على المملوك، وأذلوا الجبابرة من السلاطين والملوك، وملكوا بسطوة بلأدهم، وملأوا من خيفة اكبادهم، حتى ازالوا رسمهم واسمهم، واخرجوا دموعهم ودمهم، وتحصنوا بالقلعة والمدافع، وليس لقلعها حيلة ولا مدافع، قد ايتموا بقتلهم الولدان، وأرملوا الإماء والنسوان، وخربوا اكناف البلاد، وابطلوا معائش العباد، وعطلوا المسافرة والتجارة، وعوضوا لربحها الخسارة، كم من مسلم في حبسه مقيدون، وأي محنة بها يعذبون، كم من مراكب بنار احرقوه، كم من سفائن ببحر اغرقوه، كم من مسلم قد دخلوا في دينهم قهرا، ومنعوا طرق المسلمين برا وبحرا، أحرقوا المصحف والمساجد وعمروا في اماكنها الكنائس والمعابد، ونبشوا بظلمه قبورا، وشيدوا بحجرها قصورا، وهتكوا بين المحارم حرمة النسوان، وعذبوا المسلمين بعذاب اهل النيران، وجعلوا المؤمنين ذبيحتهم، واموالهم غنيمتهم، قد نزع الله من قلوبهم الرحمة، كأنهم لم يخلقوا الا من النقمة.[25]

O people whoever intends *jihād*, this is the occasion. Whoever aspires to the highest success this is the day. The Christians, the worshippers of idols and images have indeed entered into every locality of Malabar region. They have proliferated onslaughts and atrocities. They set forth different means of transgression and torture. They demolished Islamic edifices. They obliterated rules of governance. They have dominated over the Muslims, domination of a master over his slave. They put powerful *sultāns* and kings to disgrace, took over hegemony of their lands, filled their hearts with fear, even wiped out their

25 Qadi Muhammed bin Abdul Aziz, *Al-Khutba al Jihadiyya*, unpublished text, pp. 3-4.

> signs and names, shed their tears and blood and strengthened their position with the fortress and canons; leaving not any artifice and canons to get destroyed. They orphaned children by their murders. They widowed ladies and dames. They destroyed shadows of the land. They took away livelihoods of the people. They left traders and travellers without work; and compensated their profit with loss. How many Muslims were confined in their prisons! What a catastrophe that has been afflicted! How many vessels they did set fire! How many ships in the sea they drowned! How many Muslims were entered into their religion by force! They blocked routes of Muslims both land and sea. They burned holy books and mosques. They erected in their places churches and houses of worship. They flattened graves without any authority. They abused the women in the presence of kith and kin. They tormented Muslims like people of hell. They reduced Muslims to their scapegoats, and their wealth to their booties. Allah has indeed taken away mercy from their hearts; as though they were created out of nothing but grudge.

Then the text congratulates those who came forward to wage *jihād* and those who supported the fight by their wealth. It reminds that death is an inevitable end from which no one can escape. Running away from the battlefield is the meanest act and courting death there is the greatest honour one can achieve. It goes on inciting those around to heroic fight by illustrating the alluring rewards reserved for martyrs in the heaven.

A paragraph is set apart for elucidating special rewards assured for taking part in the maritime warfare, which is described as ten times more superior to a war in land. Every sin including debt will be forgiven to a martyr of sea, when in the case of a martyr of land, the debt has been excluded. The farmer will not feel the pain of weapon but as delicious as a chilled nectar taken by one when he is thirsty.

واحثكم على الغزو في البحر، فان غزوة في البحر افضل من عشر غزوات في البر، وكفى لغزوة البحر شرفا بقول سيد البشر، من فاته الغزو معي فليغز في البحر، ومن اجاز البحر فكأنما اجاز الأودية بقدمه، والمائد في البحر كالمتشحط في البر في دمه، وان ملك الموت يقبض روح كل شريد وغيره الا ارواح شهيد البحر، فان الله يتولى قبض ارواحهم لكرامتهم عنده على شهيد البر، ويغفر لشهيد البر الذنوب كلها الا الدين، ولشهيد البحر يغفر له الذنوب والدين، ولا يجدون ألم السلاح الا كشربة عسل، بماء بارد على الظما [26]

This text was prepared by a great scholar of Islamic theology, a mystic and Qadi of Calicut Sheikh Muhammed bin Abdul Aziz in order to rouse the valour and boost the morale of those Muslim fighters who surrounded the Chaliyam fortress to conquer it for the ruler Zamorin. The *jihād* mentioned here was not in any way to establish Muslim supremacy over the land, but in fact favouring a Hindu ruler of the land to strengthen his hands, especially his maritime power.

Al Qaseedat ul Jihadiyya

This is another valuable text found out together with *al Khutbat ul Jihādiyya* mentioned earlier in the course of the survey conducted under the leadership of this researcher, quite recently. A poem in 43 lines composed by the same author Qadi Muhammed in the same context of the war for capturing Chaliyam Fort and subsequent victory secured by the allied forces of Muslims and Nairs under the leadership of the ruler Zamorin. At the outset, he congratulates the Muslim fighters for winning this decisive victory over the Portuguese and celebrates their courage, dedication and heroism.

ألا أيها الســــادات اهل الشجاعة   ومن بهم الإســـلام حل بذروة
ويا من غدا بين الأنام مـــجاهدا   بمال وروح ثم نـــفس كريمة
لقد شاع في الآفاق صيت جهادكم   وقتلكم الأعداء في وســط لجة
فطبتم وبعتم بالجنان نفوســكم   ونلتم رضـــاء الله مع كل نعمة
واعطاكم الرحمن أجرا بلا انتها   باخرى وفي الدنيا فوز الغـــنيمة [27]

---

26 Qadi Muhammed bin Abdul Aziz, *Al-Khutba ul Jihadiyya*, pp. 7-8.

27 Qadi Muhammed bin Abdul Aziz, *al Qaseedat ul Jihadiyya* (unpublished text), lines 1-7.

O the leaders, men of courage and those
who are fascinated by Islam utmost.
O the one who turned fighter from the folk,
With wealth, spirit and his own noble self.
Reputation of their jihād *indeed spread far and wide*
for also slaying of enemies in the depth of sea.
You, done well and sold yourselves for Heaven
Won pleasure of God with all blessings together.
Bestowed by the Most Gracious unending reward
And treasures of booty in the world on other hand.

Then he turns to be an admonisher and warns those fighters who might be carried away by material motives, and they spoil divine blessings of this world and alluring rewards reserved for them in the hereafter. From the context it is understood that a small number of fighters might have misbehaved after gaining the victory by attacking some ships passing by the sea with the aim of looting the sailors belonging to their own community. The poet condemns such tendencies in emphatic terms:

وبعضهم قد باع أجر جهادهم   بظلمهم في البحر أهل السفينة
فصاروا كقطاع الطريق بأخذهم   لأموال بعض المسلمين بلجة
فمن ثم قل النصر وارتفع العدا   عليهم وكانوا غالبين بنصرة [28]
وكل يقول الحمد لله شاكرا   اذا مات عبد ظالم للبرية
لأن بظلم العبد ينقص رزقهم   كذا يرفع البركات في كل بلدة
وينزل من فوق السماء لكم بلا   ويسلب الإيمان عند المنية [29]

Some of them have sold their reward for their struggle,
They attacked shipmen in the sea.
Thus they turned into robbers by plundering

---

[28] *Al Qaseedat ul Jihadiyya.*, lines 7-9.

[29] Ibid., lines 13-15.

wealth of some believers in the depth of the sea.
So came down the success, enemies rose high
they prevailed over by (divine) assistance.
A person hostile to mankind when he dies
All say 'Al Hamdulillah' thanking Almighty.
For by hurting fellow beings their provisions grow less
Everywhere else will go high the blessings.
Calamity befalls upon you from above the heavens
And at the demise you will be stripped of your faith.

In the concluding lines he reminds that mutual admonition is the duty of every believer and clarifies that his intention while giving this advice is genuine and free from any ill-feeling. He asks for forgiveness if anybody felt otherwise.

Arabi–Malayalam Literature

Arabi–Malayalam is a unique form of expression developed by Malabar Muslims. It is Malayalam language written in sophisticated Arabic script. A number of sounds in Arabic tongue do not have corresponding phonic forms in Malayalam. Even the very fundamental terms of Islamic doctrine "Allah" and "Muhammad" cannot be transliterated retaining its purity. The Arabic alphabet comprises twenty-eight letters. Of these, thirteen letters lack phonic equivalents in Malayalam. The only solution that scholars of early Muslim generations in Kerala could find is to use Arabic script for Malayalam, and this is what has happened as a virtual inevitability. Most regional languages of India had adopted the sophisticated Arabic script in Islamic societies which gave rise to Arabi–Tamil, Arabi–Kannada, Arabi–Bengali, etc. in same manner. The languages in other cultures had undergone the similar transformation while interacting with Arabic and the original scripts of some of them had even totally surrendered to Arabic. The Pahlavi scripts of Persians, for instance, virtually became defunct by the over-riding deployment of Arabic script.[30-31]

---

30 M.N. Karasseri, *Arabic in South India,* University of Calicut, 2003, pp. 126-28.

31 Arabic–Malayalam was developed as a dialect of Muslim intelligentsia, for the purpose of communication among themselves and a separate branch of literature developed in that dialect. It was neither Arabic nor Malayalam but an admixture of both. The Muslim community, in general, was familiar with the Arabic letters and scripts. The language used by them was Malayalam but words from Arabic, Persian and Urdu languages were liberally borrowed into it. The literature of Arabi–Malayalam can be divided into prose and verse, out of which verse was more popular. It is generally known as Mappila songs (*Mappila Pāttus*) that includes hymns that eulogize the holy figures, martial songs, moral lessons, songs of praise addressed to god, historical documents of holy events, love lyrics and wedding songs.

The first work in Arabic–Malayalam verse, as per the generally accepted view, is *Muhyiddin Māla,* which is a devotional song that celebrates the greatness of Sheikh Muhyiddin Abdul Qadir of Jilan and renders the major events, especially the miraculous feats of his life. *Badar Māla, Nafeesat Māla, Manjakkulam Māla, Mamburam Māla, Malappuram Māla* and *Makhdoom Māla* are some other works of this sort.

Martial songs known as *padappāttu* is another main branch of Arabi–Malayalam verse, which was enriched by over fifty songs the most prominent being *Badar Padappāttu, Uhad Padappāttu, Makkam Fatah, Futūhu Sham, Husain Padappāttu* and *Khantaq Padappāttu,* all narrating the wars fought by Muslims in Arabia during the early period of Islamic propagation. Later these sorts of songs were also composed about local riots like that of Malappuram, Cherur and Puthangandi. The major contributions of Moyinkutty Vaidyar (1852-92) — the all time celebrity of *Mappilappāttu* — belong to this genre. Since such poems carried anti-colonial message and remained a constant source of inspiration and spirit of sacrifice, a large number of those were proscribed or destroyed by the rulers of the period.

The heroic Mappila songs composed during the colonial period in Malabar were propagated to rejuvenate the Mappila enthusiasm. For instance, the legend of *Mānāth Parambil Kunhi Marakkār Shahīd* or the *Ballad of Kottuppalli Nercha* provides a theme of martyrdom. Every year this festival is conducted by the local community of the Mappilas to cherish the memory of this martyr the hero lived at Manath in Veliyankode, near Ponnani. He had courted martyrdom fighting against the Portuguese in order to rescue a Muslim girl who had been captured by them and taken to their ship. He was the first martyr of Malabar in an anti-colonial encounter. His body was cut into pieces by a soldier, which had fallen to far-off places. It is believed that his bodily remains were kept in a small structure at Manath. The *Maulūd* or recitation of this ballad or conduct of such a song ritual is generally organized for divine blessings, cure of diseases and fulfilment of desires. The *Kottuppalli Nerchappāttu,* a ritualistic song, reflects the entire legend of heroic martyrdom of Marakkar. The narration begins according to the customary practice in the name of God and praying for His blessings.

ആദി ബിസ്മില്ലാഹി ഹംദും ഓതി ബിസ്മില്ല
            അഹ്മദ് അന്ന്ബി ആലിലും അസ്ഹാബിൽ സലാമുള്ളാ
ആദരിച്ചോതും കവിതക്ക് അതുവിയും താ അള്ളാ
            കുഞ്ഞിമരക്കാർ ശഹീദിൻ ചരിതം ഇൻശാഅള്ളാ
വെളിയങ്കോട്ടെ പതിക്ക് ഊര് മാനാത്ത് എന്നേ
            വീട്ടിൽ അബ്ദുള്ള എന്നോർ പ്രിയ പുത്രനായി
വളരെ വാത്സല്ല്യത്തിൽ മാതാവ് വളർത്തിയേ
            വേണ്ടറിവും പടതൊഴിലും കരഗതമാക്കിയേ [32]

In the name of Allah, praise be to Allah,
Peace be upon the Holy Prophet and his family.
O Allah, bestow me well being so as to complete
    the ballad of great martyr Kunhi Marakkar.
The beloved son of Abdullah, born in
    the house of Manath in the village of Veliyankode.

---

32 *Kottuppalli Nerchappattu,* lines 1-4.

With great love and affection, the mother brought him up.
He acquired knowledge and also fighting skill.

The ballad recited in *Maulūd* depicts the heroic martyrdom of Islamic scholar, who from his own wedding occasion decided to be a martyr to safeguard the honour of a Muslim girl. *Kottuppalli Māla* a ritualistic song composed by an unknown poet, reflects the entire legend of heroic martyrdom of Marakkar. The mosque and the sacred burial had created a popular culture around the historical event of a native confrontation against the Portuguese. A network of events, patterns of religious behaviours, concept of martyrdom and legends had promoted the Islamic identity and its own popular culture in the annals of history of Malabar. The Muslim community has created its own cultural environment for this purpose with supernatural events and myths.

Ramanthali Shuhadāmāla 17 in Arabi–Malayalam and *Shuhadā Moulid* in Arabic also are devotional texts bearing anti-colonial message. The Portuguese had founded a small settlement in Ramanthali village near Ezhimala of North Malabar, which was fortified and known as Kottappuram (place with fort). Since several centuries there had also been a Muslim settlement at that place. As the Portuguese were in animosity against the Muslim inhabitants the latter were exposed to constant sufferings from the new settlers. In this circumstance the Muslims decided to fight against the Portuguese and an encounter between them took place in CE 1524 at Ramanthali, in which seventeen Muslim heroes had courted martyrdoms. This incident, which was also referred in *Tuhfat al Mujahideen,* was exalted and the exploits of these heroes were recollected in a traditional *Maulūd* in Arabic and in *Ramanthali 17 Shuhadamala* in Arabic–Malayalam.

In the encounter, these martyrs were cut into pieces by the Portuguese and were deposited in a nearby well of the

Juma mosque. Finally, they were searched by the relatives who found the bodies with divine appearance and not decayed. They were given honourable burial at the place of the present Maqam where devotees used to give offerings for blessings and remedy of diseases.[33]

These sorts of *mālā*s and martial songs (*padappāttu*) had played a key role in anti-colonial struggles waged by Muslims during the British period also. They were recited in great devotion by all members of Muslim families in Malabar. Though lived in utter poverty and constant stress, such recitals provided them with a feeling of security, derived from the hope for divine blessings and the supernatural powers of saints, martyrs and other holy men. The Muslims had never been superior to their adversaries with regard to number of soldiers, provisions, arms and ammunitions. In spite of that they had achieved impressive victory in the battles they fought at various stages of Islamic history and the legends of such victories narrated in the songs extended consolation to the womenfolk who were remaining inside their houses in an environment of perpetual apprehension and concern, whereas their male counterparts were indulged in constant struggle against the mighty British imperial forces.

K.K.N. Kurup has conspicuously put it:

> Mappilas as a community encouraged the rituals of uprisings through its popular institutions. The institution like Jarems, Mouluds, Nerchas, Mosques, Thangals and Mussaliars and their popular ballads and songs of particular occasions had brought in close association of the rebels. The rebels' martyrdom had taken place in acute social frustration and in several cases it was narrated that they

---

33 K.K. Asainar, *Charitram Thamaskaricha Porattam*, Ramanthali Muslim Jama'ath, 2007, pp. 18-20.

had no alternative. It can be rightly pointed out that religion and the identity of the community were brought out together with the question of land, the means of production, in an agrarian society and its fast changing tenure system and regulations. Their anti-feudal character was inspired from religious sentiments and promoted through a ritualistic approach. It also promoted anti-British sentiments as the entire socio-political system had adversely affected the life pattern of the rural poor of the Mappila community. The struggles against injustice and social oppression in the long run had created an awareness and consciousness in the community against the land lords and the British. The institutions which promoted this awareness and social memory later played considerable role in providing a historical background of the great rebellion of 1921 in this region.[34]

Umer Qadi and Mamburam Thangals

Hazrat Umar Qadi (1765–1857) of Veliyankode, a *sūfī* saint born in 1765 in a family reputed for scholarship in Islamic theology and was educated under Mammi Kutty Qadi of the Makhdum family of Ponnani who initiated him to Qadiriyya order of Sufism. He had written several tracts and *fatwās* both in prose and poetry on various aspects of religion.

It was believed Umer Qadi had possessed supernatural powers with the ability to disappear from a police lock-up and also to force the police to act according to his desires. He was not only a *sūfī* with miraculous capabilities, but a great critic of the British and their administrative system. His landed properties in Veliyankode were heavily assessed by the revenue officials. He had even protested against such collections and openly declared that he would not pay tax to

34 K.K.N. Kurup, *The Legacy of Islam*, Kerala, pp. 70-71.

British for God's land. He never paid land revenue, but his friends had fulfilled this obligation. After their death, the village headman demanded the payment from Umer Qadi. He scolded them as servants of the imperialists who had slain Tipu Sultan and destroyed many native rulers. When a complaint was filed before the Revenue Divisional Officer, Umer Qadi was brought before him for trial. The officer Neebu asked him:

> Are you Umer Musliar of Veliyankode who rebels against the British authority and refuses to pay taxes?

He replied affirmatively. Then Neebu threatened him to confiscate his wealth and banish him out. Umer Qadi replied in a defiant tone:

> I will never pay you tax for god's land. You may exercise your authority; I am ready to face any situation.

When the officer threatened him again, he became furious, jumped up and spit on the face of the officer shouting 'ماذا تقول يا بطال' (what do you mumble, you stupid?). Subsequently he was sentenced for imprisonment for a long period.[35] During the lifetime, he was highly respected by the Hindus and Mappilas as a divine personality. After his death in 1857 he became a cult figure among the rural folk of Malabar and a symbol of defiance and negation of tax to the imperialist regime.

Mamburam Thangals of Tirurangadi played an important role in regenerating an anti-British consciousness, in the minds of Malabar Muslims who were greatly exploited by the British rulers. Sayyid Alavi Thangal (d. CE 1844), who was born in Tarim (Yemen), had arrived Calicut in CE 1767 as a boy of

---

35 Veliyankode Mahallu Committee, *Hazrat Umar Qāsiyude Jeeva Charitravum Kraikahan* Veliyamkode, 1999, pp. 38-49.

seventeen and settled at Mamburam where his maternal uncle was also a scholar and theologian. His tract *"al saif al Battār Liman Yuwāli al Kuffār"* expounds the attitude that a Muslim must adopt towards oppressive foreign rulers everywhere in the world. This tract that called for an uncompromising fight against the aggressors till the end was widely circulated in Malabar which inspired Mappilas to direct action against the British authority. Mamburam Thangal who had a large number of followers was an ambassador of Hindu–Muslim harmony. On the other hand, he had personally involved in anti-Britisih Mappila uprisings of 1801 and 1817. It is also believed that he had taken part in anti-British battle of Cheroor in 1843 in a miraculous manner, fought sitting on horseback and his leg was wounded by a gunshot of the enemies.

His son and successor, Sayyid Fadl Pookoya Thangal (d. CE 1901) who had established the Jama'ath Mosque of Mamburam inherited anti-British feelings of his father. He issued a number of *fatwā*s on theological questions and propagated anti-colonial message urging the believers to wage war against the British. His most important contribution is *Udddat al Umara wal Hukkām fi Ihānat al Kafarati wa Abadatil Asnām,* a collection of nine small works including *Tanbīh al Ghafileen, al Durr al Mandoom,* etc. which incited the believers to open fight against the colonial rulers. He was very much an architect of Hindu–Muslim unity and wielded great influence among both the sections. Hence, the authorities saw in him a big threat to their sovereignty and forced him to leave the country. He was sent in exile to Arabia in 1852 together with his family and later passed away in Constantinople in 1901.[36]

---

36 Moyin Hudawi Malayamma and Mahmood Panangangara, *Mamburam Thangal: Jeeviham Athmeeyatha Porattam,* Darul Huda Chemmad, 2009, pp. 67-87.

Muhimmat al Muemineen written by Aminummantakath Pareekkutty Musliar is another text that shows the involvement of *ulamās* of Malabar in anti-colonial struggle against the British, compiled in the context of Khilafat Movement. This work clearly stated that it was the duty of every Muslim to struggle against the imperial forces who were oppressing Muslims all over the world and confronting Islamic caliphate in Turkey. This treatise was signed by the author and testified by the prominent *ulamās* of the period. This was lithographed at Muhyil Garaib Press of Thalassery in 1921 and widely circulated in all Muslim populated areas. Due to the explosive nature of the text it was proscribed by British authorities who issued a notification in Madras Gazette which declared that anybody possessed a copy of this was liable to be sentenced for five years' imprisonment. The author later escaped to Mecca in disguise and carried on his anti-British writings there also.

In fact, these writings in Arabic and Arabi–Malayalam had to deliver a message to the Muslim community of Malabar, when they had been in a difficult situation created by the foreign aggressors in their colonial exploitations. They had not only brought commercial rivalry but also religious fanaticism to the Malabar Coast. There had been no justifications for their unwarranted lootings, destruction of men and wealth and atrocities in Malabar. As a community, Muslims had to resist these oppressions in the light of the holy Koran and its policy of *jihād*. But it was not to convert Malabar into an Islamic state. But, it was to safeguard the interest of the local ruler. It shows that it was the duty of a Muslim to support the native ruler. *Jihād* was an instrument for this motivation. The Arabic literature from Malabar, particularly from sixteenth to nineteenth centuries reveals the true spirit of anti-colonialism and propagates an ideology of consistent resistance.

References

MANUSCRIPTS (UNPUBLISHED)

Kottuppally Nerchappattu by on unknown poet.

Musliar, Aminummantakath Pareekutty, *Muhimmat al Mu'mineen.*

Qadir, Muhammed bin Abdul Aziz, *Al Khutbat al Jihadiyya.*

Qadir, Muhammed bin Abdul Aziz, *Al Qaseedat al Jihadiyya.*

Sayyid, Alavikoya Thangal, *Al Saif al Battar liman Yuwali al Kuffar.*

Seyyid, Fadl Pookoya Thangal, *Thanbih al Ghafileen.*

Sheikh, Zainuddin bin All al Ma'bary, *Tahrid Ahl allman ala Jihadi Abadat al sulban.*

Sheikh, Zainuddin bin Muhammed al Gazzali, *Tufat al Mujahideen.*

OTHER SOURCES

Abu, O., *Arabi Malayala Sahitya Charitram* (Malayalam).

Arabic in South India, Calicut: Department of Arabic, University of Calicut, 2003.

Assainar, K.K., *Charitram Tamaskaricha Porattam* (Malayalam), Ramanthali: Ramanthali Muslim Jama'at, 2007.

Aziz, Muhammed bin Abdul, *Al Path al Mubeen* (ed. and tr. to Malayalam by Mankada Abdul Azeez).

Kurup, K.K.N., 2006, *The Legacy of Islam* (Kerala), Kannur: Samayam Publications.

Malayamma, Moyin Hudawi and Mahmood, Panangangara, *Mamburam Thangal: Jeevitham athmeeyatha porattam* (Malayalam), Darul Huda Islamic Academy, Chemmad.

Muslim Lokam Yearbook 1423 (vol. 2), Datanet Publications, (Malayalam), Tirurkad, 2002.

Sheikh, Zainuddin Makhdum, *Tuhfat al Mujahideen* (English), tr. Husain Nainar, Calicut: Other Books, 2006.

Sheikh, Zainuddin Makhdoom, *Tuhfat al Mujahideen* (Malayalam), tr. and commentary C. Hamza, Calicut: Al-Huda Book Stall, 1999.

Vallikkunnu, Balakrishan, *Mappilappattu oramukha padhanam* (Malayalam), Calicut: Poonkavanam Publications, 1999.

Veliyamkode Mahallu Jama'ath Committee, *Hazrat Umer Qaziyude Jeeva Chartitravum Kritikalum* (Malayalam), Veliyamkode: 1999 Veliyamkode Mahallu Juma'ath Committee.

4

The Eighteenth-century Calcutta in the British Manuscript Records

Ranjit Sen

THE British official records preserved in various archives in India and England are the indispensable sources for the writing of the history of Calcutta. Many years ago when H. Beverley[1] wrote the history of Calcutta he lamented that he had to depend entirely on official papers because private family papers were not available. Situations did not change since then so that when A.K. Ray wrote his *A Short History of Calcutta Town and Suburbs*[2] he had to face the same difficulty. The result of this is that since the time of these two authors the most of the narratives on Calcutta had to depend on diverse sources varying from Long's *Selections*[3] to Wilson's *Early Annals*[4] and *Old Fort William.*[5] We have no city records for Calcutta in the

---

1 Beverley was the first man to write a connected history of Calcutta.

2 This history was printed as a part of the *Census of India 1901*, vol. VII, part 1.

3 Rev. J. Long, *Selections from the Unpublished Records of Government from 1748-67 Inclusive,* Calcutta, 1869.

4 C.R. Wilson, *Early Annals of the English in Bengal,* vols. I & II.

5 C.R. Wilson, *Old Fort William in Bengal,* Calcutta, 1906, vols. I & II.

first half of the eighteenth century and the history of the city for that period was studied only in association with the history of Bengal in general. Even then references to Calcutta were scanty. Till the battle of Palasi Calcutta had little importance to Persian chroniclers so much so that in the *Seir ul Mutaqharin*[6] and the *Riyaz us Salatin*[7] or in the earlier text *Ain-i-Akbari*[8] and the later text *Tarikh Bangla*[9] Calcutta gets a very casual and occasional mention.

Calcutta's urbanization in the first half of the eighteenth century was not a phenomenon which could draw the attention of the Nawābs. Hence Persian chroniclers had little interest about the event. The Nawābs noted with concern whether Calcutta grew as a base for political power and became a rival of Murshidabad. The military might of the British was well known in the first half of the eighteenth century so that the Nawābs took appropriate measures to keep in check the British efforts to build a fort in Calcutta. The idea was to checkmate the formation of a nucleus of political power in Calcutta and keep the English much within the precincts of their trading. The Nawābs' dictum was that the English should stay as traders and must not have political and territorial ambitions.

---

6 Sayid Ghulam Husain Khan, *Seir-ul-Mutaqharin,* 3 vols., Calcutta, 1789.

7 Ghulam Hussain Salim, *Riyaz-us-Salatin* (Bibliotheca Indica Series), Calcutta: Asiatic Society Press, 1902.

8 Abul Fadl, *Ain-i-Akbari,* vol. I, tr. Blochman, 2nd edn., revised by D.C. Phillot (Bibliotheca Indica Series), Calcutta, 1939, vols. II & III, tr. H.S. Jarret, revised and further annotated by Sir Jadunath Sarkar in 1949 and 1948 respectively in Bibliotheca Indica Series, 1867-77.

9 Ṡalimullah (tr. Francis Gladwin), *Tārīkh-i-Bānglā* contained in A *Narrative of Transactions in Bengal,* etc., Calcutta: Bangabasi Press, 1906.

The result of this was that the administrative records on Calcutta remained as parts of a broad and wide set of records called the *factory records* of the East India Company. Such records are not available in India and scholars have to sit at the India Office in London to glean information from such records.

We have two great historians who wrote the history of Bengal in the first half of the eighteenth century and in their writings Calcutta gets oblique references. The first among these scholars was Sir Jadunath Sarkar who while editing the *History of Bengal*, vol. II[10] wrote extensively on the history of the Bengal Nawābs in the first half of the eighteenth century. He relied mainly on the Persian chronicles noted above. Hence Calcutta did not find any separate section for its mention in his writing. Deriving from Persian sources he gives us the information that during the time of Murshid Quli Khan, Calcutta grew as a rich hub of a business class which amassed money out of their association with the various East India trading companies in Bengal. He says that the indigenous wealth thus developed within Calcutta[11] got a wide support from the 'patent of rights' which the Surman Embassy brought back to Calcutta from Delhi in 1717. This was how, according to Jadunath Sarkar, Calcutta got its start.

Abdul Karim, our second author, who wrote the history of the first quarter of the eighteenth century[12] had the

---

10 The book was published from the University of Dacca in 1948.

11 Jadunath Sarkar names two other cities where such wealth was concentrated namely Chinsurah and Hugli — Jadunath Sarkar (ed.), *History Bengal*, vol. II, The University of Dacca, 1948, p. 418.

12 Abdul Karim, *Murshid Quli and His Times*, The Asiatic Society of Pakistan Publication No. 12, Dacca, 1963.

opportunity to look into the English records at the India Office Library. Delving into *Bengal Public Consultations* vols. I-VI[13] he finds ample information as to how the English East India Company organized its position in Calcutta during the rule of the most powerful Bengal Nawāb, Murshid Quli Khan and how the Nawābī administration contested the English pretension to jurisdiction in the city and places around.[14] From the British records only we come to know that even during the time of Murshid Quli Khan (1700-08 and 1710-27) the English used to consider Calcutta and other two villages adjacent to it as "settlement of Great Britain in Calcutta".[15]

The British viewpoint that Calcutta was their purchased property and hence their *'estate'* began to flourish from this time and it gained momentum as time went on and as the Nawābī administration came to be fraught with many vicissitudes in its declining career. The English conviction that they were settled in their own territory where they had sovereign rights to deal with its subjects had been the one point that was contested by the Bengal Nawābs but from which the English did not budge even for a moment. It was in this British spirit of acquisition that Calcutta got its commission to grow. This spirit of the English is known only from contemporary British manuscript records available at the India

---

13 *Bengal Public Consultations*, Range I, vols. I-VI:
Vol. I: 29th July, 1704 – 28th November, 1709
Vol. II: 1st December, 1709 – 10th January, 1715
Vol. III: 14th January, 1715 – 8th December, 1718
Vol. IV: 15th December, 1718 – 22nd January, 1722
Vol. V: 4th January, 1722 – 31st December, 1724
Vol. VI: 4th January, 1725 – 15th January, 1729.

14 See Abdul Karim, op. cit., ch. IV.

15 Abdul Karim, p. 136.

Office and the British Museum.[16] It was not that the Nawābs were not aware of this. The British *Consultations* give us ample insight as to how the Nawābs sought to contain British ambitions.[17] Their main effort was to impose revenue demands on the English and to confine their *vakīls* as a measure to put pressure on them. This was the first primary stage of Calcutta's gradual emergence as the base from which the future city could grow. This phase was marked by a conflict between the Bengal Nawābs and the English over the latter's effort to make the city a well-secured settlement insulated from the watch of the Nawābs. Our main source of information for Calcutta for this

---

16 Apart from the *Bengal Public Consultations* noted above we have other records that give us an insight into the mechanism of the British mind in the first quarter of the eighteenth century. Among these important are the following:

(A) *Abstract of Letters from "Coast" and "Bay"*, vols. I and II:

Vol. I: 18th May, 1703 – 13rd May, 1715

Vol. II: 20th June, 1715 – 28th January, 1728

(B) The innumerable volumes of *Home Miscellaneous Series* documents which go in hundreds.

(C) *Orm MSS, India*, vols. I-IX.

(D) *Persian Copies with English Translations of Firmans and Sunnuds Granted to the Dutch Companies* preserved at the British Museum.

(E) *Letters (Home) Sent by the Court to India,* vols. 1-6:

Vol. I: 13th January, 1703 – 18th March, 1708

Vol. II: 24th March, 1708 – 23rd November, 1710

Vol. III: 9th November, 1710 – 7th October, 1713

Vol. IV: 23rd January, 1713 – 18th December, 1717

Vol. V: 20th December, 1717 – 31st March, 1722

Vol. VI: 5th April, 1722 – March, 1730.

17 Sukumar Bhattacharya in his book *The East India Company and the Economy of Bengal,* Firma KLM, 1969, ch. II deals with this problem.

phase has till date been the British manuscript records available in London.[18]

The British manuscript records of the first half of the eighteenth century inform us as to how Calcutta prepared herself to meet the challenge of the Nawābī rule both by dint of arms and also through diplomatic appeasement. In 1726 a charge of defrauding the Nawāb of his revenue through the abuse of the *dastak* was brought against the Company. The Company's *vakīl* was confined at Murshidabad and was whipped. The English retaliated: "they issued orders that no Moors' ships, vessels or boats were to be allowed to pass by the Fort, and adopted measures for the enlistment of additional forces from among the 'Europeans, Portuguese and others as quickly as possible'." Other measures to propitiate the Nawāb were also undertaken.[19] Thus long before the battle of Palasi the English in Calcutta had developed the potentiality to exercise their military might in defence of their interests in the country. From a position of strength the English Company made their overtures to the Nawāb thus:

---

18 Apart from the *Bengal Public Consultations, 1704-1740,* Range I. Nos. 1-14 the following *Factory Records* preserved at the India Office (Commonwealth Relations Office), London are important in situating Calcutta in the history of Bengal in the first half of the eighteenth century.

(i) *Factory Records, Kasimbazar,* 1733-40; Index No. 5.
(ii) *Factory Records, Dacca,* 1735-48; Index No. 2.

Those who worked on this phase of the history of Bengal have extensively depended on the *Home Miscellaneous Series* documents preserved at the India Office. Of these volumes, the most important are the vols. 69-71 which contain *Consultations and Diary of the Surman Embassy.* The volumes 629-30 are equally important because they have in them the *Manuscript Collection of Charters and Treaties, etc.* and the *Hasb-ul-hukms and Farmans of the Year 1717.*

19 Sukumar Bhattacharya, op. cit., p. 27.

> As long as their servants were urder confinement, they could not hearken to any proposals, but on having their freedom in an honourable way and the demands on the towns entirely laid aside they would readily consent to making the Nawāb a handsome present, and as soon as they were advised of their releasement they would permit the boats to pass and repass the river.[20]

This was one report we have from the *Consultation* of 1727. Calcutta by the first quarter of the eighteenth century had become so powerful as to prevent native shipping in the river and hold the country trade at ransom. That was when the most powerful of the Bengal Nawābs Murshid Quli Khan was in the office of both the Dīwān and the *Nāzim*[21] and held almost an absolute power to deal with the foreign traders. Where

---

[20] Sukumar Bhattacharya, op. cit, 28. This incident is known from the *Consultations* of 27 February, 1727.

[21] The provincial administration of the Mughals was divided into two major departments. One was the finance department and the other was the executive department. The finance department was held by the *dīwān* who controlled all matters relating to land, land-revenue, customs and civil justice. The *dīwān*'s office was called the *dīwānī*. The other part of the administration was looked after by the *nāzim* or the *nawāb* who was superior to the *dīwān* and controlled the general administrative part of the executive government, the army and the criminal justice. The department which the *nāzim* controlled was called the *nizāmat*. Officially the *dīwān* was to report to the *nāzim*. But Murshid Quli Khan was exempted from this and was advised by the Emperor Aurangzeb himself that he should report to the Imperial Government which was wherever the Emperor was. As a result of this system neither the *nawāb* nor the *dīwān* could revolt against the Imperial Government at Delhi because the *nawāb* had under his control army but no money and the *dīwān* had with him all money but no army. This was the system of checks and balance which the imperial Mughals imposed upon the provincial governments at the periphery.

then did the English get their power from to challenge the authority of the Nawāb? The answer lay in the fact that they were pre-Murshid Quli Khan in their station in Bengal. They purchased the three villages of Sutanati, Govindapur and Kalikata in 1698, two years before Murshid Quli Khan arrived in Bengal.[22] This was the aftermath of the revolt of Sobha Singh and Rahim Khan which shattered the peace of the Mughal government in Bengal. Abdul Karim writes:

> The rebellion of Subha Singh and Rahim Khan demonstrates the weakness of the Mughal government in Bengal. Not only did the *subāhdār* remain inactive, but the *faujdārs* immediately responsible for the suppression of the rebellion showed extreme cowardice. The rebellion at the same time proved the superiority of the armed strength of the European traders. In fact, the progress of the rebellion to the east of the Ganges was checked by the Dutch arms at Chinsurah. The fortified posts of the Europeans afforded shelter to many people and government servants who had been dispossessed of their positions by the rebels.[23]

It was in this situation that Ibrahim Khan, the then Nawāb of Bengal, allowed the European traders to fortify their settlements.[24] The English were thus entrenched on the soil of Calcutta much before Murshid Quli Khan could anchor his position as a *dīwān* in the country. Calcutta was thus commissioned into its career in a very troubled period of

---

22 Wilson, *Old Fort William in Bengal,* vol. I, p. 39.

23 Abdul Karim, *Murshid Quli and His Times,* p. 2.

24 "Ibrahim Khan ordered them [the European traders] in general terms to defend themselves. Taking advantage of this order, the European companies fortified their factories and thus were established Fort William in Calcutta, Dutch Fort in Chinsurah later on named Fort Gustavas and Fort Orleans in Chandernagore." — Ibid.

Mughal history in Bengal. The story of this rise of the city in the troubled days of its transitional history is partly available in the *Tārīkh-i-Bānglā* and the *Riyāz-us Salātin.* Abdul Karim who had in passing discussed this phase of the history of Calcutta had relied mainly on these two books and Wilson's book *Old Fort William in Bengal* (vol. I). As against him Sukumar Bhattacharya taking cue from two contemporary British records[25] gives us the information that while in the first two decades of the eighteenth-century English trade in the country increased by leaps and bounds their actual station in Bengal was ill defined. On the growth of English trade Bhattacharya writes:

> The development of the Company's trade is also evident from the number and tonnage of ships dispatched annually to the East. From an annual average of eleven ships of about 300 tons dispatched for the five years from 1708-09 to 1711-13, the number rose to twenty-one ships of about 490 tons in the quinquennium from 1735-36 to 1739-40. While in 1708-09 out of ten ships dispatched from the Britain only four were bound for the 'Coast and Bay' that is, the eastern coast of India, in 1739-40 out of the thirty-nine ships so dispatched nineteen were bound for the eastern coasts, and of these nineteen ships no less than nine were specially earmarked for Bengal.[26]

The disparity between the growing trade and the territorial and political station of the English in Bengal became apparent as early as the time of the death of the Alamgir. From the *Consultations* of 1708 Bhattacharya finds the British station as

---

25 These records are (a) Charles Hardy, *Register of Ships Employed in the Service of the United East Indian Company,* published by the East India House in 1799, and (b) *Consultations,* 22 October 1708 and 27 November 1708.

26 Abdul Karim, op. cit., pp. 16-17.

the one awkwardly placed vis-à-vis their trade in Bengal. He observes:

> The position of the English in Bengal at the time of Aurangzeb's death was ill defined. Though they had got the *zamīndārī* rights and a fortified settlement in Calcutta, they found that the provisions of the *farmāns* which they had hitherto obtained hardly gave them any security and stability to their trade. The provincial authorities, in fact, ignored the *farmāns* on various grounds.[27]

From this disparity in the positions of the English as traders and as estate managers emerged the dynamics of their aspirations for an imperial *farmān* that would give them the privileges necessary to cover up the gap in their position. Salimulla's *Tārīkh-i Bāngla*[28] gives us information as to how the Nawābī administration addressed itself to the English aspirations of the time but the working of the English mind and their agenda of action are available mostly in the *Home Miscellaneous Series* volumes and their *Consultations* of the time.[29] Between Aurangzeb's death in 1707 and the grant of the Imperial *farmān* in 1717 there was a very hectic period of activities and tensions for the Company in Calcutta. Attempts were made to find a corridor to the Emperor in Delhi so that their desire for trade privileges could be fulfilled. But their expectations went beyond trade. In a communication to Ziyauddin Khan, Lord High Steward of the Household of the Emperor Shah Alam they expressed their desire to have mints for their own and when the *farmān* was framed and eventually

---

27 Abdul Karim, op. cit, 17.

28 This book was translated by Gladwin (1788).

29 Sukumar Bhattacharya made a marvellous use of the *Home Miscellaneous Series,* vols. 69-71, 628-30 to study the antecedents of the Surman Embassy which reached Delhi in 1715.

granted it was found that territorial acquisition was also in the list of the Company's requisitions to the Emperor.[30] The Company was keen in removing its trade barriers but it was equally aware that the time was not unripe to press further for territorial possessions.

The death of the Emperor Aurangzeb had created uncertainties in the Bengal body-politic. The new *dīwān* was busy organizing the revenue administration of the country which was in doldrums. There was none in the provincial administration to keep vigilance on the activities of the foreign traders. Between 1708 and 1710 Murshid Quli Khan was transferred from Bengal and there was a power vacuum in the whole of the eastern part of the Mughal empire. The English wanted to take advantage of this situation. The English mind was clearly revealed in the *Home Miscellaneous Series* records and the *Consultations* and the *Factory Records* of the time. Advantage seeking was in the very way of the Company's factory officials in Calcutta from the beginning. The mastery over the three villages of Sutanati, Govindapur and Kalikata was not achieved through a direct deal with the *zamīndārs* of these places but they were acquired through a stratagem. The factory records from Calcutta show that the Company's administration at the outset

> had tried to rent the villages from the *zamīndārs* of the place. An offer of a 'quarter part more than the revenue bring in at present' to the *zamīndārs* was made to give the lands to the Company in lease. The offer was not accepted on the pleas that it would not be possible to resume the lands if the *zamīndārs* wished to do so, because the Company was a powerful body. Negotiations for a lease having failed, a

30 *The Home Miscellaneous Series*, vol. 69 gives us the major source for these developments of the period.

> mission was sent to prince Azim-ush-Shan with suitable presents. The prince was then the *subāhdār* of Bengal. He permitted the Company the acquisition of the three villages and ordered the *zamīndārs* to make over the rights and title to the Company.[31]

A weak and greedy *nawāb* succumbed to the temptation offered by the English. M. Huq relying on the contemporary factory records has brought into light as to how the contradiction between an irascible *nawāb* and reluctant *zamīndārs* was resolved through the use of force from the top. He writes:

> The Prince, actually deputed an officer to see that his order was carried out. The *zamīndārs* were still unwilling to make over the lands and contemplated complaining to the Emperor about the injustice of being ordered by the prince to part with land they had so long in their possession. The Company was, however, very anxious to have the lands, and was prepared to pay more. The threat of complaint to the Emperor did not, however, materialize; and ultimately the *zamīndārs* yielded.[32]

This whole picture comes out from one set of *Factory Records*[33] which are read in association with C.R. Wilson's *Fort William in Bengal* (vol. I). The seventeenth-century factory records are not available in the Indian archives and as such the story of the rise of Calcutta in the first half of the eighteenth century remains to be an incomplete story of urbanization in the eastern part of Mughal India. All English factory records for the first quarter of the eighteenth century give us the picture of the

---

31 M. Huq, *The East India Company's Land Policy and Commerce in Bengal 1698-1784*, Dacca: Asiatic Society of Pakistan, 1964, p. 18.

32 Ibid.

33 This is *Factory Records*, Calcutta, 3.

acquisitive spirit of the English. Starting from prevailing upon the Nawāb with a rich present in 1698 down till the grant of *dīwānī* in 1765 the entire English agenda in Bengal were one of a powerful drive toward making their settlement in Calcutta an insulated zone of influence. Our three authors under discussion, Sukumar Bhattacharya, Abdul Karim and M. Huq testify to the fact that all through the English attempt was to prevail upon the superior authority to cross over the barriers put up from time to time by subordinate officials. When *zamīndārs* did not yield to the Company's terms the inevitable strategy was to prevail over the Nawāb and when the Nawāb seemed to be a hurdle before them they went to Delhi to approach the Emperor. They knew that Indian princes had one vice in common namely greed and accordingly rich and costly presents were offered to the rulers so that they bent before the demands of the Company. One advantage received from the rulers eventually became only the stepping stone for the wringing of the next concession. Abdul Karim writes:

> In July 1698 the English received from the Prince a letter patent, on payment of Rs. 16,000 allowing them to purchase from the owners the right of renting the three villages of Calcutta, Sutanuti and Govindpur.[34] The establishment of Fort William and the right of renting the villages, which the Calcutta Council always called the *zamīndārī* right gave the English a secure foothold in Bengal. From the position of mere traders, the English became partners in the administration and co-sharer of rights and privileges with other Mughal subjects. The English, during the last half of the eighteenth century, were to take full advantage of the position thus achieved by the favour of the prince.[35]

---

34 For details see Wilson, *Old Fort William in Bengal,* vol. I, p. 39.

35 Abdul Karim, op. cit., pp. 2-3.

Our dependenee on British manuscript records dwindle when we arrive at the age of Alivardi Khan. K.K. Datta's study titled *Alivardi and His Times*[36] was based not so much on official records as on Persian literature, contemporary British narratives, Bengali literary sources, memoirs and the like. While discussing the bibliography of his book K.K. Datta narrates a five page-list of Persian records whereas only a few sentences he devotes on the manuscript records of the British for the period when Alivardi was the Nawāb of Bengal. Occasionally he refers to British *Consultations,* particularly for the 1740s and very often resorts to *Letters to and from the Court of Directors.* Sources vastly diverse used in his book left little room for British manuscript records. It is also important to note that Calcutta does not occur as a principal theme in any event of the time. It only shows that the English in Calcutta remained subdued under Alivardi Khan. He was the last guardian of the old Mughal order which crumbled under his successor. Since the English East India Company did not have a direct confrontation with the Nawāb and since the country was traumatized by the Marāṭhā invasion and Afghan insurrection the British in Calcutta did not venture to go into any experiment either with their trade or with their territorial ambitions.

British manuscript records surfaced into primacy again when Brijen Gupta wrote his book *Sirajuddaullah and the East India Company, 1756-1757 Background to the Foundation of British Power in India.*[37] Among other records he used *Bengal Correspondence, Fort William Council to the Court of Directors, I.O. Home Series Documents, Letters Written to the Select Committees at Fort St. George, Madras and Fort William, Calcutta* and so on. As

---

36 The book was published by the World Press, Calcutta, 1963.

37 The book was published by E.J. Brill, Leiden, 1966.

we approach the middle of the eighteenth century we find at our command a plethora of memoirs and personal anecdotes written by a host of Englishmen that help us in understanding the inner logic of the working of events. Thus we have accounts left by Holwell,[38] Bolts,[39] Dow,[40] Orme,[41] Vansittart,[42] Verelst,[43] Watts,[44] Scrafton,[45] Pattullo[46] and many other personalities who actually participated in the India affairs on behalf of their own country. Their writings, mostly in the nature of memoirs, provide such windows to the development of the time as one will miss in the routine narratives of British official records. None of their writings relates specifically to Calcutta but they do narrate events that either sprouted from Calcutta or had a Calcutta specificity. While writing on the times of Alivardi

38 John Zephania Holwell, *India Tracts,* 3rd edn., ed. T. Becket, London 1774.

39 William Bolts, *Considerations on India Affairs,* 3 vols., London: J. Dodsley, 1772-73.

40 Alexander Dow, *A History of Hindustan translated from the Persian* (*of Firishtah*)), 2 vols., 2nd edn., London: T. Becket, 1770.

41 Robert Orme, *Historical Fragments of the Mogul Empire,* London: Wingrave, 1805 and *A History of the Military Transactions of the British Nations in Indostan,* vols. I-II, London: John Nourse.

42 Henry Vansittart, *A Narrative of the Transactions in Bengal from 1780 to 1764,* 3 vols., London: J. Newberry, 1765 and *Original Papers Relative to the Disturbance in Bengal 1759-64,* London: J. Newberry, 1785.

43 Harry Verelst, *Rise, Progress and Present State of the English Government in Bengal,* London: J. Nourse, 1772.

44 William Watts, *Memoirs of the Revolution in Bengal,* London: A. Milar, 1764.

45 Luke Scrafton, *Reflections on the Government &c. of Indostan,* London: A. Milar, 1760.

46 Henry Pattullo, *An Essay upon the Cultivation of the Lands, and Improvements of the Revenues of Bengal,* London, 1772.

Khan, K.K. Datta did not find it necessary to refer to these texts very often. That was because till his time Calcutta was very much steeped in the old world surrounded by the Nawābī territories and overwhelmed by the Nawābī administration.

In the course of its first sixty years of its existence Calcutta had two crowning moments when it drew applause from the Nawābs. The one was in the immediate aftermath of the Shobha Singh rebellion when the English had just acquired the villages on the bank of the river and when the people of the neighbourhood crowded in Calcutta for shelter. The second one was at the time of the Marāṭhā invasions in the 40s of the eighteenth century when once again Calcutta provided a sanctuary to the harassed people of the countryside. Besides these two moments till the time of Siraj-ud-Daullah in 1757 Calcutta had always been watched by very powerful Nawābī vigilance. From 1717 onwards the Nawābī vigilance on Calcutta was tightened. This was because of two reasons. First, that year Murshid Quli Khan became the Nawāb of Bengal and he combined in his own hands the powers of both the Dīwān and the Nawāb. Thus he became free from the interference of a jealous Nawāb at the head and could concentrate on the activities of the English Company in Calcutta. Second, the procurement of a *farmān* by the Company from the Emperor was not taken with grace by the Bengal Nawāb. The Emperor granted the Company the right to purchase thirty-eight riparian villages around Calcutta but their territorial ambition was frustrated by the Nawāb himself. This was the time when individual Englishmen did not rise into prominence so as to be able to leave their memoirs. Naturally we have to rely mostly on British manuscript records for the activities of the English in Calcutta.

Calcutta was at the centre of interests of foreign travellers and we have a host of such travellers who left their accounts on the city.[47] Jadunath Sarkar while writing the history of Bengal under Murshid Quli Khan[48] takes recourse to the observations of Sebastean Manrique to discuss the economic condition of the country. Manrique visited the country in the previous century and his observations have been judged by Sarkar to compare the information gained from Persian sources. When Manrique came, he says, rice was sold at eight maunds a rupee. The same price continued hundred years later so that there had not been a rise on the effective demand of the commodity in the country. The reason of this, Sarkar says, people had no money in their hand. This was because there was no sufficient metallic reserve in the country with which money could be minted. This fiscal dearth in Calcutta has been recorded by K.K. Datta drawing information from British manuscript records.[49] In 1747 the English Council in Calcutta was suddenly embarrassed by acute dearth of finance which they needed for their trade. They were bent on borrowing money from the country bankers then available in Calcutta and Murshidabad, the house of the Jagat Seths, Anandiram and Srikrishna. Just at that time Rs. 50,000 were sent from Surat to the house of Srikrishna and Anandiram through a bill of exchange. This money was sent in favour of the Calcutta Council and the Indian bankers handed over the money to the Kashimbazar factory of the English. These details

---

47 For a study of travellers' accounts see Ketaki Kushari Dyson, *A Various Universe: A Study of the Journals and Memoirs of British Men and Women in the Indian Subcontinent 1765–1856*, Delhi: Oxford University Press, 1978.

48 Jadunath Sarkar wrote on the history of Murshid Quli Khan and his times in Bengal in the *History of Bengal*, vol. II, Dacca University, 1948.

49 The manuscript records he relies on are the *Letters to the Court for the Years 1744, 1746, 1748* and so on.

of the Indian finance is normally not available in Persian literature which concern themselves mostly with the political developments of the country.

For the financial history of the city in particular and the country in general for the eighteenth century we have no alternative but to trust English official records. From the time of Murshid Quli Khan to that of Alivardi Khan the history of the finances in the country was essentially the history of the Jagat Seths.[50] Some minor banking houses operated in Calcutta and Patna. But they were of little help to the English. Sometimes in the middle of the 1740s there was an acute financial crisis in Calcutta. The Company was in great need of money for their investments. Merchants in Calcutta and Kashimbazar who had dealings with the English were angry because the Company's debt to them for the previous year had not been cleared of. The House of the Jagat Seth was angry because it had not got back the money it had lent to the various English factories in the country. There was demand for money from everywhere — Dakha, Kashimbazar and other principal factories at various places. The ship *Bomabay Castle* brought some bullion to Bomaby and a share of it was sent to Calcutta. But that was inadequate to meet the demands of the Jagat Seths alone, not to speak of the requirements of other factories scattered all over. The demand from Dakha was pressing and the Calcutta Council advised the Kashimbazar Council to borrow money from the Jagat Seths and relieve the distress of Dakha. The Kashimbazar Council borrowed Rs. 25,000 from the Jagat Seths and sent it to Dakha. But the entire sum proved to be much below than what was needed.

---

50 For the history of the Jagat Seths see J.H. Little, *House of Jagat Seth*, with an Introduction by N.K. Sinha, Calcutta Historical Society, 1967.

For these financial dealings between the Company and the native merchants and bankers our indispensable source of information for the first half of the eighteenth century has been the contemporary British official records. A perusal of these records shows that during one decade before the battle of Palasi the English were very much distressed because of their financial stringency. They were looking for new sources of wealth. It was this hunt for wealth that led the Company to join hands with the Seths and the important political magnates of Murshidabad to bring about a revolution in the political structure of the country. The whole section of the financial stringency of the Company during the period of Alivardi Khan had been based by K.K. Datta on the contemporary manuscript British records available in London. The story of the financial crisis of the company can also be studied from the standpoint of the House of Jagat Seths because the Seths were the principal bankers of the state. This study has been made by J.H. Little with information derived mainly from *Bengal Consultations* for the period.

The eighteenth-century works on India give us an insight as to why the finance deficit was so acute in the economy of Bengal in the eighteenth century. The British official records only tell us as to how the Company's trade staggered because of the lack of money in trade and commerce. They do not explain as to why that happened. For the cause of adverse fiscal happenings we have to look elsewhere. The *nawābs* used to send their tribute to Delhi in bullion. This left little bullion to be minted into coins and the currency in circulation was therefore very poor. We give below one eighteenth-century observation on the point.

> As the King's revenue and other money are annually sent to the Mogul's Court at Delhi, the money is sent in new coined sicca rupees; therefore not only the bullion, but also the

> rupees of other provinces imported into Bengal in course of trade, are every year new coined in the Bengal mint; and this sweeps away almost all the silver, coined or uncoined, which comes to Bengal; it goes to Delhi from whence it never returns to Bengal, so that after such treasure is gone from Muxadabad there is hardly currency enough in Bengal to carry on any trade, or even to go to market for provisions or necessaries of life, till the next shipping arrives to bring fresh supply of silver.[51]

Scarcity of specie thus vitiated the robustness of Bengal's economy. This was not only a phenomenon of 1750 when the above observation was recorded. It dated far back as early as the time of Murshid Quli Khan when Bengal's economy was as capital-short as it was on the eve of the battle of Palasi and the drain of specie was the main cause for this. Relying on Inayet-Ullah's *Akham-i-Alamgiri*[52] Jadunath Sarkar analyses this endemic fiscal malady of Bengal's economy in the following way:[53]

> Aurangzeb's letters to 'Azim [us-Shan] show that the Bengal surplus revenue was despatched to the imperial camp in coins, as bills of exchange could not be obtained for such vast sums and the rate of discount also was high. This unceasing drain of silver from Bengal, amounting on an average to one krore of rupees every year, kept the volume of true money in circulation here extremely small and the price of local produce very low.[54] Hence, it is no wonder that

---

51 Mandeville's Letter, dated 27 November 1750 quoted in Sir James Steuart, *Principles of Money*, 1772, p. 63.

52 Inayet-Ullah, *Akham-i-Alamgiri* (Rampur and Patna MSS., Jadunath Sarkar writes that this is the "Most useful for Murshid Quli Khan"— *History of Bengal*, p. 506, Bibliograhy).

53 Jadunath Sarkar, *History of Bengal*, p. 417.

54 This observation on the prices of local produce has been made on the basis of French reports from Chandernagore.

> while Sebastean Manrique about 1632 found rice selling at Murshidabad at four to five maunds a rupee, ninety years later, in Murshid Quli's time, the 'price of rice there was still commonly four maunds'.[55]

This picture of the drain of wealth from Bengal is a knowledge derived from contemporary reports, English, French and Persian — all mainly from written texts. English official records mostly give us pragmatic data and seldom there is any attempt to understand any phenomenon in its over-all perspective. Specific events and their immediate perspectives — these are normally the two major aspects which qualify British records to be worthy of our trust. Even then in the absence of private papers, which we in this country are very lukewarm in preserving, British records provide the backbone of every effort we make to write a connected history of Calcutta and also of Bengal for the last few centuries. Jadunath Sarkar lamented that no attempt was ever made to write a continuous history of Bengal before the end of the eighteenth century when the Muslim rule had already become a thing of the past. Pioneers who laboured to link fragments into an integrated history of Bengal had to work virtually in a desert which the field of historical information presented to them. Sarkar writes:

> No continuous history of the province of Bengal was written in the Persian language before 1788, that is more than one generation after the passing away of the Muslim rule, and the book named the *Riyaz-us-Salatin* is meager in facts, mostly incorrect in detail and dates, and vitiated by loose traditions, as its author had no knowledge of many of the standard Persian authorities who had treated Bengal as a part of their general histories of India.[56]

---

55 This part of the observation is made on the basis of evidences supplied by Salimullah's *Tārīkh-i-Bānglā.*

56 Jadunath Sarkar, *History of Bengal,* vol. II, Bibliography, p. 501.

Thus British records stepped in where Persian literature seemed to be infirm in providing support to our historical understanding of the past. Could there be any ancillary support for our historical quest for the past of the province besides Persian literature? Sarkar's answer is a categorical "no". Here is he on the point:

> Again we miss during the Muslim period (1200–1757) the wealth and variety of inscriptions which illuminate the life of the province during the preceding Hindu period. The extant Arabic and Persian inscriptions found in Bengal merely record the names of the builders of mosques and tombs and their dates. During the many centuries when Bengal was a part of the empire of Delhi, the only mention of the province in the historical chronicles of Delhi occurs when something abnormal happened there, as in fact Bengal affairs had no 'news value' to the royalty and courtiers of Delhi. In this barren desert of historical ignorance the only oasis is the reign of Jahangir, for which a special Bengal history was written to the dictation of Mirza Nathan (entitled Shitab Khan) who was serving there all the time. . . . At the very end of our period we have the *Life of Alivardi Khan* (*Ahwal-i-Mahabat Jang*) by Yusuf Ali, and the equally valuable personal records of Sayyid Karam Ali and Sayyid Ghulam Husain Tabatabi. Only two Muslim travellers have left any description of Bengal, however, slight; they are Ibn Battuta (*c.* 13) and Abdul Latif (1608).[57]

The entire period of Muslim rule in Bengal is thus a no-information age to a modern historian. The imperial official records were indifferent to Bengal and therefore to Calcutta as well which had no special relevance to the Mughal governance of the Empire. Since the give-and-take between this peripheral state of Bengal and the core administration at

57 Jadunath Sarkar, *History of Bengal*, vol. II, Bibliography, p. 501.

Delhi had been much below the routine official transactions that used to take place between the centre and states in other parts of India there did not grow any letter-book in the Bengal Nawābī administrative system. Ancillary support was totally weak in the provincial record-keeping system in Bengal. Sarkar notes:

> Nor has Muslim rule in Bengal bequeathed to us any letter-book, such as are plentiful for Mughal India outside this province. No history or memoir was written in Sanskrit or the provincial dialect during this age; hence one source of light familiar to us during the Hindu period is totally wanting our second volume [of the History of Bengal].
>
> Therefore, the historical inquirer is thrown upon the histories of the central government of Delhi for authentic information and dates relating to Bengal, however, scanty they might be. For long periods, this source fails us altogether and our only resource is the coins of the local sultans. These, for the earlier and more obscure centuries are of crude workmanship, and often mutilated by the marginal deletion of the date where clearness is of the utmost importance, and a few inscriptions on mosques and tombs. For the rest, the student is enveloped in the twilight of local traditions and legends of saints' shrines (which came to be written down very late, only in the eighteenth century). These require critical examination and correction before they can find a place in a sober history.[58]

The above statement makes our position clear. We land at the eighteenth century with no great tradition of historical records on which we can fall back and rely. Calcutta's origin is only shrouded in mystery. We cannot trace its origin as an ancient site of urbanization although its existence was noted in local

---

58 Sarkar, op. cit., pp. 501-02.

traditions. Persian literature is silent about this site to a very large extent and its potentiality to grow as an urban centre was never noted as an event to reckon with. Its mention in the *Ain-i-Akbari* was more of a passing reference than of a noteworthy of cognizance in the geopolitical development of the region. So long as Dhaka was the capital of Mughal Bengal Calcutta was a non-entity. The presence of the Portuguese in the Bay of Bengal did not allow the sea-board to be linked to the commercial, political and territorial ambitions of any other foreign powers in eastern India. In 1632 the Portuguese were driven out from Hughli by Shahjahan and the entire sea-board became clear of the control of any extraneous powers. This led to a vacuum on the sea. It was in this vacuum that the English could build their maritime strategic nexus between Madras on the one hand and Calcutta on the other. Taking Madras to be the base the English from the middle of the seventeenth century began to rivet their attention on Calcutta. Chittagong was their original attraction but being baffled there they now found Calcutta as its substitute and the Madras–Calcutta sea-board link became the strategic nexus by which they could now contain the eastern flank of the Mughal empire. The rapidity with which Clive could move from Madras at the beginning of 1757 and recapture Calcutta from the control of the Nawāb only showed that the Mughal empire, already weak in its maritime defence, had no answer to the overseas manoeuvre of the English. In any case from the middle of the seventeenth century south Bengal became the hub of foreign Companies and the age of factory records began to burst forth. The historian's elation starts at this point. Sarkar writes:

> After the middle of the seventeenth century, we begin to get light of another kind from the records of the English factories in Bengal and the diaries of their agents. Bengali literature,

> especially that produced by the Vaiṣṇavas, touches only the social side.[59]

This is how from the middle of the seventeenth-century British manuscript records, mostly the factory records, became one of the most illuminating sources of history for Bengal and also for Calcutta in the modern age. Our dependence on factory records comes to an end with the period that was ushered in by the battle of Palasi. A.K. Ray writes:

> From 1758, the English were superior to the *subāhdār*, and altogether out of reach of any landlord.[60]

Since then our dependence on Persian records also comes to an end. We have then at our disposal a vast corpus of Company's administrative records such as the *Select Committee Proceedings* and other documents of governance and revenue and trade transactions like the *Proceedings of the Board of Revenue* and the *Proceedings of the Board of Trade* supported by the *Proceedings of the Calcutta Committee of Revenue* and innumerable such other official documents.[61] Our writing of the history of the great city of Calcutta from this time on comes to stand on a stable foot. This was colonial Calcutta. For her antiquity we have no records. It is lost in obscurity and guess.

---

59 Sarkar, op. cit., 502.

60 A.K. Ray, *A Short History of Calcutta (1902)*, Calcutta: Riddhi-India, 1982, p. 57.

61 For a detailed list of such documents refer to Ranjit *Sen Metamorphosis of the Bengal Polity (1700-1793)*, Calcutta: Rabindra Bharati University, 1987, Bibliography.

5

A Comparative Study of Bengali, Hindi and Malayalam Rāmāyaṇa

Indra Naṭh Choudhuri

THE two great epics of India — *Rāmāyaṇa* (1500 BCE) and *Mahābhārata* (1000 BCE) — are epics born out of archetypal myths and have become a part of the collective consciousness of the people.

Both are epics of the people and composed over a long passage of time not by one poet but by many poets for the purpose of the oral transmission by singers and story tellers.

There are evidences available that these were legends, folk songs and stories composed by common people by the countryside, which later became an epic when collected and built up by a great poet or a band of poets.

Here names of poets are mere excuses, otherwise these two epics like the Gaṅgā and the Himalayas are parts of the great land. They reflect the ethos and the psyche of a group of people, in a given temporal frame with a universal content.

I once asked Thakazhi Sivasankara Pillai in a television interview when he was in his prime glory, "Does he still have some wish which is yet to be realized?", he immediately replied, "Yes, I have still a wish left, I want to write like Vyāsa." In other words, he wanted to be a narrator — an oral narrator like Vyāsa or Vālmīki who narrated the history and tradition of this great country.

Here history does not denote merely events that took place in the past but events that would always happen and repeat themselves in certain circumstances and therefore the recitation of *Rāmāyaṇa* or *Mahābhārata* is a part of the process of self-renewal and regeneration. In other words they relate to the past but do not cling to it — through continuous retelling they become an eternal present.

In the Indian tradition Itihāsa (history) is coupled with Purāṇa "that which is old and still new" or "that renews the old". In the other usage Purāṇa stands for that which is ancient, eternal and primordial?

Kṛṣṇa in *Bhagavad-Gītā* is known as *purāṇa puruṣa*, the eternal man. Similarly, the Uṣā Devatā in Veda is known as *punaḥ punarjayamāna purāṇi*, the eternal ever existent. In other words, Purāṇa reveals the eternal principles or the archetypes around which a story or myth is woven. This self-renewing, eternalizing aspect of *Rāmāyaṇa* or *Mahābhārata* very much appeals to the Indian mind.

Rāmāyaṇa is *kāvya* (poetry). Vālmīki himself calls it a *kāvya*: *kṛtsnam rāmāyaṇam kāvyam* but it is mythical poetry. It is *kāvya* so it entertains and through its myths it gives archetypal significance. It teaches while it entertains.

In *Rāmāyaṇa*, the archetypal myth is depicted in the form of a war on a cosmic level between light and darkness. The two terms "divine" and "demonic" do not necessarily mean good and bad; they are two conflicting life philosophies and disclose the struggle between the body and beyond the body or what Albert Schweitzer calls, world assertion and world negation.

Greatness of a man in Indian context is determined by his conviction that he would have to make a journey from attachment to non-attachment, from worldliness to spirituality. In the Hindu way of life the concept of the hero is developed on the basis of this theory; those who renounce enjoy.

Rāma is depicted not simply as a man but as a superman (*puruṣottama*) far above the run of a common man, unique in the achievement of *karma* and the fulfilment of *dharma* — such is the Rāma of Vālmīki whose character tells us as how a man by his action can reach divine hood. Rāma renounces everything at the moment of his glory of his coronation and goes to the forest. It is not pre-deterministic fatalism but an eternal quest for truth.

The Pāṇḍavas vanish ultimately in the Himalayas, after the Great War. Buddha and Mahāvīra renounce the joys of the world and go for penance to the forest. Aśoka at the height of his victory in the Kaliṅga War renounces fighting.

The same myth envelops Mahatma Gandhi walking down the streets of Calcutta bringing solace to people beleaguered by communal riots and ignoring celebrations of India's freedom at midnight. Service and renunciation are the two ideals of these heroes, which the Indian psyche has been beholden to for centuries.

Rāmāyaṇa is accepted by many as *Guru-Saṁhitā,* i.e. a scripture but more than that it is both *Sakhī-Saṁhitā* and *Kanta-Saṁhitā,* i.e. it has an ethical purpose as an epic, but the lesson is not stated — rather it is presented in a pleasing way and the implicit meaning is to be inferred.

It is because of this quality *Rāmāyaṇa* has retained the enduring quality of a great piece of literature with multiple meaningfulness. As a result the human experience embedded in this epic has become a potential text for new encounters and new contexts.

Epic writers of different Indian languages like Kṛttivāsa in Bengali, Tulsīdāsa in Avadhī Hindi or Ezhuthachan in Malayalam and others have gone to the theme which proceeds in a circle: separation; conflict; return, and again separation to fulfil the poetic obligation and interpreted it with their own points of view and in the process made it a multi-dimensional book of entertainment and wisdom.

Most of the translation activities of these two epics from Sanskrit into different emerging Indian languages in the medieval period were not verbatim target languages. Since these translations are connected with text and languages within the same culture, deviations were not only tolerated but also welcomed and encouraged too.

In fact, most of these medieval poets of different languages were scholars of Sanskrit also, and hence there were no inhibition on their part to deviate from the original text and recreate new episodes and anecdotes because they thought they had the right to add or subtract as these epics belonged to them.

The poets/writers attempting bhāṣā renderings of Sanskrit texts treated both the languages as their "own" languages. They had a sense of possession in respect of the Sanskrit heritage.

The whole medieval Bhakti movement of poetry in India had the desire of "translating" the language of spirituality from Sanskrit to the languages of the people.

In the process they created a space of creative freedom to produce viable, fully localized texts, especially based on *Rāmāyaṇa*, *Mahābhārata* and *Bhāgavata*. The result was that we have a living translation and not a dead paraphrase with a visible absence of the anxiety of authenticity on the part of these translators.

The medieval *bhāṣā* scholars sought to liberate the scriptures from the monopoly of a restricted class of people and saw to it that these translations become a means to reorganize the entire society. The appropriation of the story by the *bhāṣā* writers of the medieval time and then presentation of it in multiple versions display their social aspirations and intellectual concerns.

It also informs us about the way different versions subscribe to the epicentral part of the *kathā* and also the way the tradition — both *loka* and Śāstra — allows space to divergent versions. All the divergent and even radical versions like the *Kāśmīrī Rāmāyaṇa* by Divakara Prakasha Bhatta or the Buddhist version of *Rāmāyaṇa*, the *Daśaratha Jātaka*, and many others are articulated with the energy of folk life.

Even a classical poet like Tulsīdāsa valorizes the role of *lokamata* (public opinion) (II.258) as an important guide of human behaviour and without considering the opinions prevalent in *loka* it is not possible to take a proper decision in crucial moments. In Indian context it is *loka* which talks of social protest, dissent and bitter sarcasm.

Kṛttivāsa (CE 1398-1461), Tulsīdāsa (CE 1532–1623) and Ezhuthachan (between CE 1475 and 1575) were part of the *Rāmāyaṇa* tradition in their respective languages.

While both Kṛttivāsa and Tulsīdāsa were inspired by Vālmīki's *Rāmāyaṇa,* Ezhuthachan chose *Adhyātma Rāmāyaṇa* of Vyāsa as his basic text for recreating the Rāma story.

Though Ezhuthachan made wise use of Vālmīki's *Rāmāyaṇa* in narrating certain episodes he was primarily inclined to describe the philosophical and devotional aspects of Rāma who is mentioned in *Adhyātma Rāmāyaṇa* as the infallible *Brahman* unlike in Vālmīki where Rāma is a superhuman (*puruṣottama*) and described as *sarvaguṇapeta naracandramā* — a human moon possessing all the qualities but he is not a god.

Rāma acts and suffers like a glorified human being; a man who is sometimes subject to human foibles but who ultimately through his deeds reaches the state of divine hood.

For Kr̥ttivāsa and Tulsīdāsa Rāma is *Param Brahman* right from his birth and emerges as the god of the devotees, as an *avatāra*, who descends in this world in the form of a human being to establish the rule of *dharma* (righteousness) in the society and hence Tulsīdāsa describes Rāma as the *maryādā puruṣottma* (an ideal man), who is an embodiment of truth and morality and Kr̥ttivāsa transforms Rāma into a kind-hearted god-like good Bengali youth admired and adored by his followers and devotees. One may try to find in congruency or contradiction in their presentation of godhead and manhood together.

In fact, in that era of devotional poetry the human life and the divine life, worldly and other-worldly, the mundane and the spiritual were so intermingled with each other that in the small circle of human life, one experienced the expanse of the divine; in the worldly life of Rāma, the divine is experienced.

Ezhuthachan combines the twin aspects of divinity and humanness without prejudicing either because for him Rāma is god in human form (*amānuṣa*). He shows humanlike behaviour of Rāma to prove that he is an ideal for both god and man.

If he is more sympathetic and powerful than the gods, he is also more far-sighted and generous than man. This is the uniqueness of Ezhuthachan's Rāma who is superior from the angle of humanity and divinity and the same time one can find a beautiful cohesion of the two aspects in Rāma's character.

Kṛttivāsa, unlike Tulsī and Ezhuthachan, seems to be quite proud of his creation because he points out repeatedly that his poetry tastes like nectar.

Tulsīdāsa, on the contrary, presents his work with utmost humility. Though he says that for his own happiness he has created his *Rāmāyaṇa* but in fact it is meant for the welfare and happiness of many (*bahujana hitāya* and *bhaujana sukhāya*).

Tulsī's *Rāmāyaṇa* begins with the question of Devī to Śiva, "How are people to be saved in the Kaliyuga?" Śiva responds to her question by saying that they will be saved by hearing the story of Rāma and hence through the heroic virtues and values upheld by Rāma, the poet proposed a new system of values and ideals, based on the Sanātana Dharma, the eternal righteous conduct for individuals and the society.

The very fact that *Adhyātma Rāmāyaṇa* of Ezhuthachan is the "song of a bird" (*kilippaṭṭu*) demonstrates that he wanted to be anonymous to prove his humility.

In the ancient Indian tradition the humbler the poet and freer he was from an ego, the more he chose to be impersonal. Avoiding conceit was both a means and end of spiritual life. His entire text is a Vedāntic allegory with accent on the philosophical and devotional aspects.

There are three very distinctive aspects of these three poets which distinguish them from one another. Kṛttivāsa, a poet rooted in the soil of Bengal, is more inclined to present a harmonious domestic picture of Bengali life. He thinks to live in harmony is a sign of culture and discord is anarchy. Whereas in Tulsīdāsa the family saga is presented on an enormous canvas and transformed into a text of universal appeal though underscoring the position of *loka* and *loka-dharma*. Ezhuthachan, on the contrary, makes it a highly philosophical text but at the same time a lively attractive text by infusing in it the splendour of poetic beauty without any erudition.

Kr̥ttivāsa makes it very clear that the aim of his writing this *Rāmāyaṇa* poem in Bengali was to make this divine creation (*deber sr̥jit*) accessible to the common man.

But his common men are all Bengalis of the village life. The Rāma episode was taken by the Bengalis to suit their particular social need. It gives more importance to local thought, keeping at the same time the universal value intact.

The sound, music, cadence and vitality of Sanskrit words and sentences have been utilized by Vālmīki. But Kr̥ttivāsa has used a language which is sweet and mellow and so near to us and which is very much rooted in the soil and acceptable to peasants and unlettered people of the rural Bengali society.

The farcical and devotional elements predominate in the Bengali *Rāmāyaṇa*. To please his rural audience Kr̥ttivāsa introduces many grotesque and exaggerated topics in his work, at many times he has made witty and ironical remarks and laughed with his audience.

It is full of fun and mirth. All the details of the wedding ceremony of Rāma and Sītā are based on a typically Bengali wedding ceremony with Bengali customs and Bengali cuisine. Sītā, the wife of a kṣatriya, became a Bengali housewife.

In fact, all the characters of the Bengali *Rāmāyaṇa*, though retain the original names, are in reality Bengali men and women. The Bengali *Rāmāyaṇa* carries a typically Bengali domestic picture, which is not to be found in the Sanskrit text.

Tulsīdāsa writes the *Rāmacaritamānasa* for the upliftment of the Hindu society in Avadhī, a language under the broader umbrella of Hindi of northern India. The text exists at multiple level as a religious, spiritual, philosophical, literary and folk (*loka*) text simultaneously. But his primary intention is to portray, through the character of Rāma, the eternal human values of service and renunciation which are essentially the attributes of *bhakti*.

Rāma tells Śabarī that of all the relations *bhakti* is the highest form to him and that a person having all great attributes but without *bhakti* is like a cloud without water.

Tulsī's *bhakti* becomes an instrument of unification of the Hindus by bringing the Śaivites and Vaiṣṇavites of the south and north together. Tulsī makes Rāma worship Śiva and Śiva worship Rāma. His main focus, however, is on to establish the supremacy of *loka* and *loka-dharma*.

In Indian tradition *loka* (folk) and Śāstra (classical) are always complementary and not binary opposites as in the Western tradition great and little traditions are.

In the introductory chapter of *Mahābhāṣya*, Patañjali clearly pronounces, *prayukto lokārthaḥ* and accordingly *loka* is the authority of word, meaning and the relationship between them and not the classical rules.

Loka is one of the important guides of human behaviour and *loka-mata* (views of common people) constitutes a significant part of behaviour before *nṛpanaya* (polity) and even *nigama nicoḍa* (essence of the Vedas) and the view of the wise (views of wise).

In this way existing both in *loka* and learned traditions, the text has performed its function as a holy book of ethics for ages with the motive of common people's welfare as said by Tulsīdāsa:

> There is no religion except for the well-being of others. There cannot be a bigger sin than inflicting pain on others.

Ezhuthachan's *Rāmāyaṇa*'s accent is on the philosophical and devotional aspects of life. The entire text becomes a Vedāntic allegory to express

1. devotion to god.
2. awareness of ultimate spiritual truths.

   But more than that

3. it is an expression of great poetry with felicity.

It is primarily because of his amazing command over the vocabulary and the intensity of his emotional fervour that the text with several spiritual discourses dealing with the doctrine of Vedānta and the idea of *bhakti* (devotion) to Viṣṇu does not tend to become dry, prosaic and monotonous, and remains ever lively.

Such philosophical discourses formed the poet's forte which was used to inspire people to follow the spiritual path and the understanding of the doctrines of Vedānta.

The happenings in the life of his characters are the springboards for his philosophical flights and exposition of his devotional fervour, *bhakti*. It is this devotional spirit which gives Ezhuthachan's poetry its principle of unity and dynamism.

Almost every alternate page of Ezhuthachan's *Adhyātma Rāmāyaṇa* contains a *stotra* (hymn) which displays his command over the spring of Malayalam language, diction, his deep sense of sound and rhythm, poetic imagery, his high poetic imagination and the use of different sentiments like pathos and valour. It gives the work the status of great poetry and makes him a pioneer in ushering a renaissance in Malayalam literature and turns it into a high and mighty literary text.

All these three *Rāmāyaṇa*s are not translations but transcriptions and constantly go on adding a little here and dropping a passage there, all the while recreating the original texts of Vālmīki or Vyāsa.

Let us take the example of the counter (not anti) hero Rāvaṇa to realize the minds and point of views of these three great poets. In Vālmīki's *Rāmāyaṇa,* Rāvaṇa (*rākṣasa* king) is a great hero no doubt, but is abominably barbarous and a veritable sinner.

But Kṛttivāsa adds one notable peculiarity to Rāvaṇa's character, i.e. devotion which he shows to Rāmacandra. While he comes to fight with Rāma, Rāvaṇa is much pleased to witness Nārāyaṇa in him. He becomes joyful when he thinks that he will be able to enter heaven if he is killed by Rāma and discloses his identity to Rāma just before his death that he was in his previous birth a *bhakta* of Viṣṇu.

Ezhuthachan's Rāvaṇa is a noble hero, a great devotee of Śiva, a fine musician and a great lover. While wooing Sītā he shows his nobility and his intense love for Sītā but Vālmīki makes Rāvaṇa blow his own trumpet making him a common place lover speaking in an undignified language.

Ezhuthachan's Rāvaṇa falls at Sītā's lotus-feet, praises her virtues, announces his passion for her and tells her that Rāma has no regard for her as he is *nirguṇa,* dispassionate and unattached.

Ezhuthachan and in the modern times Michel Madhusudan Datta in Bengali treated Rāvaṇa almost like a Greek tragic hero. He accepts his end as a dignified person knowing well that his death in Rāma's hand will make him attain *mokṣa.*

Tulsī's description of Rāvaṇa is that of a vile, demonic person. He calls him sometimes wretched and who is blinded by pride boasts about his valour before Mārīca and his wife Mandodarī.

Aṅgada calls him a vainglorious wretch and Vibhīṣaṇa calls him, perverse. While dying Rāvaṇa's false pride and his despicable nature become visible in his outburst, "Where is Rāma that I may challenge and slay him in battle?"

As said earlier all the three *Rāmāyaṇa* poets go on adding and subtracting from the original texts to create their own *Rāmāyaṇa*s.

Surprisingly, all of them fight shy of describing erotic contexts and hence in Ahalyā's episode Vālmīki, free from any kind of moral inhibition, reveals that Ahalyā could recognize Indra and out of curiosity agreed to the amorous proposal of Indra (Ādi 48.19). Whereas, all these three poets show Ahalyā as loyal to her husband and could not recognize Indra who came in the disguise of her husband and seduced her. There are two reasons for it:

1. By the time Kṛttivāsa, Tulsī and Ezhuthachan came to sing *Rāmāyaṇa,* the Vālmīki's heroic romance with his description of human realities of life were substituted by *bhakti,* towards Rāma who had, by that time, been deified as an *avatāra.* As a result the erotic contexts and the so-called crudities in characters around Rāma are obliterated.

2. In view of the moral susceptibility of the audience of the medieval time Ahalyā is shown as loyal to her husband and unable to recognize Indra.

This kind of moral propensity becomes apparent at a time of moral deterioration in the society and freedom of the writer to describe the human mind is restricted. After the war, Sītā is asked by Rāma, in a state of exaspera-tion, to come on foot and not in a palanquin to meet him.

The Sītā of Vālmīki, daughter of a kṣatriya king, a very outspoken and strong critic of anything wrong taking place around her, somehow manages to bear this insult but is unable to keep her calm when Rāma suggests her to marry any other person. Sītā though keeping her calm says strongly that a low person of debased nature talks like this and thinks all females are of low nature (Yuddha 116.5).

With reference to Kṛttivāsa, Sītā turns into a fragile, soft and a paragon of feminine virtue and beacon light of chastity as a result in that situation Sītā could only say, "The vicious Rāvaṇa only touched me when he was carrying me off. Why do you think of me as an ordinary woman?"

Tulsīdāsa cleverly engineers it by a statement of Rāma, "Vibhīṣaṇa bring Sītā walking on foot so that monkeys gaze on her as they would gaze on their mother" and absolves him from any kind of cruelty towards Sītā. Tulsīdāsa further says that Rāma, however addresses Sītā with some reproachful words and Sītā without any opposition bows to her husband and asks Lakṣmaṇa to kindle a fire for her so to perform the sacred rite.

Ezhuthachan following *Adhyātma Rāmāyaṇa* introduces the concept of Māyā Sītā — the illusory or shadow-Sītā — who disappears into fire before the golden deer episode, leaving only her shadow.

Tulsīdāsa also accepts this conceptual innovation (Araṇya, *dohā* 20). In *Adhyātma Rāmāyaṇa,* Sītā emerges from the fire at the end of the war when the shadow-Sītā enters it as has been planned. This new concept seems to perform two objectives: (a) to exonerate Rāma from the charge of the fire test he ordered for Sītā, and (b) also to vindicate Sītā from the accusation of having lived in another man's house for a while.

But the drama does not end here; it continues even after Rāma's return to Ayodhyā with Sītā and his coronation he banishes Sītā to please his subjects and accord a higher place to public opinion than to the feelings of his own heart.

Rāma's *dharma* is planted far above love and hatred, even above justice and unfairness; to abide by it he must allow injustice, and if necessary, the killing of Vāli and Śambūka, when Rāma thinks they had both violated the Śāstras, and he follows his kingly *dharma* by punishing the guilty.

Rāmāyaṇa, as Romila Thaper says, does not belong to anyone moment in history, for it has its own history, which is embedded in the many versions, which were woven around the theme at different time and places.

But A.K. Ramanujan rightly urges us to view different tellings neither as totally individual stories nor as "divergences" from the "real" version by Vālmīki, but as the expression of an extraordinary rich set of resources existing, through out history, both within India and wherever Indian culture took root.

Hence all these different tellings retain their own individuality and at the same time are related to each other by their use of *ākhyāna*s (anecdotes), *upākhyāna*s (traditional stories), *saṁvāda*s (discourses on *nīti* (morality)), *dharma* (ethics) and the expression of *rasa* as well as by their narration of the story in a leisurely way to become "a second language of a whole culture area".

Rāmāyaṇa provides Ezhuthachan with the language to fulfil his social obligations of poetry and awaken the spirit of renaissance through *bhakti*. Or it provides Kṛttivāsa the scope to intermingle Śāstrīya or classical norms of poetry with the *loka* style of emotional expression, or lends Tulsīdāsa the ability to start a debate between *jñāna*, *yoga* and *bhakti*.

But in all these *Rāmāyaṇa*s the locus is Rāma himself who is at times a superman, unbending, single-minded performer of duty as described by Vālmīki or at other times, a tear-sodden, separation-stuck lover created by later poets like Kālidāsa, Bhavabhūti, Kr̥ttivāsa and many others and we, the all time readers, go on compounding these different images of Rāma and make out of them a hero admirable both in his human and divine aspects.

6

श्रीमद्भागवतमहापुराण की टीकाओं की प्रकाशित एवं अप्रकाशित पाण्डुलिपियाँ

प्रो. गङ्गाधर पण्डा

पुराण शब्द का निर्वचन

यास्क के निरुक्त के अनुसार पुराण की व्युत्पत्ति है – पुरा नवं भवति – अर्थात् जो प्राचीन होकर भी नया होता है ।

> पुरति अग्रे गच्छतीति पुरा ।

> तुदादिगणे पुर अग्रगमने धातो औणादिके दैवादिकात् अच् प्राणने पचाद्यचि कृते पुराणम् ।

वायुपुराण (1.203) के अनुसार पुराण की व्युत्पत्ति है – 'पुरा अनति' – अर्थात् प्राचीनकाल में जो जीवित था । पद्मपुराण (5.2.53) के अनुसार यह निरुक्ति इससे किञ्चित् भिन्न है – 'पुरा परम्परां वष्टि कामयते' – अर्थात् जो प्राचीनता की अर्थात् परम्परा की कामना करता है, वह पुराण कहलाता है । ब्रह्माण्डपुराण की इससे भिन्न एक तृतीय व्युत्पत्ति है – 'पुरा एतत् अभूत्' – अर्थात् प्राचीन काल में ऐसा हुआ ।

पुराण अध्ययन की आवश्यकता

पुराण चतुर्दश विद्याओं में से एक है ।

> अङ्गानि वेदाश्चत्वारो मीमांसा न्यायविस्तरः ।
> धर्मशास्त्रं पुराणं च विद्या ह्येताश्चतुर्दश ।।

पुराणों में वेद के अर्थों का उपबृंहण है । उपबृंहण का अर्थ है किसी तथ्य की पुष्टि

करना तथा उसका विस्तार करना । बृंह् धातु का अर्थ वर्धन करना होता है । फलतः वेद के मन्त्रों द्वारा प्रतिपादित अर्थ का, सिद्धान्त का तथा तथ्य का विस्तार तथा पोषण पुराणों के श्लोकों में किया गया है । अतएव भागवत ने अपने को निगम-कल्पवृक्ष का गलित, सुपरिपक्व, एवं मधुरतम फल माना है । ग्रन्थ के अन्त में वह अपने को सर्ववेदान्तसार बतलाता है ।[1]

इतिहासपुराणाभ्यां वेदं समुपबृंहयेत् ।[2]

इस वचन के अनुसार पुराणों के साथ इतिहास वेदों का उपबृंहण करता है । राजशेखर ने इतिहास से रामायण और महाभारत को स्वीकार किया है । तदनुसार एक नायक होने से रामायण को परक्रिया और बहुनायक होने से महाभारत को पुराकल्प कहते हैं ।[3]

पुराण रचनाकाल

पारम्परिक मत

पुराणं सर्वशास्त्राणां प्रथमं ब्रह्मणा स्मृतम् ।
अनन्तरं च वक्त्रेभ्यो वेदास्तस्य विनिर्गताः ।।

उपर्युक्त श्लोक अनेक पुराणों में प्राप्त होता है । इससे शास्त्रों का स्वरूप और इनके आविर्भाव के क्रम का ठीक-ठीक ज्ञान होता है । सृष्टि-क्रम का विस्तार होने पर ब्रह्मा ने सनक-सनन्दन, वसिष्ठ आदि मानसपुत्रों को उत्पन्न किया । ब्रह्मा ने इन्हें पुराण और वेदों को पढ़ाया । इसके बाद वसिष्ठ आदि ने अपने शिष्यों को पढ़ाया । इस तरह शास्त्रों के पठन-पाठन की परम्परा चल पड़ी, जो आज भी चलती आ रही है – वेदपुराणाध्ययनं गुर्वध्ययनपूर्वकम्, अधुनाध्ययनवत् ।

द्वापर के अन्त में पुराण की अध्ययनपरम्परा में विशृङ्खलता आ गई थी । इसका एक कारण यह भी था कि ब्रह्मा का स्मरण किया हुआ पुराण बहुत विशाल था । उसमें सौ करोड़ श्लोक थे । मत्स्यपुराण का वचन है –

पुराणं सर्वशास्त्राणां प्रथमं ब्रह्मणा स्मृतम् ।
नित्यं शब्दमयं पुण्यं शतकोटिप्रविस्तरम् ।।[4]

---

1. भाग. 12.12.15 ।
2. महाभारत आदि. 1.264 ।
3. परक्रिया पुराकल्प इतिहास गतिर्द्विधा ।
   स्यादेकनायका पूर्वा द्वितीया बहुनायकाः ।। – काव्यमीमांसा अ. 2
4. मत्स्य. 3.3

इन सौ करोड़ श्लोकों को पढ़ पाना तब कठिन हो रहा था; क्योंकि मनुष्य की आयु और बुद्धि का अधिक ह्रास हो चुका था । आज कलियुग में ब्रह्मा-स्मृत उस विशालकाय पुराण का पढ़ पाना तो और भी कठिन हो गया है । अतः भगवान् की ज्ञानराशि के अवतार वेदव्यास ने चार लाख श्लोकों में ब्रह्मा द्वारा स्मृत पुराण का संक्षेप कर दिया । आज जो पुराण हमारे समक्ष है, इसके शब्द व्यास जी के बनाए हुए हैं । अब तक ब्रह्मास्मृत पुराण का कोई संस्करण उपलब्ध नहीं हुआ है । इसीलिए कहा गया है कि सत्यवतीपुत्र कृष्ण द्वैपायन व्यास ने अष्टादश पुराण का निर्माण कर सम्पूर्ण भारताख्यान की रचना की है ।

अष्टादशपुराणानि कृत्वा सत्यवतीसुतः ।
भारताख्यानमखिलं चक्रे तदुपबृंहितम् ।। – मत्स्य. 53.70

अथर्ववेद (11.7.4) के अनुसार पुराण वेदों जैसे अपौरुषेय हैं – 'ऋचः सामानि छन्दासि पुराणं यजुषा सह ।'

अर्वाचीन मत

स्मृतियों में पुराण को विद्यास्थानों में अन्यतम माना गया है । मनुस्मृति के अनुसार श्राद्ध के समय पुराण के पाठ को पुण्यवर्धक कार्य माना जाता है । याज्ञवल्क्यस्मृति जपयज्ञ की सिद्धि के लिए वेद तथा इतिहास के साथ-साथ पुराण के स्वाध्याय को महत्त्व प्रदान करती है । दार्शनिक ग्रन्थकार भी पुराण के प्रामाण्य पर आग्रह दिखलाते हैं । वात्स्यायन, शबरस्वामी, कुमारिल भट्ट, आदि-शङ्कराचार्य तथा विश्वरूप – पुराण की वेदानुगामिता को प्रमाण कोटि में स्वीकार करते हैं । अतः पुराणों के रचनाकर्ता इन आचार्यों के पूर्ववर्ती होना निश्चित है । महाभाष्यकार पतञ्जलि (द्वितीय शती ई.पू.) पुराण के आख्यानों से परिचित जान पड़ते हैं । बाणभट्ट (सप्तम शती) ने वायुपुराण के पाठ की चर्चा करके उसके स्वरूप का परिचय दिया है, वह सम्प्रति प्रचलित वायुपुराण से भिन्न नहीं है । अरबी ग्रन्थकार अलबेरुनी ने अपने भारत-विषयक ग्रन्थ में पुराणों से बहुत-सी सामग्री ग्रहण की है, जो उन पुराणों में आज भी प्राप्त होते हैं । इस प्रकार भारतीय साहित्याकाश में पुराण का अभ्युदय वैदिक युग से गुप्तकाल तक हुआ होगा, यह तथ्यपूर्ण प्रतीत होता है । सातवीं शताब्दी के बाणभट्ट ने वायुपुराण का उल्लेख किया है । अतः अधिकाधिक दसवीं शताब्दी तक सभी प्रमुख पुराण लिखे गए होंगे; यह अर्वाचीन विद्वानों का अभिमत है ।

पुराणों की वर्ण्य वस्तु एवं लक्षण

आख्यानैश्चाप्युपाख्यानैर्गाथाभिः कल्पशुद्धिभिः ।
पुराणसंहितां चक्रे पुराणार्थविशारदः ।। – विष्णु 3.6.15

अर्थात् आख्यान, उपाख्यान, गाथा एवं कल्पशुद्धि (धर्मसूत्र, गृह्यसूत्र एवं शुल्बसूत्र) के समस्त विषय पुराणों में वर्णित हैं ।

पुनश्च पुराणों का मुख्य वर्ण्य विषय पञ्चलक्षण है – सर्ग, प्रतिसर्ग, वंश, मन्वन्तर तथा वंशानुचरित ।

सर्गश्च प्रतिसर्गश्च वंशो मन्वन्तराणि च ।
वंशानुचरितं चैव पुराणं पञ्चलक्षणम् ।। – अग्नि 1.14

भागवत के अनुसार पुराणों के दश लक्षण हैं –

अत्र सर्गो विसर्गश्च स्थानं पोषणमूतयः ।
मन्वन्तरेशानुकथा निरोधो मुक्तिराश्रयः ।। – भागवत 2.10.1

विद्वानों ने उक्त दश लक्षणों को पूर्वोक्त पञ्चलक्षणों में अन्तर्भावित कर रखा है ।

पुराणों का विभाजन

पुराणों को सामान्यतः सात्त्विक, राजसिक, तामसिक रूप से तीन भागों में विभाजित किया गया है । विष्णुसम्बन्धित पुराणों को सात्त्विक, ब्रह्मासम्बन्धित पुराणों को राजसिक और शिवसम्बन्धित पुराणों को तामसिक पुराण कहते हैं । इन सभी को मिलाकर महापुराणों की संख्या अठारह है ।

इनके नाम इस प्रकार हैं ।

मद्वयं भद्वयं चैव ब्रत्रयं वचतुष्टयम् ।
अनापलिंगकूस्कानि पुराणानि प्रचक्षते ।। – देवी भाग. 1.3.21

मद्वय से मत्स्य और मार्कण्डेय, भद्वय से भागवत और भविष्य, ब्रत्रय से ब्रह्म, ब्रह्माण्ड और ब्रह्मवैवर्त्त, वचतुष्टय से वराह, विष्णु, वामन और वायु के साथ अग्नि, नारद, पद्म, लिंग, गरुड, कूर्म और स्कन्द पुराण आते हैं । परवर्ती काल में उपपुराण एवं औपपुराण भी लिखे गए हैं, इनकी संख्या भी प्रत्येक की 18 है ।

भागवत महापुराण

श्रीमद्भागवत 12 स्कन्धों में विभाजित है । दशम स्कन्ध पूर्वार्द्ध एवं उत्तरार्द्ध के रूप में दो भागों में है । प्रमुख विषयों में विष्णु के अवतार का वर्णन, चतुर्दश मन्वन्तर एवं भूगोल का वर्णन जिसमें भूः, भुवः, स्वः, जनः, मह, तपः सत्य के साथ अधोलोक अतल, वितल, सुतल, महीतल, तलातल, रसातल एवं पाताल एवं उनमें निवास करने वाले देव, दानव, राक्षस, मनुष्य एवं अन्य प्राणियों का वर्णन है । इतिहास वर्णन के अन्तर्गत सूर्यवंश, चन्द्रवंश, कलिवंश आदि वर्णित हैं एवं विभिन्न ऋषियों के वंश भी विस्तार से वर्णित हैं । इसके अतिरिक्त विभिन्न नद-नदी, विभिन्न पर्वत, शाक्तपीठ, शैवपीठ एवं गाणपत्य पीठों का एवं अन्य तीर्थस्थानों का वर्णन भी उपलब्ध है । पुनश्च समस्त वैदिक दर्शन भी अत्यन्त रोचक ढंग से इसमें वर्णित हैं । साहित्य, भाषा एवं आलङ्कारिक दृष्टि में यह पुराण सर्वोत्कृष्ट है, इसलिए फलश्रुति के रूप में कहा गया है कि –

> धनञ्जये हाटकसंपरीक्षा रणाजिरे शस्त्रभृतां परीक्षा ।
> विपत्तिकाले गृहिणी परीक्षा विद्यावतां भागवते परीक्षा ॥

श्रीमद्भागवतमहापुराण की प्रमुख टीकासम्पत्ति

1. *श्रीधरस्वामी की भावार्थदीपिका*

इनकी टीका के विषय में यह प्रसिद्धि है –

> व्यासो वेत्ति शुको वेत्ति राजा वेत्ति न वेत्ति वा ।
> श्रीधरः सकलं वेत्ति श्रीनृसिंहप्रसादतः ॥

इससे यह जान पड़ता है कि ये नृसिंह भगवान् के उपासक थे । इनका आविर्भाव काल 1300-50 ई. अर्थात् चौदहवीं शताब्दी का मध्यभाग माना जाता है ।

2. *वंशीधर की भावार्थदीपिकाप्रकाश*

श्री वंशीधर द्वारा निर्मित यह टीका वंशीधरी के नाम से भी जानी जाती है । इसमें श्रीधर स्वामीकृत भावार्थदीपिका की अद्वैतपरक व्याख्या प्रस्तुत की गई है ।

3. *श्रीराधारमणदास गोस्वामी की दीपिनी*

श्रीराधारमणदास गोस्वामीकृत दीपिनी टीका श्रीधरी की अद्वैतमतावलम्बिनी व्याख्या प्रस्तुत करती है ।

4. *श्री वीरराघवाचार्य की भागवतचन्द्रिका*

इनका समय चौदहवीं शताब्दी माना जाता है । रामानुज के मतानुसार भागवत के रहस्यों की जानकारी के लिए यह टीका अनुपम है । ये सुदर्शन सूरि के अनुयायी थे ।

5. *श्रीविजयध्वज की पदरत्नावली*

द्वैतमत के प्रतिष्ठापक श्रीमध्वाचार्य ने भागवत के रहस्यों के उद्घाटनार्थ "भागवत-तात्पर्यनिर्णय" नामक ग्रन्थ लिखा था । परन्तु यह वस्तुतः व्याख्या नहीं है अपितु मूल ग्रन्थ भागवत पर आधारित अन्य एक ग्रन्थ है । इस मत के अनुकूल प्रसिद्ध टीकाकार विजयध्वज हैं । जिन्होंने अपनी पदरत्नावली में भागवत की द्वैतपरक व्याख्या की है ।

6. *श्रीमद्जीवगोस्वामी का क्रमसन्दर्भ*

जीवगोस्वामी भागवत के अनुपम मार्मिक विद्वान् थे और इस पुराण के गूढ अर्थ की अभिव्यक्ति के लिए उन्होंने षट्सन्दर्भ नामक छः सन्दर्भों की पृथक् रचना की है । यह क्रमसन्दर्भ एक प्रकार से उनका सप्तम सन्दर्भ है । अपने पितृव्य रूप गोस्वामी तथा सनातन गोस्वामी की आज्ञा से निर्मित होने के कारण इन्होंने इस ग्रन्थ को रूपसनातनानुशासनभारतीगर्भ की संज्ञा दी है । जीवगोस्वामी की यह टीका सम्पूर्ण भागवत के ऊपर है । व्याख्यान की दृष्टि से यह बड़ी मार्मिक, प्रामाणिक तथा तलस्पर्शिनी है ।

7. *विश्वनाथ चक्रवर्ती की सारार्थदर्शिनी*

विश्वनाथ चक्रवर्ती चैतन्य सम्प्रदाय के मान्य आचार्य थे । उन्होंने ही भागवत की यह सुबोध टीका निबद्ध की है, जो श्रीधर स्वामी, प्रभु चैतन्य तथा उनके गुरु के व्याख्यानों के सार संकलन करने के कारण सारार्थदर्शिनी नाम से विख्यात है । यह टीका श्लोकों के मर्म को समझने में नितान्त कृतकार्य है ।

8. *शुकदेव की सिद्धान्तप्रदीप*

निम्बार्क मतानुयायी शुकदेवाचार्य ने भागवत की यह नई टीका लिखकर निम्बार्काचार्य के सिद्धान्तों का प्रकाशन किया है, क्योंकि आचार्य निम्बार्क की लिखी भागवत की कोई व्याख्या नहीं मिलती है । शुकदेवाचार्य की सिद्धान्तप्रदीप टीका तो सम्पूर्ण भागवत पर है, परन्तु इस मत के अन्य आचार्यों ने भी दशम स्कन्ध के रासलीला आदि प्रसंगों की बड़ी सरस व्याख्या प्रस्तुत की है । टीका के आरम्भ में इन्होंने अपने प्राचीन आचार्य श्रीहंस भगवान्, सनत्कुमार, देवर्षि नारद तथा निम्बार्काचार्य को नमस्कार किया है ।

9. *वल्लभाचार्य की सुबोधिनी*

वल्लभाचार्य ने शुद्धाद्वैत मत के अनुसार अपनी प्रसिद्ध टीका सुबोधिनी लिखी है । यह समग्र भागवत के ऊपर उपलब्ध नहीं होती है ।

10. *पुरुषोत्तमचरण गोस्वामी की सुबोधिनीप्रकाश*

पुरुषोत्तमचरण गोस्वामीकृत सुबोधिनीप्रकाश में श्रीवल्लभाचार्य विरचित सुबोधिनी टीका की शुद्धाद्वैतमतावलम्बिनी व्याख्या प्रस्तुत की गई है ।

11. *गिरिधारलाल गोस्वामी की बालबोधिनी*

बालप्रबोधिनी गोस्वामी गिरधरलालकृत यथानाम-गुण वाली है । इसमें न केवल स्कन्धों के विषयों का, अपितु अध्यायसम्बन्धी विषयों का भी सूक्ष्म विभाजन प्रस्तुत किया गया है ।

12. *सुदर्शन सूरि की शुकपक्षीया*

सुदर्शन सूरि श्रीरामानुज के श्रीभाष्य पर श्रुतप्रकाशिका के रचयिता हैं । ये विशिष्टाद्वैतमत के विशिष्ट आचार्य हैं । इनकी टीका आकार में लघु होने पर भी भावप्रकाशन में अत्यन्त गम्भीर है ।

13. *श्री सनातन गोस्वामी की बृहद् वैष्णवतोषिणी*

श्री सनातन गोस्वामी की बृहद् वैष्णवतोषिणी टीका प्राचीनतर है । यह चैतन्यमहाप्रभु के अनुयायियों की टीकाओं में अधिक प्रामाणिक मानी जाती है । यह केवल दशम स्कन्ध पर ही उपलब्ध होती है ।

14. *श्रीहरि की हरिभक्तिरसायन टीका*

भागवत के दशम स्कन्ध के पूर्वार्द्ध पर हरिभक्तिरसायन टीका के रचयिता श्रीहरि हैं । ये एक महनीय कवि तथा भक्त हुए हैं । इनकी उक्त टीका पद्यात्मक है । यह साक्षात् टीका न होकर भी प्रभावशाली एवं मौलिक ग्रन्थ प्रतीत होता है, जिनमें भागवती लीला को कोमल पदावली में ललित रूप में विन्यास किया है ।

इन टीकाकारों की भागवत के एक-एक पद पर अति विस्तृत व्याख्या अपनी परम्परा के अनुसार ही है । स्थाली-पुलाकन्याय से भागवत के प्रथम श्लोक के प्रथम पद "जन्मादि" की व्याख्या निम्न प्रकार से दर्शाई गई है ।

1. भावार्थदीपिका - विश्वस्य जन्मस्थितिभङ्ग

2. भावार्थदीपिकाप्रकाश – अद्वैतपरकव्याख्या होने से इसमें शिव और विष्णु को एक माना गया है ।

   यो हरिः स शिवः साक्षाद्यः शिवः स हरिः स्मृतः ।
   शिवस्य हृदयं विष्णुः विष्णोश्च हृदयं शिवः ।
   ईषदप्यन्तरं कृत्वा रौरवं नरकं व्रजेत् ।।

3. वीरराघवः – जीवजडजातीयत्वशङ्का घटपटादिभ्य एव व्यावर्तयति, वैजात्यं न सिध्यति जीवादिभ्यो ब्रह्म व्यावर्तयति ।

4. जयध्वजीयटीकापदरत्नावली – यतो इमानि भूतानि जायन्ते, येन जातानि जीवन्ति अहं सर्वस्य प्रभवो मत्तः सर्वं प्रवर्तते । स्रष्टा पाता तथैवात्ता निखिलस्यैक एव तु ब्रह्मैव जगत्कारणत्वम् ।

5. जीवगोस्वामी – सृष्टादिशक्तिमत् तत्त्ववाचित्वात् । स ब्रह्मणं सृजति, रुद्रेण विलापयति । अत एव विवृत्तम् ।

6. विश्वनाथचक्रवर्ती – हिरण्यगर्भः समवर्तताग्रे भूतस्य जातः पतिरेक आसीत् ब्रह्मणः पारतन्त्रम् ।

7. सिद्धान्तप्रदीपः – तदात्मानं स्वयमकुरुत तदैक्षत बहु स्याम् । इत्यादिश्रुति-प्रोक्ताद्यतो हेतोः अस्य विश्वस्य जन्मादि जन्मस्थितिभङ्गमोक्षं भवति तमित्यर्थः ।

8. भागवतभावार्थप्रकाशिका – जन्माद्यस्य यतः अस्य प्रत्यक्षादिसकल-प्रमाणसन्निधापितस्य जगतो जन्मादिजन्मस्थितिभङ्गं यतो भवतीति तं सत्यं धीमहीति सम्बन्धाः ।

भागवतमहापुराण की विभिन्न परम्परा के अनुसार उपलब्ध अन्य प्रकाशित एवं अप्रकाशित टीकाएं

अद्वैतमत सम्प्रदाय

- जयोल्लासनिधि – अप्पय दीक्षित, श्रीवत्सगोत्र, श्रीवासध्वरि के पुत्र, अड्यार, चेनै, तमिलनाडु ।
- बोधसुधा – आनन्दपूर्ण विद्यासागर मुनि, ग्रन्थपुर ।

- सारसंग्रह – उत्तमबोध यति, ग्रन्थपुर, इसमें श्रीधराचार्य मतों की समीक्षा की गई है ।

- प्रकाश – जगन्नाथ ।

- अमृततरङ्गिणी – ज्ञानपूर्ण यति, कोलकाता विश्वविद्यालय, कोलकाता, इस पर ब्रह्मविद्याध्वरि की टीका भी है ।

- कृष्णपदी – राघवानन्द, कृष्णानन्द मुनि के शिष्य, आड्डयार, बरौदा, देशमङ्गलम्, ग्रन्थपुर, किल्लिमङ्गलतु मन, मैसूर, तिरुपति, रविवर्मा संस्कृत ग्रन्थमाला, संस्कृत कालेज, त्रिपुनितुरा, 1973 ।

- सर्ववेदार्थप्रकाशिका प्रकाशिनी – रामनारायण दास, भवानीदास के शिष्य ।

- भावार्थ-दीपिका – श्रीधरस्वामी आड्डायार, इलाहाबाद अलवर, अमेरिका, आन्ध्र विश्वविद्यालय, आवणप्प्रभु मन, बड़ौदा, भरतपुर, मुम्बई विश्वविद्यालय, BORI, बर्नेल, चन्दौसी, क्रांगोनोर, ढाक्का, दाहिललक्ष्मी, दरभंगा, देंशमङ्गलम्, देवप्रयाग, असम, ग्रन्थपुर, किल्लिमङ्गलतु मन, किजक्कुम्भागतु मन, कुमारपुरम्, कुरुक्षेत्र विश्वविद्यालय, लखनऊ संस्कृत परिषद्, मद्रास विश्वविद्यालय, मैसूर, नादुविलमठम्, नागपुर विश्वविद्यालय, नासिक, नेपाल, ओसमानिया विश्वविद्यालय, पलियम्, पेरिस, पथवारि, प्रतिवादिभयङ्कर, प्रयाग, पुतुवामन मन, राजपुर, RASB, RORI, टेक्केमठम्, RSVP तिरुपति, त्रिपूणितुरा, उदयपुर, वङ्गीय परिषद्, विश्वभारती, VRI वृन्दावन, VVBISIS होशियारपुर ।

- भावार्थदीपिकाप्रबोधिनी - BISM ।

- भावार्थदीपिकाप्रकाश – काशीनाथ उपाध्याय, मुम्बई विश्वविद्यालय, वेलणकर, RASB, RORI ।

- भावार्थदीपिकाभाव – नारायणदेवाचार्य, संस्कृत कालेज, बनारस ।

- पदयोजना अथवा अर्थरत्नमाला – भवदास अथवा भगवद् दास, अड्डयार, टीका-राघवानन्दतीर्थ, टीका-वंशीधार, चौखम्बा संस्कृत प्रकाशन, दिल्ली ।

- श्रीधरीकण्टकोद्धार अथवा भावार्थदीपिकाभाव – शिवराम, मुम्बई वि. वि. वेलणकर, जयपुर ।

- सुखानन्दिनी – सुखानन्द BISM ।

- चूर्णिका – अप्पाजी पण्डित, भारद्वाज गोत्रीय, गुण्डमालीय वंश, चेनु भट्ट

के शिष्य, मैसूर मुनिभावप्रकाशिका, कृष्णगुरु, भारद्वाज गोत्र, नृसिंह गुरु के पुत्र, अड्डयार, आन्ध्र विश्वविद्यालय, मद्रास, मैसूर ।

- शुकपक्षीया – गोपाल, बाधूल गोत्र, BHU, देशिक आड्यार ।
- तत्त्वप्रदीपिका – नारायण यति TCD ।
- शुकहृदयरञ्जिनी – नृसिंहसूरि, भारद्वाज गोत्र, वासुदेव गुरु के पुत्र, श्रीनिवास देशिक के शिष्य ।
- भागवतार्थतत्त्वदीपिका – भाष्यकारसूरि कौण्डिन्यगोत्र, वेङ्करार्य के पुत्र, तिरुमलवेङ्कटाचार्य के शिष्य ।
- नारायणीव्याख्या – रामानुजाचार्य RORI ।
- चन्द्रचन्द्रिका – वीर राघवाचार्य, श्रीशैलाचार्य के पुत्र एवं शिष्य, आड्यार, मैसूर ।
- मुनिभावप्रकाशिका – वीरराघव, आड्यार वीरराघवीय वीरराघवाचार्य, मधुकरवाणी प्रेस ।
- शुकतात्पर्यरत्नावली – वीरराघव अथवा अमृतकवि, वत्सगोत्र, अहोविल के पुत्र, मैसूर ।
- भागवततात्पर्यचन्द्रिका – वेङ्कटकृष्ण, कृष्णार्य के पुत्र, कौशिक गोत्र, वेङ्कटवरदाचार्य के शिष्य, मद्रास, मैसूर ।
- मणिप्रवालदीपिका – वेङ्कटराघवाचार्य, तिरुपति ।
- जयमङ्गला – श्रीनिवासाचार्य, कौशिक गोत्र, ताताचार्य के पुत्र, बर्नेल, गन्धपुर, व्याख्या - सुदर्शन सूरि, आन्ध्र विश्वविद्यालय, RORI ।
- शुकपक्षीया – सुदर्शनाचार्य, उपनाम वेदाचार्य, वाग्विजय के पुत्र, आड्यार, मैसूर, ओसमानिया, RORI, RSVP, उदयपुर ।
- शुकभावार्थकाशिका – सुन्दरराज, वरदार्य के पुत्र, श्रीवत्सगोत्र, मैसूर ।

द्वैत सम्प्रदाय

- तात्पर्यनिर्णय – आनन्दतीर्थ, उपनाम पूर्णप्रज्ञ, अन्यनाम, मध्वाचार्य, अड्यार, बड़ौदा, BORI, बर्नेल, मद्रास, धारवाड़, मैसूर, शृंङ्गेरी, त्रिपुनित्तूरा, उदयपुर प्रकाशित, टी. आर. कृष्णाचार्य ।

टीकाएं –

भागवततात्पर्यटीकासंग्रह, तिरुपति ।

भागवततात्पर्यदीपिका, ग्रन्थपुर ।

भागवततात्पर्यप्रबोधिनी, सुपेरकर ।

तात्पर्यदीपिका, BHU, वर्णेल, RORI वाई ।

तात्पर्यबोधिनी, TD ।

दीपिका, Trav. University, BHU, बीकानेर, मैसूर ।

प्रकाशिका, कृष्णपुर ।

प्रबोधिनी, बर्णेल, TD ।

प्रमेयैका – विजयध्वज MD ।

प्रमेयचन्द्रिका – आनन्दतीर्थ ।

विवरण – कट्टे हिम्माचार्य, मैसूर ।

मणिप्रकाश – वेदगर्भ नारायण, उपनाम पुट्टाचार्य, मैसूर ।

मन्दबोधिनी – शेषाचार्य, चालाद्रि नरसिंहाचार्य के शिष्य ।

तात्पर्यनिर्णय प्रकाश/प्रमेयमणिमाला – श्रीनिवासतीर्थ, बड़ौदा, बीकानेर, कृष्णपुर धारवाड, मैसूर, पेशावर ।

तात्पर्यटिप्पणी – चट्टी जनार्दन, वेङ्कटाद्रि के पुत्र वेङ्कटाचार्य के शिष्य ।

भावप्रकाशिका/दुर्घटभावदीपिका – नरसिंहाचार्य, जयपुर ।

- पदरत्नावली अथवा विजयध्वजीय – विजयध्वजतीर्थ महेन्द्र तीर्थ के शिष्य, बर्नेल, अलवर, बड़ौदा, बीकानेर, मुम्बई ।
- सज्जनहिता – चट्टि वेङ्कटाद्रि ।
- मन्दनन्दिनी – व्यासतत्त्वज्ञ ।
- पदमुक्तावलि – लिङ्गेरि श्रीनिवास ।
- टिप्पण – सत्यधर्म तीर्थ ।
- दुर्घटार्थप्रबोधिनी – सत्याभिनवयति, BORI कृष्णपुर ।

शुद्धाद्वैत सम्प्रदाय

- तत्त्वदीपिका, VVBISIS ।
- तत्त्वार्थदीपिका, BORI ।
- तत्त्वमञ्जरी, ASB ।
- निबन्धविवरण, New DC ।
- दीपिका, BORI ।
- बालप्रबोधिनी, RASL ।
- सुधा, RORI ।
- भागवतटीका, उत्कल पद्यानुवाद के साथ ।
- राधावल्लभी – राधावल्लभ, कवीन्द्राचार्य ।
- सुबोधिनी, अड्यार, अमेरिका, BORI, देशमङ्गलम् BORI, प्रयाग, BORI बड़ौदा, BBRAS, BORI कवीन्द्राचार्य, BORI, VORI, तिरुपति, उदयपुर, मुम्बई विश्वविद्यालय ।

  टीकाएं –

  प्रकाश-पीताम्बर – यदुपति के पुत्र, मुम्बई, विश्वविद्यालय ।

  भागवत निर्णय – पुरुषोत्तम के पुत्र, जोधपुर ।

  प्रकाश-पुरुषोत्तम – पीताम्बर के पुत्र, जयपुर ।

  भागवतस्वरूपविषयकशङ्कानिरास – पुरुषोत्तम, मुम्बई ।

  सुबोधिनी योजना निबन्धः – बालकृष्ण, उपनाम-लालूभट्ट, RORI, BORI ।

  पुष्टिमार्गप्रकाशिका – मुम्बई ।

  सुबोधिनीलेख – उदयपुर ।

  वृत्तिप्रकाश-विट्ठलदीक्षा अथवा विट्ठलेश्वर, वल्लभाचार्य के पुत्र ।

मीमांसकाद्वैत सम्प्रदाय

टीका = अनन्तदेव/अनन्तोपाधयाय, BORI ।

भागवततात्पर्य – खण्डदेव, SB New DC ।

- अमृततरङ्गिणी – लक्ष्मीधर नृसिंह के पुत्र एवं अनन्तानन्द रघुनाथ के शिष्य।

रामानन्दीय सम्प्रदाय

- भावार्थदीपिकासंग्रह – तीर्थस्वामी।
- भावार्थदीपिका प्रकरणक्रम संग्रह – तीर्थस्वामी।
- भागवतमञ्जरी – तीर्थस्वामी, BORI।
- भागवताशय – रामानन्दतीर्थ, अद्वैतप्रकाश में उल्लिखित।

अचिन्त्यभेदाभेद सम्प्रदाय

- अन्वितार्थ प्रकाशिका – रामतेज पाण्डेय, चौखम्बा, दिल्ली।
- आनन्दवर्षिणी, BHU।
- चन्द्रिका, NPS।
- हर्षिणी, तोषिणी, सारार्थदर्शिनी, SB, New DC।
- तोषणीसार – काशीनाथ उपाध्याय, BISM।
- भूषण, VRI।
- अन्वितार्थप्रकाशिका – गङ्गासहाय, रामधन के पुत्र, Ptd।
- तोषिणीसार – गोकुलनाथ, CPB।
- भूषण-गोपाल, RASB Ptd, गणपतकृष्ण प्रेस, मुम्बई।
- व्याख्यालेश – गोपालशर्मा, उपनाम गोपालचक्रवर्ती, श्रीधरस्वामी की टीका पर आधारित, RASB।
- निध्यार्था – गोपालभट्ट, RORI।
- चित्सुखी – चित्सुखाचार्य, टीका जीवगोस्वामी, VRI।
- वृहत्क्रमसन्दर्भ – जीवगोस्वामी।
- क्रमसन्दर्भ – जीवगोस्वामी, अलवर, BORI, OSM, पथावरी, उदयपुर, विश्वभारती, VRI।

- लघुवैष्णवतोषिणी – जीवगोस्वामी, बृहद्वैष्णवतोषिणी पर आधारित, मुम्बई, जयपुर, औध पथावरी, RASB, RORI ।
- भागवतनिर्णयसिद्धान्त – दामोदर, BHU ।
- वैष्णवानन्दिनी – बलदेवविद्याभूषण ।
- साम्प्रदायिकसारार्थकदर्शिनी – बलभद्र, NPS ।
- वैष्णवतोषिणी – रघुनाथदास, BHU ।
- तत्त्वसार – राधामोहनशर्मा, RASB ।
- दीपिकादीपन – राधारमणदास, जीवनलाल के शिष्य, BHU ।
- भावार्थदीपिका – वंशीधरगोस्वामी, VRI ।
- भागवतसारार्थदर्शिनी – विश्वनाथ चक्रवर्ती, बैजनाथ के पुत्र, बरौदा, अलवर, उदयपुर, लखनऊ, RORI, SSPC ।
- सिद्धान्तप्रदीप – शुकसुधी, VRI ।
- चैतन्यमतचन्द्रिका – श्रीनाथ पण्डित, RASB ।

श्रीमद्भागवतमहापुराण पर आधारित अन्य ग्रन्थ

1. भागवतकथा संक्षेप – बल्लभाचार्य, लक्ष्मण भट्ट के पुत्र, RORI ।
2. तत्त्वदीप अथवा तत्त्वार्थदीप – बीकानेर, BORI ।
3. तत्त्वदीपशास्त्रार्थनिरूपण, RORI ।
4. तत्त्वप्रदीप अथवा प्रकाश – वल्लभाचार्य, BHU ।
5. तत्त्वदीपप्रकाशसंग्रह निरूपण ।
6. तत्त्वदीप निबन्ध योजना – पुरुषोत्तम, BORI, SB New DC Ptd. ।
7. तात्पर्यार्थ निरूपण, SB New DC ।
8. तात्पर्यचन्द्रिका – वेङ्कटकृष्ण, कृष्णार्य के पुत्र, VVRI, BISM, RORI ।
9. गूढार्थदीपिका – धनपति सूरि, रामकुमार के पुत्र, SB New DC RORI ।
10. भागवत उपायत्वविचार, जयपुर, France ।

11. भागवत एकश्लोकी, NPS, RORI, जयपुर ।
12. भागवतकथा – मध्वद्वारा उल्लिखित ।
13. भागवतकथा कथन क्रम, SB New DC ।
14. भागवतकथाभूषण, RORI ।
15. भागवतकथासंग्रह, मैसूर ।
16. भागवतकथा साप्ताहिक – राममूर्ति शास्त्री पौराणिक, वाराणसी ।
17. भागवतकथासार, SB, New DC ।
18. भागवतकल्पद्रुम, मुम्बई ।
19. भागवतकल्पद्रुमनिकुञ्ज, मुम्बई ।
20. भागवतकुसुमाञ्जलि, कमलकुञ्ज, कोलकाता ।
21. भागवतकौमुदी, RASB ।
22. भागवतक्रोडपत्राणि, जयपुर ।
23. भागवतगीतावली – सनातनगोस्वामी, अलवर ।
24. भागवतगुटिका, VRI ।
25. भागवतगुरुमुखी, विश्वभारती ।
26. भागवतगूढपद्यानि, BORI ।
27. भागवतगूढार्थ, VRI ।
28. भागवतचतुःश्लोकी, बड़ौदा, BHU, BISM ।
29. भागवतसार, मैसूर ।
30. भागवतचित्र, जयपुर ।
31. भागवतचूर्णिका, आनन्दाश्रम, BISM, RSVP ।
32. भागवतचूर्णिकातात्पर्य, BORI ।
33. भागवतज्योतिषयोर्विरोधपरिहारः, BOSM, RORI, बड़ौदा ।
34. भागवतदानप्रयोग, SB New DC ।

35. भागवतद्वयनिर्णय, SB New D.C. ।
36. भागवतद्वयव्यवस्था – काशीनाथ भट्ट का शिवानन्द, SB New DC ।
37. भागवद् द्वात्रिंशत् प्रश्नोत्तरी – गोविन्दरामव्यास, SB New DC ।
38. भागवतद्वादशस्कन्धार्थदिग्दर्शन, SB New DC, VSVS, Poona ।
39. भागवतधर्म, MD ।
40. भागवतध्यान, नागपुर, Uni ।
41. भागवतनमस्कार श्लोक, Adyar ।
42. भागवतनान्दी श्लोक, Adyar ।
43. भागवतनाममाहात्म्य – पुरुषोत्तमदेव ।
44. भागवतनिबन्ध अथवा तत्त्वदीप – वल्लभाचार्य ।
45. भागवतनिर्णयसिद्धान्त, Adyar ।
46. भागवतपचीसी, कुरुक्षेत्र ।
47. भागवतसमुच्चय, पुरुषोत्तमसहस्रनाम, कृष्णपुर ।
48. भागवतपाञ्चरात्रागम – कवीन्द्राचार्य ।
49. भागवतपुरश्चरणपूजनविधि, सौराष्ट्र ।
50. भागवतपूजनक्रम, उदयपुर ।
51. भागवतप्रकरण, RORI ।
52. भागवतप्रकरणाध्यायविभाग, VVRI ।
53. भागवतप्रकाश, RORI ।
54. भागवतक्रमप्रकरण, नासिक ।
55. भागवतप्रबन्ध – नारायण पण्डित ।
56. भागवत प्रबन्धन संग्रह, VRI ।
57. भागवत प्रशंसवाचना, MD ।
58. भागवतप्रसाद, SB New DC ।

59. भागवत प्रामाण्यविचार ।

60. भागवत फलश्रुति, RASB ।

61. भागवतभक्तिचिन्तामणि – दामोदर दास, उत्कल ।

Abbreviations of the Institutions for Manuscripts on Bhāgavata-Mahāpurāṇa

BHU: Banaras Hindu University, Varanasi.

BORI: Bhandarkar Oriental Research Institute, Poona.

GOL: Government Oriental Library, Madras.

KTP: K.T. Pandurangi, Dharwar.

MLBD: Motilal Banarsidass, Delhi.

NCC: New Catalogue Catalogorum.

NPS: Nagari Pracharini Sabha, Varanasi.

OSM: Orissa State Museum.

RASB : Royal Asiatic Society, Bengal.

RORI: Rajasthan Oriental Research Institute.

RSVP: Rashtriya Sanskrit Vidyapeetha, Tirupati.

SSPC: Sanskrita Sahitya Parishad, Culcutta.

TCD: Descriptive Catalogue of the Sanskrit in Curator Office Library, Trivandrum.

VRI: Vrindavan Research Institute, Vrindavan.

VVBISIS: Visweswarananda Viswa Bandhu Institute of Sanskrit and Indological Studies.

VVRI: Vishveswarananda Vedic Research Institute, Hosiarpur.

WIHM: Welcome Institute for the History of Medicine.

7

पाण्डुलिपियों में आयुर्वेद

श्याम सिंह राजपुरोहित

संस्कृत साहित्य का इतिहास जैसा कि सर्वविदित-सर्वज्ञात है, उपलब्ध सभी दूसरे साहित्यों के इतिहास से अति प्राचीन है। इस साहित्य का प्रारम्भ वेदों से होता है। विश्व में उपलब्ध समस्त साहित्य में वेद आर्य साहित्य के सर्वाधिक प्राचीन ग्रन्थ हैं, एवं समस्त ज्ञान-विज्ञान के आदि-स्रोत भी हैं। आयुर्वेद का मूल भी वैदिक सूक्तों में पाया जाता है। भारतीय धार्मिक अनुश्रुति के अनुसार सभी विद्याएं ब्रह्मा से उत्पन्न मानी गई हैं। सब विद्याओं का स्रोत वेद ही हैं व वेद के प्रणेता ब्रह्मा है। आयुर्वेदिक ग्रन्थों की अनुश्रूति भी यही है कि आयुर्वेद शास्त्र का प्रारम्भ ब्रह्मा से हुआ है।

ब्रह्मण हि यथाप्रोक्तमायुर्वेदं प्रजापतिः ।
जग्राह निखिलेनादावश्विनौ तु पुनस्ततः ।।
– चरक, सूत्र 1.4

ज्ञान के अवतरण के विषय में निरुक्तकार (यास्क) ने एक सुन्दर सन्दर्भ दिया है – सबसे प्रथम ऐसे ऋषि हुए जिन्होंने धर्म का साक्षात्कार स्वयं किया था, उन्होंने अपने पीछे आने वालों को उपदेश द्वारा मंत्रों को दिया या सिखलाया। उसके बाद ऐसे लोग हुए जिनके लिए मात्र उपदेश ही पर्याप्त नहीं थे। अतः उन्होंने अपनी सुविधा हेतु ग्रन्थ-प्रणयन की परम्परा कायम की। इसी के परिणामस्वरूप समस्त वेद-वेदांग आदि ग्रन्थ के रूप में हमारे समक्ष आए।

साक्षात्कृत धर्माणः ऋषयो बभूवुः।
तेऽवरेभ्योऽसाक्षात्कृतधर्मेभ्यो उपदेशन मंत्रान् संप्रादुः।।

उपदेशायग्लापन्तोऽवरेविल्वग्रहणायेमँ ग्रन्थ समाम्नासिषुः।
वेदं च वेदांगनि च।। – निरुक्त

इससे स्पष्ट है कि प्राचीन काल में शिक्षण की श्रुति परम्परा ही रही है लेखन कला बाद में विकसित हुई है।

ग्रन्थ-प्रणयन से पूर्व के युग को प्रवचन युग कहा जा सकता है। इसके लिए पाणिनि व्याकरण के दो सूत्र उल्लेखित किए जा सकते हैं – "तेन प्रोक्तम्" (पा० 4.3.101) एवं "कृते ग्रन्था" (पा० 4.3.116) प्रवचन अथवा उपदेश में अर्थ या प्रतिपाद्य विषय की प्रमुखता रहती है। शब्दों के पूर्व-पश्चात् की नहीं। ग्रन्थ-प्रणयन में शब्दों के चयन एवं उनके उचित क्रम का पूरा स्थान रहता है। ग्रन्थ शब्द ग्रथित-ग्रन्थित अर्थ को बताता है। प्राचीन पुस्तकें ताड़-पत्र या भोज-पत्र पर लिखी जाती थी इनके बीच में छेद कर इन्हें गुम्फित किया जाता था, इसी से ये ग्रन्थ कहलाते थे। प्रवचन के लिए आज व्याख्यान शब्द का प्रयोग होता है एवं ग्रन्थ-प्रणयन के लिए पुस्तक या पुस्तक-लेखन। पुस्तक का अर्थ पहलवी भाषा में चमड़ा है। भारतवर्ष में ताड़ या भोज-पत्र पर लेखन-कार्य किया जाता था तथा ईरान में चमड़े पर।

उपनिषद् व गीता में भी श्रवण व मनन का वर्णन आता है –

आश्चर्य वद् वद्ति कश्चिदेन – गीता 2.29

अन्येत्वेवंमजानन्ता श्रुत्वाऽन्येभ्य: उपासते।
तेऽपिचातितरन्त्येव मृत्युं श्रुतिपरायण:।।
– गीता 13.25

श्रोतव्यो मनतव्यो निदिधासितव्य:।। – छान्दोग्योपनिषद्

इस समय का साहित्य दो तरह का पाया जाता है, एक वह जिसका संबंध साक्षात किसी व्यक्ति-विशेष से होता है। जैसे सुश्रुत संहिता में – सुश्रुत पूछने वाला और दिवोदास कहने वाले है। दूसरा वह – जिसका संबंध किसी व्यक्ति-विशेष से नहीं होता जैसे वैदिक वाङ्मय। आयुर्वेद का उपलब्ध साहित्य प्रथम प्रकार का है इस साहित्य में किसी को कर्ता नहीं माना जाता उसे प्रवक्ता ही कहा जाता है जैसे – "यथोवाच भगवान् काश्यप:" चरक संहिता में – "शिष्यमग्निवेशम ब्रवीत्" आदि वचन ।

इसके बाद के काल में श्रुति व लेखन दोनों परम्परा रही, प्रवचन भी होते थे व ग्रन्थ-प्रणयन भी।

काल-क्रम से परिस्थितियों में परिवर्तन होने के कारण विचार-विनियम, विचार-प्रदर्शन, स्वपक्ष-स्थापन, परपक्ष-दूषण कार्यों के लिए लिपि की आवश्यकता हुई जिससे जनसाधारण तक अपने विचार पहुँचाए जा सकें।

ग्रन्थ-रचना की दृष्टि से ऋग्वेद संहिता एक ही समय की प्रतीत नहीं होती इसका दशम मण्डल परवर्ती लगता है। अथर्ववेद सबके बाद का वेद है, आयुर्वेद का संबंध इसी से है। काश्यप ने आयुर्वेद को पांचवा वेद बताया है –

ऋग्वेद यजुर्वेद सामवेदाथर्ववेदेभ्य: पंचमोऽयमायुर्वेद: ।। – काश्यप

सुश्रुत संहिता का प्रारंभ ही आयु शब्द का लोप कर "वेदोत्पत्ति" नामक अध्याय से किया गया है। विद् धातु का अर्थ है ज्ञान। जिससे आयु का ज्ञान हो, वह आयुर्वेद है – "आयुरस्मिन् विद्यतेऽनेन वा आयुर्विन्दति इति आयुर्वेद:" आयुर्वेद में वेद नाम रहने से इसकी उत्पत्ति ब्रह्मा से ही मानी गई है – "त्रिसूत्रं शाश्वतं पुण्यं बुबुधे यं पितामह:" – चरक। वेदों में आयुर्वेद की चर्चा स्थान-स्थान पर मिलती है। इसी प्रकार वेदों की पुष्टि करने वाले ब्राह्मण ग्रन्थों उपनिषदों में भी आयुर्वेद का विषय स्थान-स्थान पर मिलता है।

ऋग्वेद में भेषज शब्द आता है – "भिषक्तमं त्वा भिषजाशणोमि" (ऋ 2.7.16) वेदों में बहुत से शब्द रोगवाचक, औषधवाचक मिलते हैं। देवताओं के चिकित्सक का नाम अश्विनी है यह युगल है। इनके लिए तथा वरुण और रुद्र के लिए भिषक् शब्द वेदों में मिलता है। ऋग्वेद काल में वैद्यक एक व्यवसाय था। वेद में एक गृहस्थी का वर्णन है जिसमें घर का एक सदस्य कारु (बुनने वाला) है, दूसरा सदस्य भिषक् (चिकित्सक) है, माता कूटने का धंधा करती है। भिषक् का लक्षण भी ऋग्वेद में दिया है – जहां पर औषधियाँ राजा की समिति-सभा के सामने एकत्रित होती है, उसको भिषक् कहते हैं –

यत्रौषधि समग्मत राजान: समितावित। विप्र: स उच्यते भिषग्
रक्षोहामीवचातन: – ऋ० 10.97.6

औषध एवं भेषज में अंतर –

औषधं द्रव्यसंयोगं ब्रवते दीपनादिकम्।
हुतव्रततपोदानं शान्ति कर्म च भेषजम्।। – काश्यप संहिता

ऋग्वेद संहिता में आयुर्वेद से संबंधित कुछ मंत्रों का विवरण इस प्रकार है – वृद्धावस्था में जीर्ण हुए च्यवन ऋषि का अश्विनीकुमारों से पुन: यौवन प्राप्ति (ऋ० 1.116.10; 1.117.13)। दासों द्वारा अग्नि और जल में फेंकने पर भी बचे हुए दीर्घतमस् ऋषि का पुन: दास द्वारा सिर और छाती के काट देने पर अश्विनीकुमारों द्वारा जीवन देकर दस युगपर्यन्त बिना वृद्धावस्था के जीवित रहना (ऋ० 1.158.4.6)। युद्ध-क्षेत्र में खेल राजा

की पत्नी विश्पला की शत्रुओं द्वारा टांग काट दिए जाने पर अश्विनीकुमारों द्वारा लोहे की जांघ जोड़ना (ऋ० 1.116.15)। अश्विनीकुमारों द्वारा दधीच ऋषि के सिर को अलग करके घोड़े का सिर लगाना व मधु विद्याग्रहण पश्चात् पुनः घोड़े का सिर हटाकर दधीच ऋषि के स्वयं के सिर को लगाना (1.116, 12.1-117)। अन्धे ऋजाश्व को दृष्टिदान (1.116.16.1), बहरे नार्षद को श्रोत्रदान (ऋ० 1.117.8), नपुंसक पति वाली वध्रमती को पुत्रोत्पत्ति (1.116.13), नाना विषकृमि का वर्णन व उनका प्रतिकार (1.50.11.13), जल का भेषजत्व (10.137.61, 1.23.19), औषधियों का वर्णन (10.97.1-23), यक्ष्मा, अज्ञात यक्ष्मा, राजयक्ष्मा, हृद्रोग आदि का भी उल्लेख मिलता है।

शुक्ल यजुर्वेद-संहिता में श्लेष्मरोग, अर्श, श्वयथु, पाण्डुश्लीपद, यक्ष्म, मुखपाक, क्षत आदि रोगों का नाश करना (19.81.93/20, 5.9/25.1-9, 10.13.30.8-10) अथर्ववेद में - विशेषकर आयुर्वेद के विषय मिलते हैं, उदाहरण के लिए – तक्म (ज्वर) रोग का वर्णन तथा उसके मद (6.21.1.3) सतत, शारद, ग्रैष्म, शीत, वार्षिक, तृतीयक आदि का निर्देश (1.25.4-5, 21.1-64) तथा कामला रोग के पीले रंग को सूर्य में और पक्षियों में भेजने का वर्णन है इसके स्थान पर गाय का लाल रंग शरीर में लाने को कहा गया है –

> अनुसूर्यमुदयतां हृदद्योतो हरिमा चते।
> रोहितस्य वर्णेन तेनत्वा परिदध्मसि।।
>
> शुकेषु ते हरिभाणं रोपणकासु दध्मसि।
> अतो हारिद्रवेषु ते हरिमाणं निदध्मसि।। – अथर्व 1.22.4

अथर्ववेद में शरीर की नाड़ी तथा धमनियों का निर्देश व अस्थियों की तीन सौ साठ संख्या -

> द्वादश प्रध्यश्चक्रमेकं त्रीणिनभ्यानि क उ तच्चिकेत।
> तत्राहतस्त्रीणिशतानि शङ्कुः वः षष्टिश्च कीला अविचाचला ये।।

के रूप में शारीरिक अवयवों का वर्णन (2.33.1-7) मिलता है।

रोग प्रतिकार के विषय में मूत्राघात में शर या शलाका आदि द्वारा मूत्र का निकालना (1.3.1-9) सुख प्रसव तथा प्रसव की विकृति में शल्य-कर्म-योनि भेदन (1.11.1-6), व्रण की जल-चिकित्सा (5.57.1-3), पकी हुई पिडका का शलाका द्वारा वेधन (7. 74.1-2) आदि प्रक्रियाएं भी वर्णित हैं।

इसी प्रकार ब्राह्मण ग्रन्थों एवं गृह्यसूत्रों में भी आयुर्वेद का उल्लेख है।

जिस प्रकार आज भी भले व्यक्ति रोग के चंगुल में फंस जाते हैं उसी प्रकार वैदिक काल में देवता भी अस्वस्थ हो जाते थे। ब्रह्मा नासूर, वरुण जलोदर, चन्द्रमा राजयक्ष्मा, पूषण दंत-रोग, इन्द्र नेत्र-रोग, कुबेर पानात्यय से पीड़ित हुए व इन सबकी चिकित्सा अश्विनीकुमारों ने ही की। अश्विनी युगल हैं यानि काय-चिकित्सा एवं शल्य-चिकित्सा दोनों में प्रवीण हैं।

बौद्धकालीन साहित्य में भी आयुर्वेद का उल्लेख है। बौद्ध यात्री इत्सिंग 671-95 ई. में भारत आया था उसने भारतीय चिकित्सा में वनस्पतियों, त्रिदोषों, रोग परीक्षा, उपवास का वर्णन किया है, चरक, सुश्रुत के वाक्यों को उसने उद्धृत किया है। लंका का राजा बुद्धदास (ईसा की चौथी सदी में) जो कि स्वयं बुद्ध का अनुयायी था, उसने भारतीय चिकित्सकों की अपने यहाँ नियुक्ति की थी। कनिष्क का राजवैद्य चरक था, इसी समस बौद्ध भिक्षु नागार्जुन हुआ जिसने रसशास्त्र को जन्म दिया। सम्राट् अशोक ने स्थान-स्थान पर आरोग्यशालाएं बनवाई थी। महावग्ग में त्रिदोष, आँख का प्रलेप, नासा रोग के उपाय, सींग से रक्त भक्षण, स्वेदन, तैल, घृत, हरड़, भिन्न-भिन्न लवण, हींग, गण्डूष, सिर में जूँ की चिकित्सा का वर्णन है। विनयपिटक में भेजज स्कन्धक नामक प्रकरण में उदर के शल्य कर्म, सिर के शल्य कर्मों का उल्लेख मिलता है।

प्रसिद्ध बावर पाण्डुलिपियाँ बौद्ध स्तूपों में कासगर में मिली थी ये गुप्तकाल में लिखी गई थीं और दक्षिण व पश्चिमी भारत में पाए जाने वाले वृक्ष ताड़ के पत्रों पर लिखी गई थीं। इन पाण्डुलिपियों में सात पाण्डुलिपियाँ ऐसी थीं जिनमें से तीन का संबंध चिकित्सा से है। इनमें नावनीतक में सबसे प्रथम लहसुन का वर्णन बहुत सुन्दर है –

न भक्षयन्त्येनमतश्चविप्राः शरीर संपर्क विनिः सृतत्वात् नावनीतम्।

लहसुन की उत्पत्ति उसके ब्राह्मणें के न खाने के कारण, खाने की विधि अष्टांगहृदय और नावनीतकम् में समान है – "द्विजा नाश्नन्ति तमतोदैत्यदेह समुद्भवात्।।" काश्यप संहिता में लहसुन कल्प में इसकी उत्पत्ति अन्य प्रकार से दी है, परन्तु स्त्रियों के लिए यह उपयोगी है यह उसमें भी लिखा है – काश्यप पृष्ठ 138 । नावनीतकम् में बहुत से योग हैं, विशेषतः आँख के रोगों के लिए। इसमें 14 अध्याय हैं, इसमें चूर्ण, घृत, तेल, वस्ति, यूष, वाजीकरण, आँख की औषध, केशरञ्जन आदि हैं। इसकी भाषा चरक-सुश्रुत के बाद की है। काश्यप संहिता के साथ नावनीतकम् की रचना बहुत मिलती है।

निघण्टु - औषध निर्माण में निघण्टु-द्रव्यगुण का बहुत महत्त्व है, चरक संहिता में पचास कषाय बताए गए हैं, प्रत्येक कषाय में दस-दस वनस्पतियाँ हैं इस प्रकार से पाँच

सौ वनस्पतियों का वर्णन किया गया है। यह औषधियाँ उस समय मुख्यत: प्रचलन में थी। इनका नाम निर्देश उपलक्षण रूप से किया है, क्योंकि संसार में कोई भी ऐसी वस्तु नहीं है जो कि औषध के काम न आए -

नानषौधभूतं किंचिद् द्रव्यमुपलभ्यते - चरक

अमंत्रं अक्षरों नास्ति, नास्ति मूलं अनौषधं।
अयोग्य पुरुषों नास्ति, योजकस्तत्र दुर्लभः ।।

इन्हीं औषधियों का वर्गीकरण करके निघण्टु बनाए गए । इनमें मुख्य निघण्टु धन्वन्तरि निघण्टु है। मदनपाल का बनाया मदन विनोद निघण्टु 1374 ई. में बना है। राज निघण्टु इसके बाद का है इसके कर्ता नरहरि थे। भाव-प्रकाश निघण्टु औषधियों का व्यापक वर्णन करता है।

आयुर्वेद शास्त्र में रसशास्त्र एवं रसौषधियों का प्रादुर्भाव रसायन चिकित्सा का विकसित रूप है। रोग व्याधि एवं अकाल जरा (असामयिक वृद्धावस्था) के नियंत्रण की पूर्ण व्यवस्था संहिताकालीन ग्रन्थों में मिलती है। संहिताकाल में रसायन प्रभाव के लिए वनस्पतियों का विशेष तथा कुछ खनिज स्रोत के द्रव्यों का भी उपयोग किया जाता था।

रसशास्त्र का विवेचन

संस्कृत साहित्य एवं आयुर्वेद वाङ्मय में रस शब्द से अनेक द्रव्यों का ग्रहण किया जाता है यथा – पारद, स्वरस जल, द्रव, निर्यास, स्वाद, हर्ष, अनुराग, ध्वनि, बालक, सुवर्ण, विष, अमृत, शुक्र, वीर्य, मधुरादि षड्रस। शरीर के सप्त धातुओं में आद्य आहार परिणाम धातुरस आदि द्रव्यों को भी रस शब्द से सूचित किया गया है।

रसो जलो रसो हर्षः रस शृंगार पूर्वकः।
स्वाद्वादिषु च निर्यासे पारदेऽपि रसो विषे।।

शृंगारादौ छले वीर्ये सुवर्णे विषशुक्रयोः।
तिक्तादावमृते चैव निर्यासे पारदे ध्वनौ।।

आस्वादे च रसं प्राहुः रस धातुश्शरीरिषु।
– शब्दार्णव

रसः स्वादे च जले वीर्ये शृंगारादौं विषे द्रवे।
बाले रागे ग्रहे धातौ तिक्तादौ पारदेऽपिच।।

– हेमः

“रस ही ब्रह्म है” - ऐसा श्रुतियों का वचन है । इस रस को प्राप्त कर पुरुषार्थ करने वाला पुरुष आनन्द को प्राप्त करता है, सिद्ध होता है, तृप्त होता है तथा परम आनन्दमय अमृतत्त्व को प्राप्त करता है -

'रसो वै स:' इति श्रुते रसो ह्येवायं
लब्ध्वा पूमान आनन्दो भवति, स सिद्धो भवति,
तृप्तो भवति, अमृतो भवति – शाण्डिल्य

वर्तमान में प्रचलित विविध चिकित्सा प्रणालियों में आयुर्वेद सबसे प्राचीन है। चरक ने इसे अनादि और शाश्वत कहा है –

सोऽयमायुर्वेद: शाश्वतो निर्दिश्यते, अनादित्वात्
स्वभावसंसिद्धलक्षणत्वात् भावस्वभाव नित्यत्वाच्य

अलबेरूनी

ग्यारहवीं शताब्दी में अलबेरूनी भारत आया तब 33 वर्षों तक भारत में रहकर संस्कृत, पालि एवं प्राकृत भाषा का अध्ययन कर भारतीय ज्योतिष, दर्शन, योग, आयुर्वेद आदि विषयों पर उपलब्ध पाण्डुलिपियों का अध्ययन किया। उसने अपने लेख में सिद्धों की कीमियागिरि का उल्लेख किया (भारत, भाग 2, पृ० 110) । इस प्रकार कीमियागिरि का रूप सिद्धों से नौवीं शताब्दी में प्रचलित हुआ जो सोलहवीं शताब्दी तक पूर्ण उन्नत अवस्था में था।

देहसिद्धि-लोहसिद्धि

औषधि से भी सिद्धिसम्पत् प्राप्त होती है। इसे आधार मानकर सम्भवत: सर्वदर्शनसंग्रह में रसेश्वरदर्शन सम्मिलित किया गया है। इसमें पारद और अभ्रक के संयोग से शरीर को सिद्ध करने का उल्लेख है। यह सिद्धि पारद के द्वारा ही मिल जाती है। पारद का संबंध शिव से तथा अभ्रक का संबंध पार्वती से बतलाया गया है। इन दोनों के संयोग से सृष्टिजन्म सिद्धि मिलती है, यह सिद्धि जन्म से प्राप्त करनी चाहिए; मरने के बाद की सिद्धि का कोई अर्थ नहीं । अत: शरीर को “दिव्यतनु” बनाना चाहिए जो बहुत वर्षों तक स्थिर रह सके। यह सफलता पारद से सम्भव है; क्योंकि वह संसार के दु:खों से पार पहुँचाता है।

संसारस्य परं पारं दत्तेऽसौ पारद: स्मृत:।

महादेव के शरीर का रस होने से इसे "रस" कहा गया है। अकेला पारद ही सिद्ध होकर शरीर को अजर-अमर कर देता है – "एकौऽसौ रसराजः शरीरं अजरामरणं च कुरुते।" पारद की सिद्धि की परीक्षा धातु सिद्धि से की जाती थी। जब यह हल्की धातु ताम्र आदि को दूसरी कीमती धातु स्वर्ण-रजत में बदल सकता था तब इसे सिद्ध समझा जाता था। तब इसका उपयोग देहसिद्धि के लिए होता था। अभ्रक और पारद के संयोग से मृत्यु और दारिद्र्य दोनों नष्ट होते हैं, अर्थात् इस क्रिया से लोहसिद्धि और देहसिद्धि दोनों मिलती हैं। ये सिद्धियां नाथ सम्प्रदाय, कापालिक, औघड़, वामपंथी तथा कौलाचार आदि सम्प्रदायों में प्राप्त की जाती है।

चरक संहिता

इसमें द्रव्यों का वर्गीकरण करते हुए औद्भिद्, जांगम और पार्थिव भेद किए गए हैं। पार्थिव द्रव्यों में छः धातुएँ बतलाई गई हैं यथा - सुवर्ण, समला, काँच, लौह, बालू एवं चूना। इसके साथ-साथ सिकता, सुधा (चुना) मनःशिला, हरताल, मणियाँ, लवण, गैरिक, अंजन आदि भी पार्थिव वर्ग में माने गए हैं।

चरक में धातुओं के सूक्ष्म चूर्ण को रजस् शब्द से सूचित किया गया है – "नवायो रजसो भाग" (च.चि. 16.70) भस्म के नाम से नहीं। मण्डूर का भी अंजन के सदृश सूक्ष्मचूर्ण का उल्लेख है यथा – "मण्डूर द्विगुणं चूर्णाच्छुद्धमञ्जन सन्निभम्" (च.चि. 16.74)। ताम्र का भी सूक्ष्मचूर्ण बतलाया है यथा "दद्यान्ताम्ररजस्तस्मै सक्षौद्रं हृद्विशोधनम्" (च.चि. 23.239) इसी तरह स्वर्ण का भी सूक्ष्मचूर्ण बतलाया है यथा – "शुद्धे हृदि ततः शाणं हेमचूर्णस्य दापयेत्" (च.चि. 23.239) ।

स्वर्णादि लौह तथा मणियों के शोधन की ओर भी आचार्य ने पहल की है इन्होंने तेल, चेल, कच, आदि के शोधन का निर्देश किया है यथा -

यथा हि कनकादीनां मलिनां विविधात्मनाम्।
धौतानां निर्मला शुद्धिस्तैलचेलक चादिभि।।

– च. सू. 5.18

इसके अतिरिक्त रक्तपित्त-चिकित्सा में अनेक प्रकार के रत्नों एवं धातुओं यथा – वैदूर्य, मुक्ता, मणि, गैरिक, मृत्तिका, शंख, स्वर्ण, आमलक, मधूदक, उदक एवं इक्षुरस के सेवन से रक्तपित्त नष्ट होता है –

वैदूर्यमुक्ता माणि गैरिकाणां मच्छांख हेमामल कोदकानाम्।
मधूदकस्येक्षुरसस्य चैव पानाच्छमं गच्छति रक्तपितम।।

– च.चि. 4.79

चरक-चिकित्सास्थान में रसायनाध्याय के तृतीय पाद में शिलाजतु का स्वतंत्र वर्णन किया गया है। विषों को निष्प्रभाव करने के लिए मणियों के धारण का निर्देश करते हुए कहा गया है –

वज्रं मरकत: सार: पिचुको विषमूषिका।
कर्केतन: सर्पमणि वैदूर्य गजमौक्तिकम।।

धार्य गरमणि यश्चि वरौषध्यो विषापहा: ।
– च.चि. 23.252

वस्तिनेत्र के निर्माण के लिए – सुवर्ण, रौप्य, त्रपु, ताम्र, रीति, कांस्य का निर्देश किया है यथा –

सुवर्णरूप्यत्रपुताम्ररीति कांस्यास्थिशस्त्रद्रुम वेणुदन्तै:।
– च.चि. 3.7

पुंसवन-संस्कार के लिए चरक में सुवर्ण एवं रजत धातु की पुरुषाकृति का निर्माण कर उसे अग्नि में प्रतप्त कर गोदुग्ध में सिंचन कर पान करने का विधान बतलाया है यथा –

कनकमयान् राजतानायसांश्च पुरुषकानग्नि वर्णानणु प्रमाणान्
दध्नि पयस्युदकाञ्चलौ वा प्रक्षिप्य पिबेदनवशेषत:पुष्येण।
– च.शा. 8.19

कुष्ठहर द्रव्यों के रूप में मन:शिला, हरताल और कासीसादि का प्रयोग निम्न सन्दर्भ में देखा जाता है यथा –

मन: शिलाले गृहधूम एला कासीसलोध्रार्जुन मुस्तमर्जा:।
– च.सू. 3.5

पारद का उपयोग कुष्ठ रोग में बतलाया गया है यथा –

श्रेष्ठं ग्रन्धकयोगात् सुवर्णमाक्षिककप्रयोगाद् वा।
सर्वव्याधिनिर्वहणमद्यात् कुष्ठी रसं च निगृहीतम्।।
– च.चि. 7.71

इससे स्पष्ट होता है कि चरकसंहिता के समय धातु और खनिजों की जानकारी थी और इनका उपयोग भी चिकित्सा में होता था परन्तु रसशास्त्रोक्त प्रक्रियाओं का प्रादुर्भाव नहीं हुआ था।

सुश्रुतसंहिता

सश्रुतकाल चरक के बाद का माना जाता है। (ई. 1000 वर्ष पूर्व) इसमें चरक की अपेक्षा धातुओं का प्रयोग अधिक स्थानों पर तथा कुछ नवीन रूपों में देखा जाता है। यथा – अंजन का अन्तःप्रयोग (सुश्रुत उत्तर° 44.38) में वर्णित है। सुवर्ण, रजत, ताम्र, पीतल, त्रपु और सीसा इनके शल्य पित्त की उष्मा से शरीर में लीन हो जाते हैं। (सु. सू. 26.20) तीक्ष्ण लौह और काललौह भेद से लौह दो प्रकार का कहा गया है। अस्त्र-शस्त्र के निर्माण में लोहे का उपयोग बतलाया है। इसके लिए "सुलोहानि" शब्द का प्रयोग किया गया है (सु.सू. 8.8)। यहाँ सुलोह से न टूटने वाला तथा धार न गिरने वाला, ऐसा तात्पर्य है। इसे हम आधुनिक युग का स्टील कह सकते हैं।

सुश्रुत ने सिंधु देश में उत्पन्न स्रोतोञ्जन को उत्तम बतलाया है। (सु.चि. 24.18) अंजन का उपयोग आँखों में आंजने के अतिरिक्त रक्तस्तमभक द्रव्य के रूप में तथा व्रणों की चिकित्सा में भी बतलाया है (सु.सू. 38.42) रक्तपित्त की चिकित्सा के लिए अंजन का प्रयोग प्रशस्त है (सु.उ. 45.31-33)।

सुवर्ण का उपयोग रसायन, मेधाशक्ति और आयुवर्धन के लिए तथा शिशु जन्म लेने पर उसे स्वर्ण चटाने का उल्लेख किया है। (सु.शा. 10.68) सुवर्ण का उपयोग सुकृत चूर्ण के रूप में वर्णित है एवं घृत-मधु के साथ इसके उपयोग का उल्लेख अनेक स्थानों पर देखा जा सकता है।

पारद के बाह्य उपयोग का स्पष्ट उल्लेख सुश्रुत में निम्न प्रकार से मिलता है –

रक्तं श्वेतं चन्दनं पारदं च काकोल्यादिः क्षीरपिष्टश्च वर्गः।
– सु.चि. 25.39

फेनाश्म (सोमल) का उपयोग सुश्रुत में सर्वप्रथम देखा जाता है। यथा –

फेनाश्मं हरितालं च व्दे धातुविषे।

इस प्रकार सुश्रुत में स्वर्ण, रजत, ताम्र, लौह, नाग, वंग, कांस्य, पीतल, ताम्रचूर्ण, कांस्यमल आदि धातुओं एवं माणिक्य, मुक्ता, प्रवाल, वैदूर्य, मणि, स्फटिक, शंख, शुक्ति एवं वराटिका आदि रत्नों तथा हरताल, मनःशिला, शिलाजतु, माक्षिक, तुत्थ, कासीस, फिटकिरी, अंजन, टंकण, रसांजन, गंधक आदि खनिजों का उल्लेख मिलता है।

अष्टांगसंग्रह एवं अष्टांगहृदय

यह तीसरी-चौथी शताब्दी का ग्रन्थ है, वृद्धवाग्भट ने सुश्रुत की भाँति धातुओं के रस,

वीर्य, विपाक आदि का वर्णन किया है। इसमें कृष्ण-लौह और तीक्ष्ण-लौह पृथक् कहे गए हैं। धातुओं के साथ पद्मराग, महानील, पुष्पराग, मुक्ता विद्रुम आदि के गुणधर्म बतलाए गए हैं। शंख, समुद्र, फेन, तुत्थ, गेरु, मैनसिल, हरताल, अंजन, रसाञ्जन, शिलाजित इन सबका उल्लेख एक साथ किया गया है। रयासन के प्रकरण में सुवर्ण का उपयोग विस्तार से बतलाया गया है (अ.सं.उ. 49) संहिताओं में प्रथम बार मूषा अग्नि संयोग द्वारा धातुओं के भस्म निर्माण की एक विधि का निर्देश अष्टांग संग्रह में देखने को मिलता है – "मूणान्तध्मार्तचुर्णिताम्" (अ.सं.उ. 16.13-14)। संग्रह और हृदय में पारद का अन्त:उपयोग देखने को नहीं मिलता। गंधक का उपयोग भी बाह्य रूप में ही किया जाता था। धातु, उपधातु तथा पारद का ज्ञान था किंतु रसशास्त्रीय प्रक्रियाओं-कल्पों का विकास नहीं हो पाया था।

सातवीं शताब्दी - इस समय की जानकारी बाणभट्ट की रचनाओं से मिलती है। बाणभट्ट ने अपने साथियों का परिचय देते हुए कहा है –

> जाङ्गुलिको मयूरकः, भिषक्पुत्रो मन्दारकः, मन्त्रसाधकः करालः, असुरविवर-व्यसनी लोहिताक्षः, धातुवादविद् विहंगमः। – हर्षरचित, प्रथम उच्छ्वास
>
> जांगुलिक (विषवैद्य या गारुड़ी), मयूरक, भिषक्पुत्र मन्दारक, मन्त्र-साधक कराल, पाताल में प्रवेश की विद्या जानने वाला लोहिताक्ष तथा धातुवाद (कीमियागिरी) को जानने वाला विहंगम – ये बाणभट्ट के साथी थे।

अलबेरूनी के अनुसार उज्जैन के राजा विक्रमादित्य (विक्रम सम्वत् के अधिष्ठाता) के राज्य में व्याडि नाम का आचार्य रहता था। उसने रस-रसायन सिद्धि के निमित्त अपनी सारी सम्पत्ति नष्ट कर दी थी, फिर भी उसे सफलता नहीं मिल सकी। असफलता से शोकाकुल उद्विग्न मन होकर वह अपने भेषजसंस्कार व्यवस्था-पत्र को लेकर शिप्रा के तट पर बैठ गया और उसके पन्ने फाड़-फाड़कर नदी में प्रवाहित करने लगा। नीचे की ओर आगे नगर की एक प्रमुख वेश्या नदी के किनारे बैठी थी, उसने लगातार बहुत से पन्नों को बहते हुए देखकर सबको एकत्र कर लिया और व्याडि के पास आकर उसके शोकाकुल होने का कारण पूछा। व्याडि ने बतलाया कि इस ग्रन्थ से मेरा सर्वनाश हो गया है । मैं अपना प्रचुर धन इन क्रियाओं के पीछे खर्च कर कंगाल बन गया हूँ। मैं चाहता हूँ कि भावी पीढ़ी इसके पीछे अपना धन व्यय न करें, अत: इसे मैं नष्ट कर देना चाहता हूँ। वेश्या ने उसे ढांढस बंधाते हुए कहा कि ऋषि-प्रणीत यह ग्रन्थ झूठा नहीं हो सकता; निश्चय ही तुम्हारी प्रक्रिया में कहीं कोई भिन्नता है। जिस कार्य के लिए तुमने जीवन का एक बड़ा अंश लगाया है उसे धनाभाव के कारण मत छोड़ो। मेरे पास

प्रचुर धन है और तुम अपने कार्य को आगे बढ़ाने के लिए इसका उपयोग करो। इस प्रकार व्याडि ने पुनः अपना कार्य प्रारम्भ किया एवं सफलता अर्जित की।

रसशास्त्रों के ग्रन्थ, ग्रन्थ-कर्ता एवं उनका काल प्रारम्भिक काल

नागार्जुन

यह काल पाँचवीं से सातवीं शताब्दी का है। "नागार्जुनेन लिखिता स्तम्भे पाटलिपुत्रके" – वृन्द द्वारा कथित यह नागार्जुन सुश्रुत का प्रतिसंस्कर्ता गुप्तकालीन है। रस-विद्या के साथ भी इनका संबंध जोड़ा जाता है। सम्भव है इन्होंने भी रसशास्त्र पर कुछ लिखा हो। किन्तु इस मान्यता के पीछे मतभेद हैं।

कुब्जिकातन्त्र

नेपाल के पुस्तकालय की छानबीन से यह ग्रन्थ श्रीहरिप्रसाद शास्त्री को मिला। इस तन्त्र की पाण्डुलिपि गुप्तकालीन लिपि में लिखी हुई थी। इसका समय 600 ई. माना जाता है। इसमें एक स्थान पर शिव स्वयं पारद के सम्बन्ध में कह रहे हैं कि गंधक से 6 बार मारित होने पर इसमें गुण-वृद्धि हो जाती है।

मदवीर्यः पारद यद्वं पतितः स्फुरितं मणिः।
मद्वीर्येण प्रसूतास्ते तावाय्यी सूनकेवहि।
तिष्ठन्ति संस्कृताः सन्ताः भस्मा षड् विप्रजारणम् ।।

पारद की सहायता से ताम्र स्वर्ण में बदल जाता है।

रसरत्नाकर या रसेन्द्रमंगल

यह दोनों ग्रन्थ नागार्जुन-रचित रसशास्त्र का सबसे प्राचीन ग्रन्थ माना जाता है। डॉ. पी. सी. राय इसे सातवीं-आठवीं शताब्दी का मानते हैं। रसरत्नाकर तथा रसेन्द्रमंगल दोनों ग्रन्थों को श्री पी.सी. राय तथा श्री जीवराम कालीदास ने एक ही माना है। इसकी दो हस्तलिखित प्रतियाँ – एक डॉ. पी.सी. राय और दूसरी स्वर्गीय श्री तनसुख राम म. त्रिपाठी के पास उपलब्ध थी। श्री राय संगृहीत प्रति के अन्त में "नागार्जुन विरचित रसरत्नाकर" तथा श्री त्रिपाठी के पास उपलब्ध प्रति के अन्त में "नागार्जुन विरचित रसेन्द्रमंगल" लिखा है। श्री जीवराम कालीदास ने गोंडल से 1924 में रसेन्द्रमंगल को प्रकाशित किया था। श्री राय ने भी अपने पास उपलब्ध अंश को प्रकाशित कराया था। दोनों के मिलान से दोनों ग्रन्थ एक ही प्रतीत होते हैं। ग्रन्थ के प्रारम्भ में आठ अध्याय होने का उल्लेख है किन्तु प्राप्त पुस्तक में चार ही अध्याय हैं। ग्रन्थ खण्डित एवं

अव्यवस्थित है। उपलब्ध अंश में पारद के अठारह संस्कार, लौहवेध, रस, उपरस और लौह का शोधन, सभी लौहों का मारण, अभ्रक-माक्षिक आदि का सत्त्वपातन तथा अभ्रक द्रुति का वर्णन उपलब्ध होता है। मन्थानभैरव तथा रोगनाशक दशमूल क्वाथ का उल्लेख भी मिलता है, जिससे इस ग्रन्थ के ग्यारहवीं शताब्दी के होने का भ्रम पैदा होता है। रसरत्नाकर तंत्र-ग्रंथों में मुख्य है तथा इसमें रसायन योगों का समावेश है। यह ग्रन्थ महायान सम्प्रदाय से सम्बन्धित है। इसमें कई स्थानों पर "प्रणिपत्य सर्वबुद्धान" शब्द आया है।

नन्दीतन्त्र

काव्यमीमांसा में "रसाधिकारिकं नन्दिकेश्वरः" कहकर रससिद्ध नन्दी को उद्धृत किया गया है। कवीन्द्राचार्य सूची के अनुसार आचार्य नन्दी ने नन्दीतंत्र की रचना की थी। इनका काल सातवीं शताब्दी माना जाता है।

रसहृदयतन्त्र

तन्त्र नाम से कहा जाने वाला वास्तविक यही प्रथम ग्रन्थ है। यह ग्रन्थ सम्पूर्ण और व्यवस्थित है। चन्द्रवंशी हैहय वंश में किरात देश का राजा मदन रसविद्या में पारंगत था। राजा मदन के राजवैद्य रसाचार्य भिक्षुगोविन्द इस ग्रन्थ के प्रणेता हैं।

काल की दृष्टि से रसहृदयतन्त्र का काल दसवीं शताब्दी माना जाता है। यदि गोविन्दभगवत्पाद को इस ग्रन्थ का कर्ता मान लिया जाए तो इस ग्रन्थ का रचना-काल सातवीं शताब्दी का उत्तरार्द्ध एवं आठवीं शताब्दी का पूर्वार्द्ध होना चाहिए ग्रन्थकार द्वारा अपने परिचय में कहे हैहय कुल की स्थिति दसवीं शताब्दी में थी।

रसहृदयतन्त्र में 19 अवबोध हैं। प्रथम अवबोध में रस की प्रशंसा की गई है। रसशास्त्र के दार्शनिक पक्ष पर सशक्त विचार व्यक्त करते हुए कहा है कि मनुष्य को धन-शरीरादि अनित्य जानकर मुक्ति के लिए यत्न करना चाहिए। मुक्ति ज्ञान से मिलती है, ज्ञान अभ्यास से होता है और अभ्यास तभी सम्भव है जबकि शरीर स्थिर हो। शरीर को स्थिर एवं अजर-अमर अकेला रसराज ही कर सकता है। लेखक को वैयक्तिक मुक्ति से संतोष नहीं है।

रसार्णव

यह रसशास्त्र का एक लोकप्रिय ग्रन्थ है। इस ग्रन्थ के कर्ता एवं समय के बारे में स्पष्ट उल्लेख नहीं मिलता, तथापि इस ग्रन्थ का समय बारहवीं शताब्दी माना जाता है। लेखक के बारे में लोगों की ऐसी धारणा है कि कोई कापालिक योगी इसका कर्ता है। कई विद्वान्

भैरवानन्द योगी को इसका कर्ता मानते हैं। यह ग्रन्थ पार्वती-परमेश्वर संवादात्मक है। इसकी भाषा जटिल है। धातुवाद एवं देहवाद संबंधी इसके विचार स्पष्ट हैं। ग्रन्थ अपने में पूर्ण है। इसके अध्यायों को पटल के नाम से कहा गया है। चौथे पटल में रसकर्म के उपयोगी एवं उपरस, लौह में काम आने वाली काँजी, विड्, धमन, लौहयन्त्र, खल्व, कोष्ठिका, वंकनाल, गोमय, ठोस ईंधन, मिट्टी के यन्त्र, मूसल, ऊखल, सँडसी, मृण्पात्र, लौहपात्र, तराजू-बाट, कैंची, कसौटी, दंशनाल, लौहनाल, मूषा, स्नेह, अम्ल, विष, उपविष आदि सम्भार लेकर कार्य प्रारम्भ करने को कहा गया है।

गोरक्षसंहिता

गोरक्षसंहिता के लेखक गोरखनाथ हैं। विद्वानों की मान्यता के अनुसार इनका काल बारहवीं शताब्दी है। गोरक्षनाथ की गणना 84 सिद्धों में हुई है। गोरक्षसंहिता 1 लाख श्लोकों में लिखी गई थी, जिसका वर्णन नवम पटल के अन्त में इस प्रकार किया गया है – "इत्याद्ये स्वच्छन्दशक्त्यावतारे शतसाहस्र्यां गोरक्षसंहितायां भूतिप्रकरणे शिवसूत्रं रसायनविधिर्नाम नवमः पटलः समाप्तः"।

काकचण्डीश्वरकल्पतन्त्र

रसरत्नसमुच्चय के 27 सिद्धों में काकचण्डीश्वर की गणना की गई है। अतः यह ग्रन्थ रसरत्नसमुच्चय से पहले का है।

रसरत्नसमुच्चय

ग्रन्थ के रचयिता ने अपने पिता का नाम सिंहगुप्त कहा है। स्वयं ग्रन्थकर्ता का नाम वाग्भटाचार्य केवल पुष्पिका भाग में मिलता है। पिता एवं पुत्र की नाम समानता के कारण अष्टांगहृदय एवं रसरत्नसमुच्चय का कर्ता एक होने का भ्रम पैदा करता है। ग्रन्थ की विषय-सामग्री एवं काल के लम्बे अन्तराल के कारण यह सिद्ध कर पाना कठिन है। ग्रन्थकर्ता के पार्थक्य प्रकट करने के लिए इन्हें रसवाग्भट के नाम से कहा जाता है। इनका काल तेरहवीं शती का है।

रसरत्नाकर

यह ग्रन्थ पार्वती-पुत्र नित्यनाथ द्वारा तेरहवीं शताब्दी में लिखा गया है। रसखण्ड, रसेन्द्रखण्ड, वादिखण्ड, रसायनखण्ड और मन्त्रखण्ड इस प्रकार यह पाँच खण्डों में विभक्त है। इस ग्रन्थ में पारद की सभी क्रियाओं का विस्तृत विवेचन किया गया है। पारद-संस्कार में उपयोगी सभी द्रव्यों का विवेचन किया गया है। वादिखण्ड में पारद के

सभी संस्कारों का विधिवत् वर्णन किया गया है। यह खण्ड 20 अध्यायों का है। इसमें माणिक्य, इन्द्रनील, मरकत, गोमेद, पुष्पराग, मुक्ता, प्रवाल, हिंगुल, सिन्दूर, सैंधव, हिंगु, वंग, घृत, कर्पूर, कस्तूरी तथा कुंकुम आदि द्रव्यों का कृत्रिम निर्माण तथा धातुवेध की अनेक विधियाँ बतलाई गई हैं।

कंकालीय रसाध्याय

इस ग्रन्थ पर मेरुतुंग ने 1386 में टीका लिखी है। अतः यह ग्रन्थ इससे पूर्व (तेरहवीं शती) का होना चाहिए। इसके लेखक कंकाल योगी है।

रसरहस्य एवं रसेश्वरसिद्धान्त

ये दोनों ग्रन्थ माधवकृत सर्वदर्शनसंग्रह में उद्धृत हैं अतः उनके पूर्व के हैं। इनके लेखक अज्ञात हैं। इनमें पारद द्वारा मोक्ष एवं शरीर को स्थिर करने की बात कही गई है।

रसकल्प

इस ग्रन्थ में गोविन्द एवं स्वच्छन्दभैरव आदि का उल्लेख आया है। ग्रन्थ का काल चौदहवीं शती है। इस छोटे से ग्रन्थ में धातुओं का शोधन-मारण ही दिया गया है। लेखक ने पुस्तक की प्रक्रिया को स्वानुभूत बताया है।

आनन्दकन्द

यह ग्रन्थ 1952 ई. में प्रकाश में आया। ग्रन्थ में विषयों के विस्तार से यह तेरहवीं शती के बाद का प्रतीत होता है। ग्रन्थ दो भागों में पूर्ण किया गया है।

रसराजलक्ष्मी

इसका काल चौदहवीं शती का माना जाता है। इसके लेखक विष्णुदेव हैं। इन्होंने रसार्णव, काकचण्डीश्वर, नागार्जुन, दामोदर, वासुदेव, भगवतगोविन्दपाद आदि को उद्धृत किया है। विष्णुदेव राजा बुक्क के राजवैद्य थे। बुक्क का समय 1354-71 ई. है।

रससार

इस ग्रन्थ का काल चौदहवीं शती का है। यह गोविन्दाचार्य द्वारा लिखा गया है। गोविन्दाचार्य कापालिक परम्परा में दीक्षित थे, ऐसा उनके द्वारा लिखित "कापालिक आचार्यों की प्रशंसा" से ज्ञात होता है। इसमें पारद के अठारह संस्कारों का वर्णन कर पारद के संबंध में अनेक तथ्यों पर प्रकाश डाला गया है। अहिफेन का वर्णन भी इसमें

मिलता है। लेकिन अहिफेन क्या है, इसके बारे में लेखक मौन है। इसे समुद्र में तैरती विषैली मछली से प्राप्त होना बतलाया है।

रसपद्धति

यह ग्रन्थ महाराष्ट्रीय बिन्दु-रचित है। बिन्दु का समय कुछ विद्वान् तेरहवीं शती का मानते हैं। रसकामधेनु और आयुर्वेदप्रकाश में इसे उद्धृत किया गया है अतः इससे पूर्व का है तथा रसरत्नाकर, रसराजलक्ष्मी और रसरत्नसमुच्चय के बाद का है। अतः कई विद्वान् इसका काल पन्द्रहवीं शती का मानते हैं। सम्पूर्ण ग्रन्थ "शार्दूलविक्रीडित" इस एक ही छन्द में पूरा किया गया है। 1925 में यादवजी द्वारा निर्णयसागर प्रेस से मुद्रित किया गया था।

शार्गंधरसंहिता

यह चौदहवीं शती का ग्रन्थ आचार्य शार्गंधर मिश्र द्वारा लिखा गया है। यह भैषज्यकल्पना का मुख्य ग्रन्थ है। इसमें रसशास्त्रीय द्रव्यों का शोधनमारण आदि बतलाया गया है।

रसचिन्तामणि

यह ग्रन्थ अनन्तदेवसूरी द्वारा पन्द्रहवीं शती में लिखा गया है। ग्रन्थ कुल 11 स्तबक में पूर्ण किया गया है। प्रथम स्तबक में पारदभस्म-निर्माण की 20 विधियाँ दी गई हैं। तथा पाँचवें और छठे स्तबक में पारद-संस्कार, बुभुक्षितीकरण, धातुओं का भस्मीकरण तथा स्वर्ण-रौप्य निर्माण की 11 विधायाँ बतलाई गई हैं। शेष स्तबकों में रसयोगों का विस्तार से वर्णन किया गया है। 1967 में इसका प्रकाशन वेंकटेश्वर प्रेस बम्बई से हुआ था।

रसरत्नप्रदीप

इसके रचयिता रत्नपालसुत रामराज है। इनका काल पन्द्रहवीं शताब्दी का माना गया है।

रसनक्षत्रमालिका

इसका काल पन्द्रहवीं शती का है तथा इसके लेखक मालवा के राजवैद्य मथनसिंह है।

धातुरत्नमाला

इसके लेखक गुर्जरदेशीय देवदत्त हैं। इनका समय सोलहवीं शती का है। इसमें यशद को खर्पर का पर्याय कहा है। इसमें धातु, रत्न आदि की मारण विधि दी गई है। स्वर्ण, रजत, ताम्र, सीसक, त्रपु और लौह इन 6 धातुओं का उल्लेख किया गया है।

रसेन्द्रचिन्तामणि

यह कालनाथ के शिष्य ढुण्ढुकनाथ की रचना है। इनका काल सोलहवीं शती का है।

रसमञ्जरी

यह शालिनाथ द्वारा लिखा गया पन्द्रहवीं शती का ग्रन्थ माना जाता है। वैसे तो यह संग्रहग्रन्थ है तथापि कुछ मौलिक विचार भी प्रस्तुत किए गए हैं। इसमें अनेक रसौषधियों का वर्णन मिलता है। ग्रन्थ लघुकाय है तथा वेंकटेश्वर प्रेस बम्बई से सं. 1978 में हिन्दी टीका सहित प्रकाशित कराया गया था जो सम्प्रति अनुपलब्ध है।

लोहसर्वस्व

इसके कर्ता आचार्य सुरेश्वर हैं। इनका काल पन्द्रहवीं शती का माना गया है। रसकामधेनु तथा आयुर्वेदप्रकाशकार ने इसको उद्धृत किया है। यादवजी द्वारा 1925 ई. इसका संशोधन एवं प्रकाशन कराया गया था। इन्होंने लौह के आठ भेद बतलाए हैं, जिनमें 4 भेदों का वर्णन किया है।

रसेन्द्रसारसंग्रह

यह ग्रन्थ सोलहवीं शताब्दी के पूर्वार्द्ध में श्रीगोपालकृष्ण भट्ट द्वारा लिखा गया था। रसद्रव्यों से चिकित्सा का विस्तारपूर्वक वर्णन इसमें देखा जाता है। रसद्रव्यों का वर्गीकरण तथा संक्षेप में द्रव्यों का शोधन-मारण भी बतलाया गया है। रसमञ्जरी और चन्द्रिका का इसमें उल्लेख है। इस पर वैद्य घनानन्द पन्त (दिल्ली) तथा रामप्रसाद वैद्य (बम्बई) की टीकाएँ हैं। इस ग्रन्थ में दिए गए रसकर्पूर के पाठ को रसप्रकाशसुधाकर और भावप्रकाश से मिलाने पर यह रसप्रकाशसुधाकर के बाद तथा भावप्रकाश से पूर्व का प्रतीत होता है। इस आधार पर कुछ लोग इसे तेरहवीं शती का भी मानते हैं।

रसेन्द्रकल्पद्रुम

यह ग्रन्थ सोलहवीं शती का है। इसके लेखक श्री नीलकण्ठ के आत्मज श्री रामकृष्ण भट्ट हैं। इन्होंने अपने ग्रन्थ में रसार्णव, रसमंगल, रसरत्नाकर, रसामृत और रसरत्नसमुच्चय से विषयों का संग्रह किया है। मुख्यतः धातुओं-खनिजों का उल्लेख किया गया है।

रसप्रदीप

इसका काल सोलहवीं शताब्दी तथा रचनाकार श्री प्राणनाथ हैं। फिरंग रोग और उसकी

चिकित्सा तथा चोपचीनी का उल्लेख इसमें किया गया है। चीनी व्यापारियों द्वारा 1535 ई. में चोपचीनी को गोआ लाया गया था। इसमे शंख द्रावक बनाने की विधि दी गई है।

रसकौमुदी

इस ग्रन्थ का निर्माण सोलहवीं शती में किया गया है। रचनाकार चन्द्रशेखर मुनीश्वर के वंशज सर्वज्ञ चन्द्रसुत ज्ञानचन्द्र शर्मा हैं। ग्रन्थ का विषय 4 अधिकारों में पूर्ण है। इसमें नवनाथसिद्धों और नवदुर्गा की पूजा का विधान बताया गया है (2150)। पारद की उत्पत्ति, गंधक तथा अभ्रकादि द्रव्यों का शोधन-मारण आदि तीसरे अधिकार में वर्णित हैं। चतुर्थ अधिकार में कुछ विशिष्ट योगों का वर्णन मिलता है। इस ग्रन्थ का संशोधन जीवानन्द के पुत्र सदानन्द शर्मा ने 1923 में किया था तथा मोतीलाल बनारसीदास ने प्रकाशित किया था। यह सम्प्रति चौखम्बा द्वारा प्रकाशित एवं उपलब्ध है इसी नाम का ग्रन्थ माधव, शक्तिवल्लभ तथा गोल्हदेव द्वारा विरचित भी है।

भावप्रकाश

इसका काल सोलहवीं शती तथा रचनाकार श्री भावमिश्र सर्वविदित है। यह निघण्टु एवं चिकित्सा के रूप में अत्यन्त प्रतिष्ठा प्राप्त ग्रन्थ है। यह दो भागों में उपलब्ध है। पूर्वखण्ड में दिनचर्या तथा रात्रिचर्या और औद्भिद, खनिज तथा जान्तव द्रव्यों का वर्णन, गुणधर्म, उपयोग विधि आदि का सुन्दर एवं सुव्यवस्थित वर्णन किया गया है।

वसवराजीय

यह ग्रन्थ पन्द्रहवीं एवं सोलहवीं शती के मध्य का है। ग्रन्थकर्ता कर्णाटक के लिंगायत मत के संस्थापक एवं प्रचारक वसवराज हैं, जो वैद्य एवं कवि दोनों रूप में प्रसिद्ध थे। ग्रन्थ का अध्याय उपकरण के नाम से कथित है। इन्होंने सतयुग में चरक, त्रेता में रसार्णव, द्वापर में सिद्धविद्या और कलयुग में वसव को प्रधान बतलाया गया है। यथा –

कृते तु चरकः प्रोक्तस्त्रेतायां तु रसार्णवः।
द्वापरे सिद्धविद्या तु कलौ वसवकः स्मृतः।।

इसमें रसकर्पूर का प्रयोग है। चरक, माधव, भैरवकल्प, वाग्भट, रसार्णव, भेषजकल्प, काशीखण्ड, कर्मविपाक और रेवणकल्प आदि ग्रन्थों के आधार पर इसे लिखा गया है। नित्यनाथ के भी कुछ योग वर्णित हैं। इन्होंने हेमादि को भी उद्धृत किया है। इसमें रसौषधियाँ अधिक वर्णित हैं। श्रीगोवर्धनशर्मा छंगाणी ने 1930 में नागपुर से इसका प्रकाशन कराया था।

रसकामधेनु

यह ग्रन्थ सोलहवीं शती में शाकद्वीपीय विप्र बलभद्रमिश्र के पौत्र हरिराममिश्र के पुत्र श्री चूड़ामणिमिश्र द्वारा लिखा गया है। इस ग्रन्थ में चार पाद हैं; यथा – उपकरणपाद, धातुसंग्रहपाद, रसकर्मपाद और चिकित्सापाद। इन्होंने अपने पूर्ववर्ती सभी रसग्रन्थों के मौलिक विचारों का संकलन इस ग्रन्थ में किया है। गोरक्षसंहिता, पुरन्दर रहस्य, शैवालभक्ष्य, कक्षपुट, रसेन्द्रमंगल आदि ग्रन्थों को उद्धृत किया है। 1925 ई. में बम्बई से श्रीयादवजी ने इसका प्रकाशन कराया था।

धातुक्रिया

यह ग्रन्थ रुद्रयामल तंत्र के अन्तर्गत मिलता है। इसका काल भी सोलहवीं शती का है। इस ग्रन्थ में फिरंग देश तथा दाहजल का उल्लेख मिलता है। ताम्र और खर्पर के योग से पीतल और वंग तथा ताम्र के योग से कांस्य बनाने की बात लिखी है। खर्पर शब्द जस्ते के अर्थ में प्रयुक्त हुआ है। ग्रन्थ शिव-पार्वती संवाद के रूप में है। इसमें एक स्थान पर शिव पार्वती से कहते हैं कि मनुष्य कलियुग में स्वर्ण के लिए व्याकुल रहेंगे। वे पारद और गन्धक के सहयोग से नकली सोना बनाने लगेंगे। सुवर्णसाधिनी विद्या जानकर लोग प्राकृतिक स्वर्ण को पूछेंगे नहीं।

निम्नांकित ग्रन्थ टोडरानन्द (आयुर्वेद सौख्य) में उद्धृत है, अत: ये सोलहवीं शती में उपलब्ध थे – रसचिन्तामणि, रसदर्पण, रसरत्नप्रदीप, रसरत्नावली, रसरहस्य, रसराजहंस, रससिन्धु, रसार्णव, रसालंकार तथा रसावतार।

बृहद्योगतरंगिणी एवं योगतरंगिणी

यह ग्रन्थ काशीवासी तैलंग ब्राह्मण आचार्य त्रिमल्लभट्ट द्वारा सत्रहवीं शताब्दी में लिखा गया था। बृहद्योगतरंगिणी ग्रन्थ में 147 तरंग हैं। इसमें आयुर्वेद के आठों अंगों का वर्णन है। इसके 41 से 43 तरंग में रसद्रव्यों का शोधन-मारण, भेद, गुणधर्म आदि वर्णित है। 1914 ई. में आनन्दाश्रम प्रकाशन, पूना द्वारा प्रकाशित किया गया है।

योगतरंगिणी

इसमें 80 तरंग हैं। यह योगों का भण्डार सदृश है। इसे चिकित्सा-प्रधान ग्रन्थ कहेंगे। सत्रहवां तरंग (अध्याय) रसविषयक है। इसमें पारद के दोष, गुण, शोधन, मारण मूर्च्छना, बन्धन आदि का वर्णन किया गया है। इन्होंने भावमिश्र और लोलिम्बराज को उद्धृत किया है तथा योगरत्नाकरकार ने भी इन्हें उद्धृत किया है। अत: यह ग्रन्थ दोनों के बीच के समय का है। यह ग्रन्थ गोण्डाल से 1956 ई. में प्रकाशित किया गया था।

आयुर्वेदप्रकाश

यह सत्रहवीं शताब्दी का ग्रन्थ है। इसके लेखक सौराष्ट्र निवासी माधव उपाध्याय हैं। इन्होंने भावप्रकाश को उद्धृत किया है। यह रसशास्त्र का एक महत्त्वपूर्ण ग्रन्थ है। इसमें विस्तारपूर्वक पारद का विवेचन किया गया है। अन्य रसाचार्यों के मत स्पष्टरूप से उद्धृत किए गए हैं। ग्रन्थ में 5 अध्याय हैं। प्रथम अध्याय में पारदविषयक सर्वात्मनाविचार, सवर्णादि निर्माण तथा लौह-परिवर्तन की विधियाँ दी हैं। दूसरे अध्याय में रसद्रव्यों का वर्गीकरण एवं विवेचन किया गया है। ग्रन्थकार का कथन है कि गुरु-चरणों में बैठकर जिन-जिन क्रियाओं को सम्पन्न किया है उन्हीं का वर्णन इसमें समाविष्ट है।

योगरत्नाकर

यह अठारहवीं शती का ग्रन्थ है। इसके कर्ता अज्ञात हैं। काष्ठौषधियों के साथ रसयोगों का भी इसमें अच्छा संकलन है। लगभग सभी रसद्रव्यों के शोधन-मारण एवं गुण-दोषों का वर्णन है।

भैषज्यरत्नावली

उन्नीसवीं शती के अन्त में आचार्य गोविन्ददास सेन ने इस ग्रन्थ की रचना की। यह एक संग्रह ग्रन्थ है। चिकित्सा की दृष्टि से यह महत्त्वपूर्ण ग्रन्थ है। इसमें सफल और अच्छे योगों का संग्रह किया गया है। लगभग सभी प्रकार की आयुर्वेदीय कल्पनाएं इसमें वर्णित हैं।

वृहद्रसराज सुन्दर

इसका रचना काल उन्नीसवीं शताब्दी का उत्तरार्द्ध तथा रचयिता मथुरा निवासी पं. दत्तराम चौबे हैं। इस ग्रन्थ की रचना पूर्ववर्ती रस ग्रन्थों के आधार पर की गई है। ग्रन्थ में स्थान-स्थान पर लेखक के मौलिक विचार भी देखे जाते हैं।

रसेन्द्रचूड़ामणि

इस ग्रन्थ का काल बारहवीं शताब्दी का है। इसके रचयिता सोमदेव हैं। रसरत्नसमुच्चय का पूर्व भाग इसी ग्रन्थ पर आधारित है। सोमदेव गोविन्दभगवत्पाद के बाद और रसरत्न के कर्ता से पहले हुए हैं। इसमें मन्थानभैरव, नन्दी, भालुकी, भास्कर, श्रीकण्ठ तथा गोविन्दभगवत्पाद के मत को नामोल्लेख सहित उद्धृत किया है। सोमदेव करवाल (भैरवपुर) के अधिपति तथा महावीर के वंशज थे, जैसा कि द्वितीय अध्याय की अवतारणा से ज्ञात होता है। सोलहवें अध्याय की पुष्पिका में इन्हें नारायणसूनु कहा गया है।

यह ग्रन्थ 16 अध्यायों में पूर्ण है। इसमें रसपूजन, रसशाला-निर्माण के प्रकार, रसशाला-संग्रहण, परिभाषा मूषा-पुट-यन्त्र, दिव्यौषधि, रसौषधि, औषधिगण, महारस, उपरस, साधारण रस, रत्न, धातु इनके रसायनयोग तथा पारद के अठारह संस्कार पूर्ण रूप में कहे हैं। यह ग्रन्थ यादवजी त्रिकमजी आचार्य द्वारा लाहौर से संवत् 1984 (1933 ई.) में प्रकाशित कराया गया है।

रसप्रकाशसुधाकर

इस ग्रन्थ के कर्ता श्री यशोधर भट्ट हैं। यशोधर भट्ट सौराष्ट्र (जूनागढ़) के रहने वाले गौड़ ब्राह्मण और पद्मनाभ के पुत्र थे। इनका काल तेरहवीं शताब्दी का है। रसरत्नसमुच्चय ने इसे बहुधा उद्धृत किया है। रसाचार्यों की गणना में यशोधन ही सम्भवतः यशोधर हैं। इन्होंने सोमदेव को उद्धृत किया है (9.11)। औषधियों के प्रकरण में शोढलनिघण्टु का अनुसरण किया है। रसरत्नसमुच्चय से पूर्व के ग्रन्थ में यह बहुत सुव्यवस्थित ग्रन्थ है। इसमें पारद के अठारह संस्कार, रसन्ध, रसभस्म-विधि, रसकर्पूर की विधि, स्वर्णादि धातु, महारस, उपरस, रत्न आदि का लखण, गुण, शोधन, मारण तथा एक सौ रसों का प्रयोग, यन्त्र-मुषा-पुटों का विवरण, वाजीकरण प्रयोग आदि रसशास्त्र के सभी विषय हैं। शुक्र-स्तम्भन के क्रम में अहिफेन, अकरकरा, मस्तकी आदि द्रव्यों का प्रयोग किया है। सवर्ण, रौप्य, मौक्तिक, प्रवाल आदि अनेक द्रव्यों का कृत्रिम निर्माण भी बताया है। कीमियागिरी की बातें जिसे यह कौतुक कहता है, इसमें हैं। ग्रन्थकार ने कहा है कि मैंने थोड़ा अनुभव किया है और शेष अधिक भाग सुना है। यह ग्रन्थ रसशास्त्र की प्रामाणिकता का आधारस्तम्भ है तथा अपने में पूर्ण है जो 13 अध्यायों में पूर्ण किया गया है। यह गोण्डल से यादवजी द्वारा प्रकाशित किया गया है; अधुना विभिन्न ग्रन्थालयों में उपलब्ध है।

संस्कृत साहित्य में आयुर्वेद

भाषा चाहे जो हो, कवि को सब विधाओं और कलाओं की जानकारी होना आवश्यक है। संस्कृत साहित्य के कवियों की भी यही विशेषता रही कि उनका ज्ञान सर्वतोन्मुखी था – कोई भी विषय उनकी प्रतिभा से नहीं बचा था। इसी से उनकी रचना में ज्योतिष, आयुर्वेद, पुराण, इतिहास सबका उल्लेख मिलता है। पाणिनी से लेकर पंडितराज जगन्नाथ तक काव्य में आयुर्वेद का वर्णन मिलता है।

पाणिनि की अष्टाध्यायी में सूत्रों के उदाहरणरूप में आयुर्वेद का उल्लेख है यथा – उपतापो रोगः (7.3.61), रुजत्यसौ रोगः; स्पृशतीति स्पर्श उपतापः (3.3.16) औषधं पिबति (5.4.37)।

अन्य रोगों के नाम भी बड़ी मात्रा में मिलते हैं यथा – अतिसार (5.2.129); अर्श (5.2.127); आस्राव (3.1.141); कुष्ठ (8.3.97); न्युब्ज (7.3.61); पामा (5.1. 100); सिध्म (5.2.97); स्पर्श (3.3.16); हृद् रोग (6.3.61) आदि।

भास ने अपने नाटकों में कई स्थान पर आयुर्वेद का प्रयोग किया है।

प्रतिज्ञायौगन्धरायण (तृतीय अंक) में भास ने यौगन्धरायण द्वारा शत्रु-देश में इन वस्तुओं को विष से दूषित करने का उल्लेख किया है; यथा –

> यौगन्धरायणः – वसन्तक! गच्ध भूयः स्वामिनं पश्य। विज्ञाप्यतां च स्वामी-या सा प्रयाणं प्रतीह प्रस्तुता कथा, तथ्याः श्वः प्रयोगकाल इति। कुतः, स्थानावगाह-यवसशय्याभागेप्वाश्रयेषूपन्यस्तौपधिव्याजो नलागिरिर्मन्त्रौपधि- नियमसम्भृतः पुराणकर्मव्यामोहितः। अनुकूल मारुतभोक्तव्यः संजितो धूपः।

अविमारक नाटक (पंचम अंक) में –

> विदूषकः – नहि घुतवचनेन पित्तं नश्यति, मम हस्तगतं कुरु।

स्वप्नवासवदत्ता (अंक चार) में –

> सुप्रच्छन्नायां शय्यायां निद्रां न लेभे। यथा वातशोणितमभिमत इवेति प्रेक्ष्ये। भोः सुखं नाम आमयपरिभूतमकल्यवर्त्तश्च।

अश्वघोष

> द्रव्यं यथा स्यात्कटुकं रसेन तच्चोपयुक्तं मधुरं विपाके।
> तथैव वीर्यं कटुकं श्रमेण तस्यार्थ्इसिद्ध्यै मधुरौ विपाकः।।
>
> – सौन्दरानन्द 16.93

कालिदास

> स्रगियं यदि जीवितापहा हृदये किं निहिता न हन्ति माम्।
> विषमप्यमृतं क्वचिद् भवेदमृतं वा विषमीश्वरेच्छया।।
>
> – रघुवंश 8.46

> दक्षस्य शापेन शशी क्षयीव, प्लुप्टो हिमेनेव सरोजकोशः।
> वहन्विरूपं वपुरुग्ररेतश्चयेन वह्निः किल निर्जगाम।।
>
> – कुमारसम्भव 9.17

सर्पदंश की चिकित्सा

तेन हि दंशच्छेद: पूर्वकर्मेति श्रूयते स तावदस्य क्रियताम्।
छेद्यो दंशस्य दाहो वा क्षतेर्वा रक्तमोक्षणम्।।

एतानि दष्टमाणामायुष्या: प्रतितत्तय:।।
– मालविकाग्निमित्र 4.4

इसी प्रकार शूद्रक की मृच्छकटिक, हाल की गाथासप्तसई, विष्णुशर्मा की पंचतंत्र, भारवि की किरातार्जुनीय, विशाखदत्त की मुद्राराक्षस, दण्डी की काव्यादर्श, बाणभट्ट की कादम्बरी, भवभूति के नाटक, माघ का शिशुपालवध, श्रीहर्ष का नैषधचरित्र आदि ग्रन्थों में भी आयुर्वेद के प्रचुर उदाहरण मिलते हैं।

राजस्थान प्राच्य विद्या प्रतिष्ठान के विपुल ग्रंथ भंडार में आयुर्वेद से सम्बन्धित लगभग 5 हज़ार पाण्डुलिपियाँ संगृहीत हैं। इनमें संस्कृत के साथ-साथ हिन्दी-राजस्थानी की पाण्डुलिपियाँ भी हैं। ये पाण्डुलिपियाँ चौदहवीं शताब्दी से लेकर उन्नीसवीं शताब्दी तक की हैं। इन पाण्डुलिपियों में माधवनिदान, वृद्धचाणक्य, शार्गंधर संहिता, आनन्दमाला, कौमारभृत्य, आयुर्वेद महोदधि, भावप्रकाश, चरक संहिता, सुश्रुत संहिता, अष्टांगहृदय, औषधिकल्प, वैद्य जीवन, वैद्यक ग्रन्थ, नाड़ीपरीक्षा, नाड़ीज्ञान, रसरत्नाकर आदि प्रमुख हैं।

8

पाण्डुलिपियों में निहित भक्ति साहित्य राजस्थान के विशेष सन्दर्भ में

डॉ. देवेन्द्र

मध्यकाल में राजस्थान में अनेक पंथ-सम्प्रदायों की स्थापना हुई। इन सम्प्रदायों में बड़ी संख्या में काव्यप्रतिभा-सम्पन्न संत-महात्मा हुए जिन्होंने अपने भावों-विचारों को कविता के माध्यम से व्यक्त किया। उनके शिष्यों-प्रशिष्यों ने इस वाणी-साहित्य के प्रति पूज्य भाव रखते हुए अपने और दूसरों के पठन-पाठन हेतु प्रतिलिपियाँ तैयार की, कराई और वाणी की पवित्रता के विचार से इन ग्रन्थों को पूर्ण सुरक्षित रूप में रखा। सम्प्रदाय में दीक्षित या इन सन्तों के सम्पर्क में आने वाले अथवा इन पर श्रद्धाभाव रखने वाले पढ़े-लिखे सामाजिक व्यक्तियों ने भी सन्त-वाणी की प्रतिलिपियाँ तैयार करने में अपना योगदान दिया और धार्मिक दृष्टि से महत्त्वपूर्ण मानकर उनकी सुरक्षा के प्रति भी सजग रहे। परिणामस्वरूप आज हमें पाण्डुलिपियों के रूप में विशाल भक्ति साहित्य प्राप्त है।

हस्तलेखों के रूप में उपलब्ध यह साहित्य पंथ-सम्प्रदायों के साधना केन्द्रों में आज भी पवित्र मानकर सुरक्षित रखा हुआ है तथा उसका पठन-पाठन भी होता है। हालाँकि अनेक धर्मस्थलों में पाण्डुलिपियों के रख-रखाव की उचित व्यवस्था न होने के कारण उनकी सुरक्षा चिन्ता का विषय है। समाज और सरकार ने भी इस प्राचीन धरोहर को महत्त्वपूर्ण मानते हुए इसकी सुरक्षा के लिए संस्थाओं की स्थापना की जिनमें लोगों के पास रखी प्राचीन पाण्डुलिपियों को उनसे प्राप्त करके हस्तलिखित ग्रन्थ संग्रहालयों में सुरक्षित रखने की व्यवस्था की गई।

राजस्थान के जिन पंथ-सम्प्रदायों का भक्ति साहित्य पाण्डुलिपियों के रूप में प्राप्त होता है उनमें कुछ प्रमुख पंथ-सम्प्रदाय निम्नलिखित हैं -

1. विश्नोई सम्प्रदाय
2. जसनाथी सम्प्रदाय
3. निरंजनी सम्प्रदाय
4. लालपंथ सम्प्रदाय
5. दादूपंथ सम्प्रदाय
6. रामसनेही सम्प्रदाय
7. चरणदासी सम्प्रदाय
8. अलखिया सम्प्रदाय
9. गूदड़पंथ सम्प्रदाय
10. भावपंथ सम्प्रदाय
11. आईपंथ सम्प्रदाय आदि।

इनके अतिरिक्त राम-भक्ति एवं कृष्ण-भक्ति सम्बन्धी साहित्य की भी पर्याप्त रचना हुई । नाथ सम्प्रदाय का भी राजस्थान में विशेष प्रभाव रहा है। जैन भक्ति साहित्य भी मिलता है।

विश्नोई सम्प्रदाय के प्रवर्त्तक जाम्भोजी की रचनाओं का प्रकाशन हो चुका है। इस सम्प्रदाय से सम्बन्धित सन्तों के साहित्य का विवेचन-विश्लेषण भी हुआ है। विश्नोई सन्तों की रचनाओं की पाण्डुलिपियाँ साधना केन्द्रों तथा हस्तलिखित ग्रन्थ संग्रहालयों में मिलती हैं।

निरंजनी सम्प्रदाय राजस्थान का एक महत्त्वपूर्ण सम्प्रदाय है। इस सम्प्रदाय की स्थिति अन्य सम्प्रदायों की तुलना में इस दृष्टि से विशिष्ट है कि इसमें किसी एक सन्त को संस्थापक या सर्वोच्च स्थान न प्रदान कर द्वादश महन्तों को समान महत्त्व प्रदान किया गया है। निरंजनी सम्प्रदाय के सन्त हरिरामदास के निम्नलिखित छन्द से यह बात पूरी तरह स्पष्ट हो जाती है -

जन हरिदास हरि सुमिर दास तुरसी तत पाया।
श्याम तजी सब श्यामता पद पूरण ध्याया।

ध्यान धरत हरि मिले नाथ मति नाथ ही गया।
कान्हड़दास कृपालु खेम पुनि खेम समाया।

मोहन भजे मुरारि दास जगजीवन सिधवर।
आनदास जगन्नाथ भए प्रभु के अनुचर।।

घाट बाध इनमें नहीं अधिकारी निज धाम के।
द्वादस महन्त निरंजनी हृदय बसहु हरिराम के।।

उपर्युक्त छन्द के अनुसार बारह निरंजनी महन्त इस प्रकार हैं - 1. हरिदास, 2. तुरसीदास, 3. श्यामदास, 4. पूरणदास, 5. ध्यानदास, 6. नाथ, 7. कान्हड़दास, 8. खेमदास, 9. मोहनदास, 10. जगजीवन दास, 11. आनदास, एवं 12. जगन्नाथ।

हरिरामदास ने स्पष्ट कहा है कि "घाट बाध इनमें नहीं" इनमें कोई किसी से छोटा-बड़ा नहीं है।

बहुत दिनों तक यह माना जाता रहा कि सन्त हरिदास इस सम्प्रदाय के प्रवर्त्तक हैं। इधर नए तथ्यों के प्रकाश में सन्त हरिदास को इस सम्प्रदाय का प्रवर्त्तक तो नहीं माना जा सकता। हाँ, निरंजनी सम्प्रदाय को व्यवस्थित एवं सुसंगठित रूप देने का श्रेय हरिदास को ही है।

इस सम्प्रदाय के सन्त-कवियों की लम्बी परम्परा है। उपर्युक्त द्वादश सन्तों में से दो-एक को छोड़कर अन्य सभी की रचनाओं की जानकारी मिलती है। इनके अतिरिक्त इस सम्प्रदाय के अन्य सन्त जिनकी रचनाएँ उपलब्ध होती हैं, इस प्रकार हैं - सेवादास, नरीदास, पीपादास, कल्याणदास, प्रेमदास, भगवानदास, मनोहरदास, हरिरामदास, आत्माराम, रूपदास, रघुनाथदास, प्यारेराम, उदयराम, कोमलदास आदि।

निरंजनी सम्प्रदाय के प्रमुख सन्त हरिदास जी की रचनाएँ प्रकाशित हो चुकी हैं। इनके जीवन और काव्य पर एकाधिक शोध-कार्य भी हुए हैं। *निरंजनी सम्प्रदाय और सन्त तुरसीदास निरंजनी* नामक अपनी पुस्तक (प्रकाशन 1964 ई.) में डॉ. भगीरथ मिश्र ने सन्त तुरसी की रचनाओं के विवेचन-विश्लेषण के साथ उनकी रचना का कुछ अंश भी प्रकाशित किया था। सन्त तुरसी पर एक शोध-कार्य डॉ. सत्यनारायण मिश्र ने किया था। *सन्तकवि तुरसीदास निरंजनी : साहित्य और सिद्धान्त* नामक उनका प्रबन्ध 1974 ई. में कानपुर से प्रकाशित हुआ था। तुरसी-रचित काव्य विशाल परिमाण में है। इनकी रचना से सम्बन्धित पाण्डुलिपि की फोटोकॉपी मुझे महामाया पीठ, नवलगढ़ के महन्त आचार्य साँवरदास जी शास्त्री से प्राप्त हुई थी। तुरसीदास जी की वाणी के सम्पादन का कार्य मेरे शिष्य डॉ. गोपीकिशन चितारा ने अपने हाथ में लिया है।

सेवादास जी की वाणी भी विशाल परिमाण में है। हाल ही में आचार्य साँवरदास शास्त्री ने इसे प्रकाशित किया है। सेवादास जी के जीवन और काव्य को आधार बनाकर

डॉ. एच.एस. मोरे ने पूना विश्वविद्यालय से शोधकार्य किया है। उनका शोध प्रबन्ध 1977 ई. में मथुरा से प्रकाशित हो चुका है।

हरिरामदास निरंजनी की एक रचना *छन्दरत्नावली* का प्रकाशन पूर्व में हुआ है। शेष साहित्य अप्रकाशित है। शोधछात्रा सुश्री नेहा बैद ने हरिरामदास निरंजनी के जीवन और काव्य पर पी.एच.डी. उपाधि हेतु अपना शोध-प्रबन्ध जयनारायण व्यास विश्वविद्यालय, जोधपुर में प्रस्तुत किया है। शोधछात्र श्री अजीत कुलश्रेष्ठ को मनोहरदास निरंजनी की लगभग सभी रचनाओं की पाण्डुलिपियाँ प्राप्त करने में सफलता मिली है। वह इन पर शोध-कार्य कर रहे हैं। आत्माराम जी की सम्पूर्ण वाणी का एक गुटका आचार्य साँवरदास जी शास्त्री से प्राप्त हुआ था। इस समय वह डॉ. रतनलाल मिश्र के पास है जो आत्माराम की रचनाओं का सम्पादन कर रहे हैं।

मंगलदास स्वामी ने काफी पहले निरंजनी साहित्य को एकत्र करने का कार्य किया था। उन्होंने विभिन्न निरंजनी "अस्थलों" में जाकर वहाँ उपलब्ध पाण्डुलिपियाँ हस्तगत कर कुचामन में संगृहीत की थीं। *श्री हरिपुरुष जी की वाणी तथा अपर निरंजनी महात्माओं की रचनाओं के अंशांश* नामक अपनी पुस्तक उन्होंने इसी सामग्री के आधार पर तैयार की थी। उनके गोलोकवास के पश्चात् यह साहित्य उसी कक्ष में बन्द पड़ा रहा। ग्रन्थों की सार-सँभाल तो दूर वह कक्ष कभी खोला तक नहीं गया। तीन-चार वर्ष पूर्व जब मुझे इस बात का पता चला तब मैंने निरंजनी सम्प्रदाय के महामंत्री आचार्य साँवरदास जी से अनुरोध किया कि उस साहित्य को सँभाला जाना चाहिए। साँवरदास जी ने रुचि ली। काफी प्रयास करने पर वह कक्ष खुल सका। उसमें रखी अनेक पाण्डुलिपियाँ दीमकों का आहार बन चुकी थीं। कई ग्रन्थों के पत्र इस तरह चिपक गए हैं कि उन्हें अलग करना असम्भव है। साँवरदास जी ने वहाँ से प्राप्त ग्रन्थों को महामाया पीठ, नवलगढ़ में ले जाकर सुरक्षित किया है।

निरंजनी सन्तों की वाणी-सम्बन्धी पाण्डुलिपियाँ राजस्थान के बाहर पंजाब, महाराष्ट्र, उत्तर प्रदेश आदि प्रान्तों में भी हैं।

दादूपंथ में भी अनेक उत्कृष्ट काव्य-प्रतिभा-सम्पन्न सन्त हुए हैं। दादूजी सहित रज्जब, सुन्दरदास बषना जी आदि की रचनाओं का प्रकाशन काफी पहले हो चुका है। रज्जब की *सरबंगी* कुछ समय पूर्व डॉ. ब्रजेन्द्र कुमार सिंहल द्वारा सम्पादित होकर प्रकाशित हुई है। डॉ. सिंहल सन्त साहित्य की खोज एवं सम्पादन-प्रकाशन में निरन्तर संलग्न हैं। जन गोपाल रचित *दादू जन्म लीला परची* प्रकाशित है। इनकी रचनाओं की पाण्डुलिपियाँ राजस्थान प्राच्य विद्या प्रतिष्ठान आदि के ग्रन्थ संग्रहालयों में बड़ी संख्या में मिलती हैं। वाजिन्द का भी कुछ साहित्य प्रकाशित हुआ है। राघौदास-कृत *भक्तमाल*

अत्यन्त प्रसिद्ध है। जगजीवनदास के लगभग 20 ग्रन्थों का संग्रह दादू महाविद्यालय, जयपुर में है। खेमदास की लगभग एक दर्जन रचनाएँ मिलती हैं। रसपुंजदास की रीति-प्रभाव वाली रचनाएँ - *चमत्कार चन्द्रोदय, प्रस्तार प्रभाकर* तथा *वृत्तविनोद* उल्लेखनीय हैं। इनके अतिरिक्त स्वरूपदास, चैनदास, ठाकुरदास, भीखा आदि संत-कवियों की रचनाएँ भी मिलती हैं।

राजस्थान में प्रादुर्भूत रामसनेही सम्प्रदाय की स्थिति इस दृष्टि से विशिष्ट है कि एक ही नाम से यह तीन अलग-अलग स्थानों में, अलग-अलग समयों में अलग-अलग सन्त-परम्पराओं के साथ स्थापित और विकसित हुआ। सम्प्रदाय के नाम के साथ स्थान का नाम जोड़कर इनका विभेद किया जाता है। रेण, सींथल-खेड़ापा तथा शाहपुरा। काव्य-रचना की दृष्टि से ये सभी अत्यन्त सम्पन्न हैं।

रेण-रामसनेही सम्प्रदाय के प्रवर्त्तक दरिया साहब की वाणी प्रकाशित है। उनके शिष्य पूरणदास की वाणी का भी प्रकाशन हुआ है। मेरे शिष्य डॉ. सतीश कुमार ने रेण-रामसनेही सम्प्रदाय से सम्बन्धित अपने शोधप्रबन्ध (प्रकाशित) में इस सम्प्रदाय के उन संत-कवियों की लम्बी सूची दी है जिनकी रचनाएँ हस्तलिखित ग्रन्थों के रूप में उन्हें सम्प्रदाय के साधना-स्थलों में उपलब्ध हुई। उनमें से कुछ सन्तों का नामोल्लेख यहाँ किया जा रहा है - किशनदास, नानगदास, सुखराम, कुस्यालीराम, हरखाराम, हेमदास, हरिदास, मेघोदास, बुधराम, सावंतराम, साहिबराम, पदुमदास, अंभाबाई, शिवकरण, रामकरण, गीधराम, साँवलदास, सहजराम, खेतादास, गंगाराम, प्रेमदयाल, सुखरामदास, सुखसारण, रामकिशोर।

रामसनेही सम्प्रदाय सींथल-खेड़ापा के प्रवर्त्तक हरिरामदास, खेड़ापा पीठ के संस्थापक रामदास सहित इस सम्प्रदाय के नारायण दास, दयालदास, हरदेवदास, पूरणदास, सेवगराम, भावनादास, जीयाराम, सालिगराम आदि की रचनाओं का प्रकाशन हो चुका है। मेरे शिष्य डॉ. हरीश कुमार को सींथल-खेड़ापा रामसनेही सम्प्रदाय सम्बन्धी अपने शोध-कार्य के दौरान बड़ी संख्या में इस सम्प्रदाय के सन्तों की पाण्डुलिपियाँ रामद्वारों तथा हस्तलिखित ग्रन्थ संग्रहालयों में उपलब्ध हुई जिनका उल्लेख उन्होंने अपने शोध-प्रबन्ध (प्रकाशित) में किया है। कुछ महत्त्वपूर्ण सन्त-कवियों के नाम हैं - पीथोदास, लालदास, राघोदास, परसराम, निर्मलदास, मनीराम, दौलतराम, कनीराम, सिंभूराम, तेजराम, उत्साहराम आदि। रामदास जी के शिष्य तथा पाली-रामद्वारा के संस्थापक सन्त निर्मलदास के जीवन और काव्य पर मेरे शिष्य डॉ. सुभाषचन्द्र भाटिया ने शोध-कार्य किया है।

शाहपुरा-रामसनेही सम्प्रदाय का काफी साहित्य प्रकाशित हुआ है। सम्प्रदाय के प्रवर्त्तक स्वामी रामचरणजी की सम्पूर्ण वाणी का प्रकाशन होने के साथ-साथ इन पर एकाधिक शोध-कार्य सम्पन्न हो चुके हैं। सन्त देवादास की वाणी भी सम्प्रदाय की ओर से प्रकाशित हो चुकी है। सन्त देवादास के व्यक्तित्व एवं कृतित्व पर डॉ. शैलेन्द्र स्वामी ने शोध-कार्य किया है। हाल ही में सन्त अमृतराम रामसनेही द्वारा सम्पादित *सन्त गिरधरदास जी महाराज की अनुभव वाणी* प्रकाशित हुई है। काव्य-रचना की दृष्टि से यह भी काफी सम्पन्न सम्प्रदाय है। अभी भी अनेक संत-कवियों की रचनाएँ पाण्डुलिपियों के रूप में ही हैं।

रामभक्ति में रसिकोपासना का प्रारम्भ राजस्थान में हुआ। कृष्णदास पयहारी के शिष्य अग्रदास पहले रामभक्त हैं जिनकी रचनाओं में रसिक-भावना मिलती है। हिन्दी में "भक्तमाल" परम्परा का सूत्रपात करने वाले नाभादास इन्हीं के शिष्य थे। इनकी रचनाएँ प्रकाशित हो चुकी हैं। रामभक्ति की इसी परम्परा में भक्त बालकृष्ण, जिनका साम्प्रदायिक नाम "बाल अली" था, की ये रचनाएँ मिलती हैं - *ध्यानमंजरी, नेहप्रकाश, सिद्धान्तवृत्तदीपिका, दयालमंजरी, प्रेमपहेली, प्रेमपरीक्षा, परतीत परीक्षा*। साम्प्रदायिक संघर्ष से जुड़ा एक नाम है बालानन्द। दशनामी शैवों का सामना करने के लिए अखाड़े की स्थापना कर इन्होंने साधुओं की सेना तैयार की। संवत् 1802 में जयपुर में लश्करी मन्दिर की स्थापना की। मन्दिर का नाम ही उसकी स्थापना का उद्देश्य जानने के लिए पर्याप्त है। भक्त मधुराचार्य संस्कृत और हिन्दी दोनों भाषाओं में काव्य-रचना करते थे। एक अलग ही तरह की विचारधारा के रामभक्त हैं सूरकिशोर। यह सीता को पुत्रीवत् मानते थे और इस नाते राम को अपना दामाद। स्वयं को जनक तो नहीं मानते थे, जनक का भाई मानते थे। इनकी रचना *मिथिलाविलास* है। अन्य रसिकरामभक्त कवियों में, जिनकी रचनाएँ हस्तलिखित ग्रन्थों के रूप में मिलती हैं, उल्लेखनीय हैं - *सियासखी, मनभावन, चन्द्रअली, रूपसरस,* आदि।

इसी प्रकार कृष्ण-भक्ति का भी राजस्थान में व्यापक प्रभाव रहा है। इस प्रभाव को समझने के लिए एक ही नाम काफी है - मीरा। जयपुर के शासक सवाई प्रतापसिंह भी कृष्णभक्त थे। राजा के रूप में सवाई प्रतापसिंह ही भक्त के रूप में "ब्रजनिधि" के नाम से जाने जाते हैं। इनकी रचनाएँ *ब्रजनिधि-ग्रन्थावली* के रूप में प्रकाशित हो चुकी हैं। इस परम्परा का एक और महत्त्वपूर्ण नाम है - रसराशि। अन्य कृष्णभक्त कवियों में उल्लेखनीय हैं निम्बार्क सम्प्रदाय से सम्बद्ध वृन्दावन देवाचार्य, जिन्होंने सलेमाबाद तथा जयपुर में गद्दियाँ स्थापित कीं। ललित सम्प्रदाय से सम्बद्ध किशोरी अलि ने संस्कृत तथा हिन्दी दोनों भाषाओं में काव्य-रचना की। हिन्दी रचनाओं की संख्या 20

के लगभग है। किशनगढ़ नरेश सावंतसिंह हरि-सम्बन्ध-नाम नागरीदास की सम्पूर्ण रचनाओं का संकलन *नागर समुच्चय* नाम से 1898 ई. में बम्बई से प्रकाशित हुआ था। तत्पश्चात् नागरीदास की रचनाएँ डॉ. किशोरीलाल गुप्त द्वारा सुसम्पादित होकर नागरी प्रचारिणी सभा वाराणसी से *नागरीदास ग्रन्थावली* के रूप में दो खण्डों में प्रकाशित हुई। हस्तलिखित ग्रन्थ संग्रहालयों में अन्य अनेक कवियों एवं कवयित्रियों की कृष्ण-भक्ति-सम्बन्धी रचनाओं की पाण्डुलिपियाँ मिलती हैं।

यहाँ सभी सम्प्रदायों के साहित्य पर इस प्रकार के विचार से चर्चा काफी लम्बी हो जाएगी। वस्तुत: सभी सम्प्रदायों की प्राय: ऐसी ही स्थिति है। कुछ साहित्य प्रकाशित और विवेचित-विश्लेषित हो चुके हैं तो बहुत कुछ अप्रकाशित और अनालोचित हैं।

अब हम उस साहित्य पर थोड़ी चर्चा करना चाहेंगे जो सीधे-सीधे ईश्वराराधन अथवा भक्त के भगवान् के प्रति निवेदन, उसके आध्यात्मिक-सांसारिक दर्शन आदि से सम्बद्ध न होते हुए भी भक्ति साहित्य का ही हिस्सा है। इस प्रकार का साहित्य भी बड़े परिमाण में पाण्डुलिपियों के रूप में मिलता है। वस्तुत: मध्यकाल में भक्ति साहित्य से सम्बन्धित कुछ नए काव्य रूप विकसित हुए। इनमें से एक है परचई काव्य। सन्तों का जीवन-परिचय लिखने की एक नई परम्परा मध्यकाल में आरम्भ हुई। इन परचई काव्यों के रचनाकार भी सन्त ही होते थे। बहुत पहले डॉ. त्रिलोकीनारायण दीक्षित ने परचई काव्य को आधार बनाकर शोध-कार्य किया था जो *परिचयी साहित्य* शीर्षक से 1957 ई. में पुस्तक रूप में प्रकाशित हुआ था। उस समय तक उन्हें केवल 15 परचइयाँ ही उपलब्ध हुई थीं। उसके बाद श्री अगरचन्द नाहटा ने *राष्ट्रभारती* पत्रिका के जनवरी और सितम्बर 1962 के अंकों में इस प्रकार की लगभग 75 रचनाओं की जानकारी दी। इधर मेरे शोधार्थी श्री पुखराज ने परचई साहित्य को अपने शोध-कार्य का विषय बनाया है और अब तक लगभग 50 परचइयों की प्रकाशित/हस्तलिखित प्रतियाँ प्राप्त कर चुके हैं। जो प्रकाशित परचइयाँ मेरे देखने में आई हैं उनमें से अधिकांश किसी एक प्रति के आधार पर बिना पाठ और अर्थ पर ध्यान दिए प्रकाशित करवा दी गई हैं। आवश्यकता इस बात की है कि इनका पाठ-वैज्ञानिक सम्पादन हो।

यह सही है कि परचइयों में अधिकांशत: सन्तों के जीवन से सम्बन्धित चमत्कारपूर्ण घटनाओं का ही वर्णन मिलता है। फिर भी इनके सूक्ष्म अध्ययन से सम्बन्धित सन्त के जीवन के महत्त्वपूर्ण सूत्र प्राप्त किए जा सकते हैं।

इसी प्रकार का एक और काव्यरूप है भक्तमाल। यह भी मध्यकालीन हिन्दी साहित्य का एक विशिष्ट काव्यरूप है। परचई में जहाँ एक ही सन्त के जीवन का विस्तार के साथ वर्णन होता है वहाँ भक्तमाल में अनेक सन्तों-भक्तों का संक्षेप में परिचय रहता

है। कुछ भक्तमालों में केवल नामावली ही मिलती है। संक्षिप्तता के कारण ही आगे चलकर भक्तमालों पर टीका लिखने की परम्परा शुरु हुई। जिनमें टीकाकारों ने सम्बन्धित सन्तों-भक्तों के परिचय को विस्तार प्रदान किया। नाभादास से प्रारम्भ हुई भक्तमाल लेखन की परम्परा आगे निरन्तर गतिमान रही। नाभादास-कृत भक्तमाल प्रकाशित हो चुका है तथा इसका विस्तृत विवेचन-विश्लेषण भी हुआ है। नाभादास के भक्तमाल पर लिखी गई प्रियादास की टीका अत्यन्त प्रसिद्ध है। इसके अतिरिक्त राजस्थान प्राच्य विद्या प्रतिष्ठान द्वारा भी कुछ महत्त्वपूर्ण भक्तमाल प्रकाशित किए गए हैं - चारण ब्रह्मदास जी दादूपंथी-विरचित भक्तमाल, राघवदास-कृत भक्तमाल (चतुरदास-कृत टीका सहित), जग्गा जी रचित भक्तमाल तथा चैनजी-कृत भक्तमाल। रामसनेही सम्प्रदाय की खेड़ापा पीठ के संस्थापक रामदास जी ने एक भक्तमाल ग्रन्थ की रचना की थी जो प्रकाशित है। खेड़ापा पीठ के द्वितीय आचार्य रामसनेही सन्त दयालदास प्रणीत भक्तमाल भी प्रकाशित हो चुका है। रामसनेही सम्प्रदाय - रेण के प्रवर्त्तक दरिया साहब-रचित भक्त-माल भी प्रकाश में आ चुका है। लेकिन ऐसे अनेक भक्तमाल अभी भी सम्प्रदायों के साधना केन्द्रों में अथवा हस्तलिखित ग्रन्थ संग्रहालयों में वेष्टनों में बन्द हैं जिनका प्रकाशन और अधययन-अनुशीलन होना चाहिए। इनमें सन्त सिंभूराम, प्रेमदयाल, सावंतराम, साहिबराम, किसनदास, गंगाराम, हरखाराम द्वारा रचित भक्तमाल उल्लेखनीय हैं। निरंजनी सम्प्रदाय की परम्परा के सन्त प्यारेराम द्वारा भी एक भक्तमाल लिखा गया जो अद्यावधि अप्रकाशित है। इसकी एक पाण्डुलिपि राजस्थानी शोध संस्थान चौपासनी, जोधपुर में है।

हिन्दी साहित्य के मध्यकाल विशेषत: उत्तरमध्यकाल में संस्कृत के प्राचीन धार्मिक साहित्य का हिन्दी में अनुवाद कर उसे सर्वसुलभ एवं सभी के लिए बोधगम्य बनाने का प्रयास भी व्यापक रूप में दिखाई पड़ता है। भक्ति एवं दर्शन से सम्बन्धित ग्रन्थों के साथ-साथ *रामायण*, *महाभारत*, पुराण आदि के काव्यानुवादों की समृद्ध परम्परा मिलती है। अनेक ग्रन्थों पर टीकाएँ भी लिखी गई हैं। यह कार्य सामान्य और दरबारी कवियों के द्वारा तो किया ही गया, सन्त-भक्त-कवियों ने भी महत्त्वपूर्ण संस्कृत-ग्रन्थों के अनुवाद किए तथा उन पर टीकाएँ लिखीं। इस प्रकार के अनूदित एवं टीका साहित्य की ओर शोधार्थियों का ध्यान प्राय: कम ही गया है। यह साहित्य पाण्डुलिपियों के रूप में सुरक्षित है। कुछ का प्रकाशन हुआ है।

प्राय: माना जाता है कि निर्गुण भक्ति-परम्परा के सन्तों को संस्कृत भाषा का ज्ञान नहीं होता था। ये कम पढ़े-लिखे होते थे। लेकिन निर्गुण भक्ति-परम्परा के साहित्य का विहंगावलोकन करने पर यह धारणा अंशत: ही ठीक मानी जा सकती है, पूर्णत: नहीं। क्योंकि निर्गुण सन्तों में से अनेक नाम ऐसे मिलते हैं जिन्होंने संस्कृत के धार्मिक ग्रन्थों

के अनुवाद किए या फिर उन पर टीकाएँ लिखीं। उदाहरण के लिए दादूपंथी सन्त जगन्नाथ दास द्वारा प्रणीत *गीतासार* तथा *योगवाशिष्ठसार* ग्रन्थ। दामोदरदास ने *मार्कण्डेय पुराण* का अनुवाद किया। निरंजनी सन्त हरिरामदास निरंजनी ने शंकराचार्य के *विष्णुसहस्रनाम भाष्य* का अनुवाद किया। इसी प्रकार भगवानदास निरंजनी ने *अध्यात्मरामायणभाषा* तथा *गीतामाहात्म्य* नामक ग्रन्थों का प्रणयन किया। रामसनेही सम्प्रदाय की खेड़ापा पीठ परम्परा के सन्त भावनादास की रचनाएँ उल्लेखनीय हैं - 1. *श्रीमद्भागवत एकादश स्कंध की टीका*, 2. *भर्तृहरि शतक त्रय*, 3. *चाणक्य नीति*, 4. *श्रीमद्भगवद्गीता*।

अब मैं पाण्डुलिपियों के महत्त्व पर थोड़ा प्रकाश डालकर अपनी वाणी को विराम दूँगा। प्रायः मान लिया जाता है कि यदि कोई कृति प्रकाशित हो चुकी है तो उसकी पाण्डुलिपियाँ महत्त्वहीन हो जाती हैं। यह निष्कर्ष पूरी तरह गलत है। पाण्डुलिपियों का महत्त्व कभी समाप्त नहीं होता। हाँ, प्रकाशन हो जाने से कृति सर्व-सुलभ हो जाती है, यह कहा जा सकता है। हालाँकि यह कहना भी सब प्रकार से सही नहीं ठहरता। क्योंकि कई बार बहुत पहले प्रकाशित किसी कृति की प्रकाशित प्रतियाँ अनुपलब्ध हो जाती हैं जबकि हस्तलिखित प्रतियाँ ग्रन्थ-संग्रहालयों आदि में सुरक्षित होने से आसानी से प्राप्त हो जाती हैं। उदाहरण के लिए जब मैं काशी हिन्दू विश्वविद्यालय, वाराणसी में आचार्य विश्वनाथ प्रसाद मिश्र के निदेशन में पी.एच.डी. उपाधि हेतु रीतिकवि मण्डन पर शोध-कार्य कर रहा था तब मण्डन की एक रचना *जानकीपचीसी* के सम्बन्ध में यह जानकारी तो मिली कि यह प्रकाशित हुई थी। लेकिन अनेक पुस्तकालयों में ढूँढने पर भी उसकी कोई प्रकाशित प्रति नहीं मिल सकी। अनेक विद्वानों, पुस्तक संग्रहकर्ताओं से भी सम्पर्क किया लेकिन सफलता नहीं मिली। जबकि मुझे उक्त रचना की एक नहीं दो-तीन हस्तलिखित प्रतियाँ उपलब्ध हुई जो मेरे अध्ययन का आधार बनीं। हालाँकि शोधकार्य पूर्ण हो जाने, उपाधि मिल जाने तथा *मण्डन-ग्रन्थावली* का प्रकाशन हो जाने के बाद मुझे *जानकीपचीसी* की प्रकाशित प्रति की जानकारी मिली, वह भी देश में नहीं, विदेश में। उसकी प्रकाशित प्रति इण्डिया ऑफिस लाइब्रेरी, लन्दन में है।

प्रकाशित भक्ति साहित्य का बहुलांश सम्बन्धित सम्प्रदायों के द्वारा प्रकाशित कराया गया है। यद्यपि अनेक सम्प्रदायों में साहित्यिक अभिरुचि के ज्ञान-सम्पन्न महात्मा हुए हैं और उनके सम्पादकत्व में यह कार्य सम्पन्न हुआ है तथापि अनेक ग्रन्थों के प्रकाशन में वह गम्भीरता दिखाई नहीं पड़ती। एक प्रति के आधार पर जैसा पढ़ा-समझा गया वैसा मुद्रित करवा दिया गया। कहीं-कहीं तो मनोवांछित परिवर्तन भी कर दिए गए हैं। कुछ छोड़ा और जोड़ा भी गया है। ऐसी स्थिति में प्रकाशित प्रतियाँ सर्वथा विश्वसनीय नहीं मानी जा सकती। इनके आधार पर किए गए अध्ययन के निष्कर्ष भी पूरी तरह

सही नहीं होंगे। उदाहरण के लिए शाहपुरा-रामसनेही सम्प्रदाय के सन्त नवलराम द्वारा प्रणीत *सर्वांगसार* ग्रन्थ सन्त गुरुमुखराम रामसनेही की व्याख्या के साथ सम्प्रदाय की ओर से प्रकाशित हुआ है। इस प्रकाशित ग्रन्थ में कृति की पूर्णता/अपूर्णता के सम्बन्ध में कुछ भी नहीं कहा गया है। सामान्यत: यही माना जाएगा कि ग्रन्थ पूर्ण है। जबकि यह सही नहीं है। शोध-छात्रा सुश्री नेहा बैद को इस कृति की एक हस्तलिखित प्रति अभय जैन ग्रन्थालय, बीकानेर में प्राप्त हुई। उसके अध्ययन से स्पष्ट हुआ कि यह ग्रन्थ प्रकाशित प्रति की तुलना में कहीं बड़ा है। सन्त गुरुमुखराम रामसनेही ने कुछ चुनिन्दा सन्तों की रचनाओं की व्याख्या कर उसे ग्रन्थ रूप में प्रकाशित करवा दिया। नवलराम ने इसमें रामसनेही सम्प्रदाय-शाहपुरा की परम्परा के सन्तों के साथ अन्य सम्प्रदायों के सन्तों की रचनाएँ भी संगृहीत की थीं। प्रकाशित ग्रन्थ में अन्य सम्प्रदायों के थोड़े से सन्तों को ही स्थान मिला। अनेक को सम्मिलित नहीं किया गया और इसका उल्लेख भी नहीं किया गया।

वस्तुत: ज्ञान का मूल स्रोत हैं पाण्डुलिपियाँ। शोधार्थियों-अध्येताओं को ठीक निष्कर्ष पर पहुँचने के लिए जरूरी है कि वे अपने शोध-अधययन का आधार ज्ञान के मूल स्रोत को बनाएँ। न कि इधर-उधर से पढ़ी-सुनी गई बातों को। द्वितीय स्रोत से प्राप्त सामग्री पर आधारित शोध-अध्ययन द्वितीय श्रेणी का ही होगा।

9

Formation of the Kashmiri Language and Some Early Kashmiri Works

Shashi Shekhar Toshkhani

THOUGH absolute historical documentation of the crystallization of Kashmiri as the regional language spoken in the Kashmir Valley is not possible, it can be said with a fair degree of certainty that it is more than 1,000 years old. Looking at its grammatical structure, vocables and phonology, it would not be wrong to claim that Kashmiri, like Hindi, Punjabi, Marathi, Gujarati, Bengali, Sindhi and other modern Indo-Aryan languages, evolved from a Prākr̥t-Apabhraṁśa substratum sometime around the tenth century. The actual processes that led to its surfacing as the regional voice of Kashmir's literary culture can be known only when the language is studied in the full perspective of its historical and cultural development. This becomes all the more important as bizarre and outlandish theories continue to be orchestrated about the descent of Kashmiri from languages belonging to totally unrelated word stocks, like Hebrew or dialects spoken in Nagaland.

We have the polyglot Kṣemendra's evidence that Kashmiri coexisted with Sanskrit for quite some time as a communicative as well as expressive medium of the people of the region before "the historical dynamic of vernacularism" finally led to its individuation as a modern Indian language that acquired a distinct identity of its own and occupied the local cultural space. He exhorts the upcoming Sanskrit poets of his time to study *bhāṣā kāvya* or poetry written in the regional dialect alongside Prākr̥t and Apabhraṁśa works. The reference to Prākr̥t and Apabhraṁśa by Kṣemendra does not pertain to the regional but standardized trans-regional forms of these languages which had come to be literalized throughout the country like Sanskrit itself. Kṣemendra, however, does not name of any *bhāṣā* poet of his time, nor does he refer to any verse written in the language. Obviously, works of all these vernacular poets are lost. Soon after we find Bilhaṇa, another noted Sanskrit poet of the eleventh-century Kashmir praise the ladies of his native land for writing poetry in Prākr̥t and Apabhraṁśa with an ease with which they wielded their own *janma bhāṣā* (mother tongue). In the twelfth century, Kalhaṇa in his *Rājataraṅgiṇī* provides an example of spoken Kashmiri in the form of the sentence *raṅgassa helu diṇṇā* (the village of Helu must be given to Raṅgā), supposed to have been uttered by a Ḍomba singer — a curious piece of linguistic evidence.

Later, in the thirteenth century, we have Śītikaṇṭha claiming to have written his *Mahānaya Prakāśa* (MNP) (Illumination of the System of the Highest Meaning), a work belonging to the Krama school of Kashmir Śaivism, as a *nuti* (hymn) in *sarvagocara deśa bhāṣā* — the regional dialect intelligible to all: *athocitr̥citam nutiṁ sarvagocarayā deśabhāṣāyā.* But it was Amir Khusro who first mentioned the name of the language as Kashmiri in his *Nūh-i-Siphir* (*c.* 1300), placing it alongside "Lahauri" in his list of Indian languages: Sindhi, Lahauri, Kashmiri, Dogri, Dhursamundari, Tilangi, Gujarati, Gaudi Bengali, Avadhi and Dehalvi.

It is highly probable that Kashmiri may have remained confined to the realm of orality for quite some time before it was committed to the written form, but one cannot achieve absolute "temporal precision" to borrow a phrase from Sheldon Pollock, regarding this historical moment. Perhaps it needed a little encouragement to come out of obscurity and become a literary language, and this was provided by the Krama school of Kashmir Śaivism. With spiritual democracy at work, the Krama school urged that the local vernacular be preferred in place of Sanskrit for exposition of its tenets. This can be evidenced in works like *Chumma Sampradāya,* or rather *Chummā Sampradāya* (*CS*) as Navjivan Rastogi calls it, and the *Mahānaya Prakāśa* (*MNP*), which are directly related to it and provide the earliest specimens of written Kashmiri.

Analysed from the point of view of both its linguistic features and esoteric contents, *CS* appears to be a much older text than *MNP* and can be assigned to the eleventh century when Krama Tantricism was supposed to have been at the height of its popularity in Kashmir. Rastogi, however, considers *CS* to be a much later work as Śivopādhyāya, an eighteenth-century Kashmiri scholar of monistic Śaivism, has referred to the cult in his commentary on *Vijñāna-Bhairava.* It is an unpublished text though Rastogi has published a version of it, very painstakingly edited by him, as an appendix in his book *Kāśmīr kī Śaiva Saṁskṛti mein Kula aur Krama.* The work was scheduled for publication by the Research and Publications Department of Jammu & Kashmir state in the early 1960s, but for unknown reasons the exercise was aborted. But late Pandit Dina Nath Yaksh, a well-known Kashmiri scholar who was working as Head Paṇḍit of the Sanskrit unit of the Department those days, gave me galley proofs of some pages containing 52-65 aphorisms together with the commentary on them. The late scholar had a personal copy of the manuscript with a commentary entitled *Chummā-Saṅketa-Prakāśa,* of which he gave a Devanāgarī transcript to Rastogi for his personal study. Both, according to Rastogi, have been authored by Niṣkriyānandanātha, an important name in the preceptorial tradition of the sect.

The text of the work, divided into 74 sections, each headed by an aphorism (*sūtra*), is not in Kashmiri alone but in three languages — Prākr̥t, Sanskrit and Kashmiri. The *sūtra* or the aphoristic heading introducing the subject is given in Prākr̥t at the top and followed by its exposition in Sanskrit, which in turn ends in an explanatory verse in Kashmiri. Of the thirty odd Kashmiri verses the manuscript contained, Rastogi deleted some while copying the transcript provided by late Paṇḍit Yaksha, considering them "as unnecessary due to ignorance". In the text edited by him there are thus no Kashmiri verses available now under *sūtra*s 19, 20, 22, 23, 24, 26, 32, 35, 37 and 39, the missing verses being indicated by him by dotted lines. The most unfortunate part of it is that Paṇḍit Yaksha had to leave Kashmir during the terrorist violence that erupted there in 1990 and his house, where he had maintained his personal manuscript library, was burned down to ashes by the terrorists along with a whole treasure of rare manuscripts he possessed. This irretrievable loss left Paṇḍit Yaksha so deeply shocked that he died. Nothing is known about the fate of the original manuscript of *CS* lying with the Jammu & Kashmir Research and Publications Department.

Though mediated by Sanskrit, and highly metaphysical in content, these verses announce the inauguration of a departure that was to be of great significance in the literary history of Kashmiri language. Rastogi identifies the Chummā sect as a sub-school of Krama Tantricism allied to the Sāhasa school. What the term *chummā* means exactly is not clear, but according to him: "*Chummā*s probably mean the physiological centres of spirituality". The mysticism and esoteric symbolism of the work express themselves in the enigmatic language of *apūja pūjā, adr̥ṣṭa darśana* and *akrama krama,* appearing to lay emphasis on internality than just outer ritual.

CS speaks in the general idiom of the Krama Tantricism and subscribes to the notion of consciousness being a cyclic phenomenon. It seems to be more inclined towards mysticism and philosophy than mere ritualistic worship. Like the Sāhasa cult, it believes in transcendence of experience based on intuitive realization of the ultimate reality through immersion of the self in the great void of absolute consciousness. Thus, in the benedictory verses following the very first *sūtra*, the author invokes Parama Śiva as the Great Sky, inaccessible and without a dwelling, in which all forms of consciousness, inner and outer, arise and submerge. He describes Śakti as the Supreme Goddess of consciousness, inseparable from Śiva, and beyond all gradation, manifesting herself as the universe of her own free will. She represents the all-pervading fullness (*pūrṇatā*) of the absolute. *CS* presents the ultimate transcendental experience as a thought-free state in which the void of consciousness merges with the non-void (*śūnyāśūnya*), with all phenomenal entities absorbed at the highest level in undifferentiated consciousness. In an explanatory Kashmiri verse at the end of the 53rd aphorism of *CS*, the author says:

vigalani śunnya āśunnya svarūpā
vividha padārathu sāthu kavalet ।
āśayu citi sadā nīrūpā
viccī viju virtha praghatet ॥

More than its cultic significance, however, the text of *CS* is important for the light it throws on the Kashmiri language when it was probably in its earliest stage of development. Unfortunately, no attention has been paid towards this by scholars so far, though I have made some effort in this direction in my book *Kaśmīrī Sāhitya kā Itihās*. Rastogi's efforts in bringing out an edited version of it and drawing attention to its characteristics as a Krama text are of great value, but he too has not discussed its linguistic aspect. Without viewing it in its proper linguistic context, he has ascribed the work to the late fifteenth century and clubbed it with Śitikaṇṭha's *MNP*. A look at its linguistic features, however, shows that the work is quite old and could belong to a period not later than the eleventh century. The u-endings of the words in the Kashmiri verses and other structural aspects show a strong Prākr̥t and Apabhraṁśa influence, but several phonetic and morphological elements of early Kashmiri too are visible — a fact of considerable linguistic interest. Subsequently, these nascent features take a more pronounced and distinct form in later works like *MNP*, *Bāṇāsura Kathā* (*BK*) and *Sukha-duḥkha-Carita* (*SDC*). This, it may be pointed out, constitutes the total corpus of the early Kashmiri works available to us in the Śāradā script. A proper linguistic study of these works can help us piece together quite a reliable, connected and authentic account of the Kashmiri language in the mid-Indo-Aryan stage of its development.

If *CS* represents the earliest form of the literarization of Kashmiri as an emerging regional dialect coming out of the cosmic shadow of Sanskrit, *MNP* documents the next stage when it had crossed the Prākr̥t–Apabhraṁśa threshold to step into a new world of "vernacular expressiveness" as a distinct linguistic entity. *MNP*, it may be necessary to mention, is not written in Kashmiri alone, the Kashmiri verses being accompanied by a Sanskrit commentary also written by the same author. There is a controversy about the date of *MNP*. While Suniti Kumar Chatterji and P.N. Pushp date it to the thirteenth century, and rightly so, keeping in view its linguistic features, George Grierson and Navjivan Rastogi push it to late fifteenth century, confusing its author Śitikaṇṭha with another Śitikaṇṭha, the author of *Bālabodhinī Nyāsa*, a commentary on Jagaddhara Bhaṭṭa's grammatical work *Bālabodhinī*. It will be clear to anyone who cares to study it linguistically that the language of *MNP* is historically older than that of *SDC*, a work actually belonging to the late fifteenth century when Sultan Hassan Shah ruled over Kashmir. The fact becomes evident immediately as we compare the two.

MNP is a work that expounds the *Mahārtha* or *Mahānaya* doctrine of the Krama Śaivism, a system which believes in the "notion of cyclic reality" and perceives cosmic emanation in terms of a sequence of *sṛṣṭi* (creation), *sthiti* (sustenance), *saṁhāra* (withdrawal), etc. corresponding to the fivefold functionality of Parama Śiva. The Krama system is believed to have originated in Uttarapīṭha which is identified with Kashmir. Female ascetics like Keyuravatī, Madanikā and Kalyāṇikā are said to have played a significant role in spreading it far and wide mainly through oral tradition. The core philosophical idea it propounds is that of *bhedābheda* (unity in diversity) underlining the basic identity of the individual self with the universal self in its dynamic aspect as Śakti. Combining metaphysics with mysticism in his work, Śītikaṇṭha regards duality or immanence as the unfolding of one transcendental reality. He perceives the ultimate reality as feminine and regards intuitive realization of the self's unity with it as the highest goal of life. This realization, according to the Krama system, is to experience pure and undifferentiated consciousness (*saṁvid*) through spiritual progression. Identical with the Goddess of Consciousness, *mahārtha* (Absolute Meaning) unfolds itself gradually through the four forms of speech: *parā* (transcendental), *paśyantī* (visioning), *madhyamā* (middling) and *vaikharī* (displayed) word. The pure universal consciousness manifests itself in *cakra*s (cycles of energy) symbolizing states of "individualized consciousness".

Śītikaṇṭha, it may be pointed out, belongs to the later phase of Krama Śaivism when esotericism and ritualism were its more predominant features than speculative thought or meditative practices. In *MNP*, he expounds on such esoteric and secret elements of the system as *mudrā, mantra, pūjā* and *pīṭha,* and the preceptorial lineage treating them as its defining features. He also acquaints us with the key Krama concepts of *pañcavāha* (five flows), *pañcaugha* (five traditions) and the theory of *cakra*s.

The conception of *kāla* (time), taken as sequence of actions connecting the "prior" and the "subsequent", also holds an important place in the Krama doctrine which has been defined not in terms of "succession of time", but "succession as time", to quote Rastogi. Transcending time and realizing reality as *akrama* (trans-sequential unity) of phenomenal existence is regarded as the ultimate experience in the Krama system. Śītikaṇṭha begins his work with singing the praise of the supreme, all-pervading, tremendously powerful, lean, Goddess Maṅgalādevī who "devours" the Bhairava of time:

devat akka kiśī paru rāji
jaga ghasmaru bhairu bhakṣet ।
nanta shatta gāsaka nerāji
śamavānyī āśaya takṣet ॥

He then describes the sequence of cosmic manifestation, explaining the process as the first pulsation of inner blissful impulse that came from the harmonious union of Parama Śiva, the Supreme Being and Parā Śakti, his supreme creative power with the world coming into existence:

parama śivas parasyau tas śaccī
pathama sapandā yo nigghātu ।
yugmā uditu sadāśiva ruccī
so viśvabīja nādas ugghātu ॥

Inquiring into the precise meaning of the term *mahārtha,* the poet begins with devoting himself exclusively to its exposition in several of a total of 14 *udaya*s (cantos), and then proceeds to explain the other concepts of Krama thought in the remaining ones.

But beyond deciphering and decoding the esoteric symbolism of what Śītikaṇṭha says about the gradual revelation of the Great Meaning, of great significance is his claim that he wrote this *nuti* (hymn of praise) of the Goddess of Consciousness in "the regional language understood by all" — *athocitarucitam nutim sarvagocaryā deśabhāṣā.* Raising Kashmiri to the status of literary language for the first time, this statement ushers a new era of vernacular transformation in Kashmir. Later in the fifteenth century Bhaṭṭāvatāra also uses the word *deśya* to describe the language of his work *BK.* But *MNP* is not exactly a literary work although it is written in verse in a four-line metre with the first and third and the second and fourth lines rhyming. Of the extant early Kashmiri works written in the Śāradā script, *MNP* is the only one which has been brought out in print. It was published by the J&K Research Department in 1918 under the Kashmir Sanskrit Texts Series.

George Grierson published a very valuable paper on the language of *MNP* in the *Indian Antiquary* in which he admitted that its verses "clearly show the lines of connection between the Indo-Aryan side of Kashmiri and Sanskrit", and that "they throw light on the various forms in Modern Kashmiri that, but for the *MNP* would be inexplicable". At the same time he attributed the predominance of Indo-Aryan vocabulary in it to its author being a *paṇḍit,* a scholar of Sanskrit. The fact is that the work clearly points to the lines along which Kashmiri language developed from the regional Prākr̥t-Apabhraṁśa.

The fourteenth century gave Kashmiri language its most celebrated icon, the great Śaivite saint-poetess whose verses, called *vāk*s have become an integral part of Kashmiri culture. Even as they continue to dazzle us with their incandescence more than 600 years after they were uttered, as they have come to us through oral tradition, they cannot be a part of this discourse. The same can be said of the verses of Sheikh Nur-ud-Din, the saint-poet who was the founder of the Muslim Rishi Order of Kashmir.

It is rather a strange coincidence that in the fifteenth century when Kashmir was passing through a very crucial period of its political history, Kashmiri literary culture was showing evidence of an unprecedented creative upsurge. Breaking its silence of centuries, the Kashmiri language was experimenting with new forms and genres of expressiveness. Śrīvara, the historian of the times tells us about a number of writers who produced literary works in the language as never before. While Yodhā Bhaṭṭa wrote *Zaina Prakāśa,* Nottha Som composed *Zaina Carit* and Bhaṭṭāvatāra authored *Zaina Vilāsa* — all panegyrics of the king, but literary endeavours none the less. All these are now lost, but fortunately Bhaṭṭāvatāra had written another work also, namely Bāṇāsurakathā (*BK*), which Śrīvara forgot to mention. And it is this work that has survived as a testimony to his poetic genius.

BK is a work of great poetic excellence — a masterpiece of early Kashmiri literature based on the Uṣā–Anirudddha love episode of *Harivaṁśa Purāṇa.* Mohib-ul-Hassan dubs it as "the first secular poem of the Kashmiri language". Its author, Avatāra Bhaṭṭa, or Bhaṭṭāvatara as he prefers to call himself, describes it as a *kāvya prabandha* (narrative poem). Avatāra Bhaṭṭa also informs us in the colophon of the work that he belonged to the Śṛgālapurī (modern Shālpur) village of the

Lār sub-division of the Kashmir Valley. More importantly, he gives us the exact date when it was composed by him — the twenty-sixth year of King Zain-ul-Abidin's reign, which comes to CE 1446. This gives *BK* the distinction of being the first Kashmiri work that is precisely dated. The poet tells us very little about his life, but we come to know from Śrīvara, the chronicler of the times, that he was held in great respect at the king's court as a great scholar of not only Sanskrit but also Persian language and literature. (Śrīvara describes him as *Śāhanāma-deśa-granthābdhi-pāragaḥ* — or "he who has gauged the oceanic vastness of the *Śāhanāmā*".) Śrīvara, however, as pointed out earlier, is silent about *BK* even as he refers to the encouragement that literary creativity in the local vernacular received during Sultan Zain-ul-Abidin's time. Apart from being work of superb poetic beauty, *BK* is immensely valuable for the light it throws, along with *SDC*, on the state of the Kashmiri language in the fifteenth century.

Written in the Śāradā script, *BK* is available only as a single copy manuscript, which has remained unpublished to this day. It was discovered in Bikaner by the famous nineteenth-century Indologist Georg Bühler when he set out on his "Search for Sanskrit Manuscripts in Kashmir, Rajputana and Central India" about which he published his famous report in *Journal of the Royal Asiatic Society*, Bombay in 1877. Bühler gave its notice under the wrong name of *Bāṇāsuravadha* and George Grierson, Suniti Kumar Chatterji and several other scholars followed him uncritically. What is even more surprising, he showed it to some Sanskrit *paṇḍit*s of Kashmir, but they expressed their inability to decipher its contents. The manuscript was acquired by the Deccan College, Pune, along with other manuscripts Bühler had discovered, and later these were transferred to the Bhandarkar Research Institute, where they are still preserved. It indeed speaks a lot about the state of scholarship in Kashmir that except some superficial and stray references here and there nobody studied this rare work all these years till 1970 when I undertook linguistic research on it for my doctoral thesis. The manuscript, I understand has now been digitized by the IGNCA.

BK has the distinction of being the first narrative poem — *kāvya pabandha* as the poet himself calls it — in Kashmiri. As required by convention, such a *kāvya* should have the obtaining of desired damsel by the hero as its theme and should display ingenuity in evoking the erotic or the heroic sentiments — and that is precisely what *BK* does in a very effective manner. The theme revolves around the twin axels of love and war, with the poet admitting to having drawn on *Harivaṁśa Purāṇa* for it — *harivaṁśas andhar vanithuy*. He, however, does not adhere to the *Harivaṁśa* storyline blindly, but demonstrates his innovative genius by introducing several changes and additions. Focusing more on character delineation and emphasizing on particular aspects which appeal to him, he changes the Purāṇic legend into a beautiful poetry with its lilting cadences and soft music holding a great appeal for the reader.

The story is simple and has a few high points. Having vanquished all his enemies, Bāṇāsura, the demon king, prays for a more fulfilling combat with a powerful rival really matching him in prowess and Śiva grants him his prayer. Meanwhile, his beautiful daughter Uṣā sees Kr̥ṣṇa's grandson Aniruddha in a dream and is at once smitten with love. She asks her close friend and confidante Citralekhā to bring him from Dwārakā by her magic for a tryst to her parlour. But as they are making love, Bāṇa's palace guards detect his presence and a battle ensues. Despite fighting valiantly, Aniruddha gets snared in Bāṇāsura's magical serpent-noose, but Kr̥ṣṇa coming to know about it rushes there to save him. The demon king is defeated in a fierce battle in which Śiva also intervenes and Aniruddha returns with Uṣā to a rousing welcome in Dwārakā.

Avatāra Bhaṭṭa displays great imagination and innovative skills in describing various situations of the story, and in delineation of character, confirming his claim of having presented a "charming narrative" (*ramaṇī ākhya*) to the readers. Replete with depictions of delicate moods of love and exciting scenes of war, *BK* is indeed a great work of poetic art. The poet seems to revel particularly in describing the physiology and psychology of erotic love, displaying at places a sense of beauty reminiscent of poets like Jayadeva and Vidyāpati. He is at his best in passages depicting amorous scenes and physical charms of the female body, as is illustrated by his descriptions of Uṣā as a ravishing beauty:

sā uṣā amar nipendas dullabha
varakāmini vadanā zan śaśi pabha ।
lata zan kṣāvun pike
puṣkara gay adā niret kṣani ake ॥

The enchanting Uṣā was difficult even for the king of gods to obtain.
With her face beautiful as the radiant moon.
He (Aniruddha) enjoyed her charms as the cuckoo bird enjoys a flower-laden creeper.
And then he went away in a moment.

No less impressive is this verse describing Aniruddha's valiant behaviour and his sense of honour when in the midst his amorous tryst with Uṣā in her parlour he is discovered by her bodyguards. In response to Uṣā's anxiety about his safety, he is shown as saying:

dhik-dhik myānes yāday jammas
vanati atsā majja kacān ।

yuddha karā namet svakammas
uṣe athachŏn iha thān ||

Shame be on my Yādava birth,
if I hide behind your beautiful tresses, O lady!
I would rather prefer to fight at this very place
though I am without any weapon in my hands.

Avatāra Bhaṭṭa portrays human emotions and states of mind like a sensitive and fully conscious artist. In *Bāṇāsura Kathā* we find a whole spectrum of moods associated with both love-in-union and love-in-separation expressed with great sensitivity. The poet's genius flashes forth in all its brilliance not only when he describes the supersensuous physical appeal of Uṣā's beauty or the gallantry of the hero Aniruddha, but also when he depicts Bāṇāsura's valorous belligerency and the wisdom and sagacity of his minister Kumbhāṇḍa or Kṛṣṇa's role in upholding the cosmic order as the divine hero.

Avatāra Bhaṭṭa displays a rare sense of verbal music with exquisite acoustic values of words finding expression all through *BK*. Numerous examples of the poet's sense of music can be quoted from the work. This music is the result of the inner accord between vowels and consonants and the effect generated by the harmonious relationship between their various combinations that the poet has created and it accentuates the prevailing mood at different places. In fact, a delightful symphony of melodies pervades almost the whole work, even as the poet's ingenuity shows itself in his employment of the short lyric to depict human sentiments and moods in different situations. There are several enthralling songs embedded in the narrative structure of the work which punctuate descriptive passages to take us into the inner emotive world of the characters. These songs, expressive of the tender feelings of love and longing, anxiety and elation, joy and sorrow, are the earliest examples of the Kashmiri short lyric form (*vatsun*) which became very popular in the succeeding years. Songs like *kar iyi so piya me nikaṭo* (when will my Love come near me) and *piyā ma gatsh mārnay* (O Love, do not go, they are out to kill you), are beautiful examples of this genre.

After *BK* another extant Kashmiri work of the fifteenth century is *Sukha-duḥkha-mohamāyā-jāla-caritam* (*SDC*), which was written by a poet named Ganak Prashast. No information about this poet is available except a reference to the fact that he wrote the work during the reign of Sultan Hassan Shah (CE 1475-85), the grandson of Sultan Zain-ul-Abidin, to whom he has addressed a poetic tribute, praising him for taking care of the country at a young age — *narpat hassan shah jayi yo nava vaya janapada rakṣiśayi.* Ganak does not appear to be his real name as he calls himself by several other names also like Saṅkyeśa, Kalaneśa and Gaṇapati. It seems that he worked as an accountant or astrologer at the court of Hassan Shah and "Prashast" was his pseudonym. Single manuscript copy of *SDC* in the Śāradā script was also discovered by Bühler from Bikaner. It is now preserved at the Manuscript Library of the Bhandarkar Research Institute, Pune. *SDC* cannot be strictly classified as belonging to the literary or poetic genre though it is composed in verse. It is actually a sort of a manual of morally correct living and is written in the form of advice doled out by the poet to a supposed friend to conduct his affairs with caution lest he is deluded by vain pleasures of the world and becomes a profligate. He is repeatedly reminded that life is transitory and nothing in the world is permanent. The "advice" covers four spheres: *jyotiṣa* (astrology), *gāruḍa* (effects and treatment of poison) and *vaidaka* (medicine), *madana śāstra* (sexology) and *yoga,* and the work is accordingly divided into four sections:

kṣe śāstra ghanē kate ko mo bujji
vaidak, gāruḍa, jyotiṣa, buddha ।
sāra sāra gāhenas pajji
hans yākhet jalo majjā duddha ॥

The Śāstras are very profound. Who can explain them?
There is the science of medicine, of toxicants and their treatment, of astrology and spiritual realization
One should try to grasp their essence
As the swan separates milk from water.

The "friend" is advised to keep the nature of the world and the vanities of life in view and avoid pitfalls.

SDC is thus a medley, a potpourri of bits of information about subjects which were probably of interest to people of his time. The work lacks depth, but perhaps its author wanted to demonstrate his knowledge about things. He himself seems to admit as much when he says:

naravara vipadi viyoga samaggi
ast no it samsāras paśca
yas atha jñāna kathi man laggi
so jananīsuta jiyin niśca

The world is wholly unreliable, full of misfortunes and partings
He whose mind is interested in this philosophical discussion, that mother's son lives in the real sense.

At several places the author of *SDC* tries to strike a philosophical pose, referring to "Vaiṣṇava–Sāṁkhya–Pāśupata" systems of philosophy and saying that only "by watering the creeper of *yoga* with the water of devotion can worldly suffering be mitigated". This may not sound exactly like poetry, but *SDC* is certainly structured as a *kāvya.* It does display certain purple patches of imagination and a sense of verbal music. Ganak Prashast often indulges in verbal artistry, embellishing his lines with alliteration, pun and other figures of speech.

Apart from its poetic flourishes, *SDC* can also be regarded as a useful source of information on Kashmiri life in medieval Kashmir covering the beliefs, interests and even superstitions of the people. It was written in late fifteenth century soon after Hassan Shah's enthronement, with the author giving its date as the year 1472 (perhaps of the Saptarṣi era), which is not much later than Avatāra Bhaṭṭa's *BK* with which its language shares many a common feature. However, oriented more towards depiction of the daily life of the ordinary people as it is, *SDC* furnishes us with a vast vocabulary prevalent in those times related to articles of daily use, edibles, common medicines and herbs, parts of body, etc. a good part of which is used even today with slight modifications. Barring poetic expressions, it shows word-forms that have nearly crystallized to their present forms in many cases. Of course, there are slight changes in spelling, even as many words have become totally obsolete.

Like *BK*, there are several *vatsun*-type songs also in *SDC*, which are interspersed throughout the narrative. These songs are not subjective or expressive of deep personal feelings or subtle emotions, but they do have a certain lyrical quality about them and throw light on the development of this genre in Kashmiri literature. One can also detect some poetic flashes in some of them here and there. As, for instance, in lines like these:

him zan tāpē viglos pāpē, kukaram citto

When I remember my bad deeds, my heart melts as snow melts in the heat of the sun.

Most rewarding is the study of *BK* from the point of view of the diachronic history of the Kashmiri language. It would be pertinent to say, even at the risk of repetition, that between them the two works, *BK* and *SDC*, can tell us a lot about the mid-Indic development of Kashmiri language and the lines along which it emerged as a modern Indian language. They can help us in tracing earlier forms of many Kashmiri words. For instance, we can come to know that the Kashmiri auxiliary verb forms were originally *kṣ*-based — *kṣi, kṣo, kṣem, kṣiyiy,* etc. suggesting that these could have developed from the Skt. root *kṣi* (meaning "to be"). As a latter development, Skt. *kṣ* changes to *ch* in Kashmiri.

The language of *BK* is predominantly suffused with Indo-Aryan elements, there being hardly one or two Persian-derived words in it. Although Persian had been declared as court language by Zain-ul-Abidin, it had not been able to make much impact at the literary or spoken language level yet. This is the case with *SDC* also, while in *CS* and *MNP* the terminology of Kashmir Śaivism is profusely employed due to the nature of the subject. Apart from the dominance of Sanskrit and Sanskrit-derived words, we have a number of words in *BK* (and also in *SDC*) whose etymology is not clear, while there is another category of words which have become totally obsolete today, although their etymology may not pose much of a problem. For example, we have words like *yākhet* (= like this, as, just as, as if — also found in *MNP*), *kākhet/kangat* (= in what manner), *tākhet* (= like this, in this manner), *javē* (= quickly, speedily), *bhut* (= a lot, lot of, in large quantity, many), etc. It will be interesting to note that some words from the rural dialect of Kashmiri, like *koḍ* (where, wither), *prāḍ* (wait — imperative), *khāḍet* (having made to mount), etc. have been used freely in *BK*. Another linguistic feature of interest is the use of several words denoting the same meaning. For instance, we have *vadi, nigadi, dappi, vāci, vanno, girl,* etc. all of which mean "he/she says". It may also be noted that in all these cases Kashmiri terminations have been attached to Sanskrit verbal bases.

In the 400 years or so from the time of *CS* to that of *SDC,* we see Kashmiri language emerging out of its Prākr̥t-Apabhraṁśa shell and acquiring a definite form and face and a personality that distinguishes it as a modern Indian language. Old word forms undergo changes to be replaced by new forms in this period, while many forms remain almost unchanged to be used as such even today. All the four works unfold the story of this entire fascinating evolutionary journey which passed through different stages. Features of early Kashmiri that appeared in *CS* in a nascent form become more distinctive and developed in *MNP* which displays a strong tendency of Prākr̥tization with its u- ending words. *BK,* on the other hand, is a record of that stage of the mid-Indic development of Kashmiri when the language had just come out of the Prākr̥t-Apabhraṁśa stage to take shape as a modern Indian language. The language of *SDC* is relatively closer to modern Kashmiri while sharing most of the characteristics of *BK.* Being a record of the Kashmiri language as it was spoken, or rather written, in the first and second halves respectively of the fifteenth century, these two works are greatly helpful in tracing the original forms of a large number of modern Kashmiri words. For instance, the present tense forms of the Kashmiri auxiliary verb *chu* occur in them as *kṣo, kṣoḥ, kṣi, kṣem, kṣes, kṣeyiyi,* etc. (modern Kashmiri *chu, chi, chim, chĕs, chi*), suggesting that these may have originated from the Sanskrit root *kṣi,* meaning "to be", "to stay", "to reside", etc. The present "*ch*"-based forms of these words seems to be the result of Skt. *kṣ* changing to *ch* in Kashmiri. Similarly we find the Kashmiri word like *hĕki, hyath, hyŏtun* in the form *śiki, śit, śiton* in *BK* and *SDC,* retaining the original *ś*. Another word belonging to this category is *śŏṭ*, its modern Kashmiri form being *hŏṭ* (throat). This is what we see prevailing in the Pogulī dialect of Kashmiri, spoken in the Pogal-Paristan region in the proximity of Bānahāl, which even today preserves the original sibilant. This is a very significant feature that requires to be studied as in modern Kashmiri Skt. *ś* mostly changes to *h*. Among the many intermediate forms of modern Kashmiri words that are found in these works, examples can be given of *ḍiṭṭho* (< Skt. *dr̥ṣṭvā*, Mod. Ksh. *ḍyūṭh, having* seen) and *ditto* (< Skt. *dattaḥ*, Mod. Ksh. *dyut*).

Most of the phonological changes that took place in the period under consideration did so much in the same manner as in other middle Indo-Aryan languages. But in many cases Kashmiri displayed its own peculiarities, being both a synthetic language like Sanskrit or rather Old Indic and analytical like the modern Indo-Aryan languages. All these works, for instance, share the tendency of elision of initial and terminal vowels, including instances of epenthesis and extensive vowel change. Thus we have *a > ā, i > a, a > u* or *ū, a > ē, a > o, ā > a, ā > i, ā > ū, i > a, i, ē, ī > ū, ī > ū, ī > ē, u > a, u > o* and so on. There is also an elision of independent consonants *c, t, d, p* and sometimes *k* also with an insertion of the glide *y* or *v*, and *r̥* changing to *a, i* and *u* (though at places it remains intact). Elision of *r* and the doubling the following consonant is also common besides conjunction and simplification of conjunct consonants with — *th > -d, - pt > t, -nm > -m/-mm, -ty > c, -dy dhy > jj* and so on. All the three — *MNP, BK* and *SDC* follow Prākr̥t-Apabhraṁśa in elision of one member of a conjunct consonant and the doubling of the remaining one. Conjunct or double consonants in modern Kashmiri have all gone as there is no way they could be written in the Persian script which followed Śāradā. Śāradā orthography has also played a part in this process as it has no diacritic marks to render the sounds of peculiarly Kashmiri vowels. Besides, *a, e, i, o* and *u* are often interchanged in pronunciation and due to scribal error, creating a lot of confusion. *R* and *r̥* are also back in Kashmiri today due to a process of re-Sanskritization. We are not in a position of discussing these changes in greater detail because that will take a long time. We would however like it to be noted that there are several words occurring in *MPN, BK* and *SDC* that are found in Hindi and other North Indian languages but are not prevalent in modern Kashmiri. For example, we have *jalo* (Hindi *jalā*), *paḍo* (Hindi *paḍā*), *caḍos* (Hindi *caḍhā*) and *gauḍe* (Hindi *ghoḍe*). All these four works of early Kashmiri are in fact packed with linguistic information which is waiting to be explored but there is no one to venture forth. It speaks volumes about the state of scholarship in Kashmir that Bühler discovered some of these texts nearly more than 150 years back but there is no scholar who cares to study them. I had taken some initiative in this direction some years back and am presently also working on a book on the beginnings of Kashmiri language and literature. I am not sure, however, whether lack of research facilities and funds will allow me to go far in completing the task. All except one of these works, viz. *MNP,* are in the unpublished and unedited form.

These early Kashmiri texts also shed very significant light on Kashmiri metrics. While in *CS* and *MNP* the quatrains used are very akin to the Sanskrit *śloka* and Prākr̥t *gāthā,* we are greatly surprised to find a whole variety of Sanskrit syllabic metres being used with great effect in *BK* and *SDC.* Demonstrating great virtuosity, the author of *BK* employs Sanskrit metres like *Mālinī, Mandākrāntā, Sr̥gdharā, Narkaṭakā, Vasantatilakam, Tanumadhyā, Toṭaka, Praharṣiṇī, Mattamayūra, Śārdūlavikrīḍitam, Catuṣkhaṇḍikā, Vaitālī, Hariṇī, Puṣpitāgrā,*

Pañcapājā and so on to structure his narrative. Some of them like *Thaddo, Phuro, Kaḍokḍyā* and *Dukkaṭikā* appear to be original Kashmiri metres as their etymology seems to suggest. *Thaddo* was perhaps a metre which was meant to be recited aloud and used at places where something needed to be emphasized, while *Phuro* was used where something needed to be said in passing. We find Sanskrit metres used again in *SDC* — which adds one more metre, *Dviphuro*, to the list — and that is the last we see of them. Although *BK* and *SDC* gave to Kashmiri such a wealth of verbal-metrical beauty, all of it has unfortunately been abandoned. Yet, this gives a lie to the fallacy that Grierson tried to spread about Kashmiri metrics by arguing that it by nature is oriented towards the Persian metrical system.

Concluding, I would like to emphasize that I consider these early Kashmiri texts as an open and important invitation to young researchers to come forward and explore an uncharted but very rich and intellectually rewarding field of historical linguistics. But is there anyone interested — that is the moot question?

10

Sanskrit on the Silk Route

Lokesh Chandra

SANSKRIT was the mind of the Silk Route, at one with the sky-void and the spring mist, the live hues of sensibility dyed in eternity, a bridge of dreams floating across cloudless skies of the sands, a symbol system that made heart pure, the spring blossoms of the devout. It was the realization of Truth, and the very being of Values. Sanskrit was to enter the profound, the inner depths. Today torn Sanskrit fragments from the Silk Route reflect the savagery of fundamentalism, the furious wrath of apostasy. They remind me of ten million Buddhist Sūtras being ruthlessly committed to fire in Buryatia, Mongolia, Kalmykia and Tuva. As Lama Sandaa related to me with tears flowing across his withered face of eighty years:

> I was forced to destroy what I revered, admired and had faith in. There's no torture more terrible than that.

Likewise, these Sanskrit fragments are tears of time. Scholars sit in their silence, forgetting the hours that follow each other, to identify tiny and large fragments as if perfecting a diamond. They are *ratnakūṭa* (heaps of jewels) in the words of Prof. Karashima. We are pilgrims to amazing centuries that have flourished and vanished.

The Global Vision of Aśoka and Central Asia

Sanskrit in Central Asia was due to the global vision of Aśoka (r. *c.* 273–232 BCE). Emperor Aśoka gave up war at Kaliṅga or *bherīghoṣa,* which was substituted by *dharmaghoṣa,* the drums of war were silenced into drums of peace. His Rock Edict XIII mentions the Hellenic kingdoms of Syria, Egypt, Cyrene, Macedonia and Epirus to which he sent missionaries to preach Dhamma. These missions embrace the three continents of Asia, Africa and Europe. In 251 BCE he sent his son and Saṅghamitrā to Sri Lanka. He sent gifts to King Devanāṁpiya Tissa including a *nandyāvarta* which has been interpreted as a gold vessel or a gold flower. It must have been a six-storeyed palace (as described in the architectural text *Mānasāra* 24.24), in keeping with the imperial style of Aśoka. The Kandahar Inscription in Greek and Aramaic (dated to 258 BCE) says that as a result of Aśoka's activity "everything prospers over the whole earth". All the four Chinese and Tibetan accounts of the foundation of Khotan associate it with the son and ministers of Emperor Aśoka. Aśoka thus initiated the presence of Sanskrit and Indian influence on what was to become the Silk Route. A collection of coins bearing Prākṛt legends on the reverse and Chinese legends on the obverse from Yotkan the ancient capital of Khotan belong to the first centuries CE. Khotan was a major centre of Mahāyāna and has yielded the earliest Gandhari Dharmapada. The Nidāna of the Eye-destruction of Dharmavardhana? (Chin. A-yu-wang-hsi-huai-mu-yin-yuan-ching) mentions Kucha as "one of the parts of his great empire which Aśoka proposed to give over to his son Kuṇāla" (Watters 1904: 1.59). The grand international far-sightedness of Aśoka enriched the Silk Route states with script, scriptures and Sanskrit. The idealized figure of Aśoka in Buddhist literature made a great impression in China. The search for the "relics of Aśoka" is a regular phenomenon, from the fourth century

CE. By his devotion and compassion for all mankind *(hitasukha* of his inscriptions) he was able to extend his sway over the whole continent of Jambudvīpa. The Chinese concluded that China being a part of Jambudvīpa had belonged to the empire of Aśoka and if investigated some traces would be found, even some holy relics themselves (Zürcher 1972: 1.277-80). So the ancient sites of Aśoka-temples and Aśoka-*stūpas* were being identified. On 25 March 394, a statue appeared near the city wall of Chiang-ling with a Sanskrit inscription. Dhyāna master Saṅghānanda from Kashmir told the monks that it had been made by Aśoka (ibid.: 279). Aśoka became a legend and the king of the Sogdians in the Tonyukuk epitaph near the capital of Mongolia is named Ašoqa. The Turks have the name Ašuq. The Russian chronicles mention the Prince of the Voguls in northern Siberia under the name Asyka. The epic folk songs of the Voguls sing of Ōšc even today. The beloved of the gods is immortal among the farthest people *(Journal de la Société Finno-Ougrienne* 1958: 60.59f.)

Central Asian Peoples in Sanskrit Literature

From *Ṛgveda* to the *Śatapatha°*, *Aitareya°* and *Pañcaviṁśa Brāhmaṇa,* to the Kāṇva recension of *Bṛhadāraṇyaka Upaniṣad,* to Pāṇini, to *Mahābhārata* and Purāṇas, to *Bṛhat-Saṁhitā, Kathā-Sarit-Sāgara,* lexicons and *Rājataraṅgiṇī* there are continuing references to the peoples of Central Asia.

TURK

Tura, Turan, Turakvāḥ, Turk. The Turks are reflected in Firdawsi as Turan (-an being a toponymic suffix as in Bamiyan). Tūra is the name of a people in *Yasht* 17.55 who are *āsu-aspa* (having swift horses).

Ṛgveda X.61.1 speaks of a prince of the Pakthas named Tūrvāyaṇa. Tura Kāvaṣeya is mentiond in a list of teachers in

Śatapatha Brāhmaṇa 10.6.5.9. He is the family priest of Janamejaya Parīkṣit in *Aitareya Brāhmaṇa* 4.27, 7.34, 8.21. He is a sage in the Kāṇva *Bṛhadāraṇyaka Upaniṣad* 6.5.4. Tura is a sage of the gods (*deva-muni*) in *Pañcaviṁśa Brāhmaṇa* 25.14.5. Turva and Turvaśa people are mentioned in *Ṛgveda* along with the Yadu.

The Sanskrit term *Turuṣka* for the Turks is found in the lexicons *Medinī, Trikāṇḍaśeṣa, Abhidhāna-Cintāmaṇi* of Hemacandra, *Rājataraṅgiṇī* and *Kathā-Sarit-Sāgara*. The variant forms are Turakāḥ, Turakvāḥ (compare Greek Tourkoi). Turakvāḥ is *tura* (fast) + *akva* (horse, compare Tocharian *yakwe,* Lat. *equus* 'horse'), keeping in view their epithet *asu-aspa* in Avesta. The form with *-ṣk-* has a parallel in the Kuṣāṇa names Kaniṣka, Huviṣka, Huṣka (Mayrhofer 1956: 1.515). The *Mañjuśrī-Mūla-Kalpa* speaks of *turuṣka taila* for petroleum. The Turks were one of the North Asian or Altaic nomads who were constantly attacking the settled agricultural peoples. They were present in Central Asia and the frontiers of India from very ancient times.

SOGDIANS

Śūlikāḥ in the plural is the name of a people in *Bṛhat-Saṁhitā* and *Mārkaṇḍeya Purāṇa* 57.41. They are Sogdians, known in Chinese as Su-lê or Sha-lei (in the Chinese text of *Candragarbha-Sūtra*). *Mahābhārata*, Purāṇas, *Bṛhat-Saṁhitā*, besides Buddhist Sūtras, also contain extensive and early references to other Central Asian peoples.

The main cities of Sogdiana were Varaksha, Samarkand, Bukhara and Panjikant. The Sogdian cities were centres of cultural excellence and artistic skills. The Sogdians translated several Buddhist Sūtras. Their ethnonym K'ang in Chinese is the initial syllable of Kām-boja. Five Sogdian translators are

K'ang Chu (CE 187), K'ang Meng-hsiang (CE 194-99), K'ang Sang-k'ai (CE 252), K'ang Sêng-hui (CE 251), K'ang Tao-ho (CE 396) and Saṅghavarman (CE 656). *Ṣaṭ-Pāramitā-Sūtra* of K'ang Sêng-hui has a résumé of the *Rāmāyaṇa*. Their endeavours in translating the Sūtras into Chinese show their deep knowledge of Sanskrit and their devotion to Buddhism. *Mātaṅgī-Sūtra* was composed in Samarkand and is extant in its Chinese translation done in the third century. Amoghavajra was born in CE 705 as the son of a brāhmaṇa of Sogdiana. He travelled to Java and thence to China with Vajrabodhi. He is one of the Eight Patriarchs of Mantrayāna in Japan. He translated several Sūtras into Chinese, of which 108 are extant in the Chinese *Tripiṭaka*.

TASHKAND

Pāṇini 3.2.20 says that *kantha* is suffixed to names of cities. It is neuter in general, but is feminine in the Uśīnara region. The *Kāśikā* commentary thereon gives the following names: Sauśamikantha, Āhvarakantha, Vīraṇakanthā, Dākṣikanthā. *Kāśikā* on *sūtra* 4.2.142 adds Mahikīkanthīyam to them. *Kāśikā* has more names on Pāṇini 6.2.124, 125: Capyakanthă, Cihaṇakanthă, Maḍarakanthă, Maḍurakanthă. Dākṣikanthā is Tashkent and Āhvarakantha can be Yarkand. The works on Central Asia do not refer to this valuable evidence. Kanthaka was the white horse on which Gautama Buddha left his father's palace. It refers to a Ferghana horse from Kantha or Samarkand. It was not understood and the spelling was altered to Kaṇṭhaka. The Pāli texts show the variant Kanthaka, but in Sanskrit only *Mahāvyutpatti* has the spelling Kanthaka.

Kaṅka is the name of a people in *Mahābhārata*, Varāhamihira's *Bṛhat-Saṁhitā* 14.4 and *Bhāgavata Purāṇa* 2.4.18, 9.20.30. In Tocharian *kāṅk* means "stone". It can refer to Tashkand, which is from *tāš* (stone). In *Mahābhārata* they occur with Śakas and Tukhāras (*śakās tukhārāḥ kaṅkāś ca*). The ethnonym *aśmakāḥ* occurs in *Mahābhārata* and *Bhāgavata Purāṇa*. *Kalpanā-Maṇḍitikā* mentions that a painter from Puṣkalāvatī visited Aśmaka to decorate a monastery (Sylvain Lévi, JA 1908: 88). Foucher (1918: 2.644) identified this place with Tashkent. In *Bṛhat-Saṁhitā* 14.22 Aśmaka is a north-western country.

Sanskrit Was the Cultural Identity of the Central Asian Peoples

Sanskrit was the language of refinement and thought, of religion and philosophy, of poetry and prose of the different peoples of various ethnicities who spoke several tongues. While the media of conversation and administration were vernaculars, written in Indic scripts, Sanskrit was *the* idiom of higher domains of intellection. More than twenty *ācārya*s from Central Asia were busy translating Sanskrit originals into Chinese, from the mid-second century to the seventh century. Fa-hsien is the first pilgrim who wrote an account of his visit to India from CE 400 to 414. He makes an interesting observation that is Shan-shan, just on the border of China, the Indian script was used for all languages of the Silk Route and the Buddhist monks studied Sanskrit and Indian books. The Lop Nor desert separates the Tun-huang area from Shan-shan (Haiyan Au-von Hinüber 2010, no. 22: 224, 240).

Yüeh-chihs: Horses to Sūtras

The Yüeh-chihs gained prominence in trans-national contacts by selling horses to the Ch'in and Han dynasties of China which had embarked on a major programme of expansion, and created four military commanderies in Central Asia. They considered the Yüeh-chihs barbarians, but the Yüeh-chihs were wise to point out their higher culture of philosophic texts and linguistic sophistication of Sanskrit. They taught Sanskrit to a Chinese prince, the first Buddhist monks went to China from their court, and they were the first translators of Sanskrit texts into Chinese. The first Buddhist monastery in China was the White Horse Monastery, redolent of the horse trade of the Yüeh-chihs. Monks came on white horses of Ferghana which became the might of China. Sanskrit was the very being of the so-called "Silk Route" which should really be called the "Sūtra Route". The Yüeh-chihs later became the Kuṣāṇas. Sanskrit manuscripts in the Kuṣāṇa script in its grand lapidary style of imperial monumental inscriptions with a head-line (*śirorekhā*) over the letters, are wearing a crown so to say. The Chinese Emperor sent Chang Ch'ien to Bactria (Da-hsia) in 128 BCE to find out the Yüeh-chihs who by then were no longer horse-dealers. The Chinese envoy took the Mahātukhāra Rāga of Sanskrit, on which martial tunes were created for the Chinese armies treading long un-inhabited terrains. Sanskrit was the proud heredity of the Yüeh-chih. The seventh-century Chinese poet Li Po wrote:

> The horses of heaven come out of the dens of the Kuṣāṇas.

The divine horses and Sanskrit *sūtra*s were the *śastra* and *śāstra* of the Yüeh-chihs.

The Sanskritization of the dynastic name Ch'in as *cīna* (चीन) for China originated with the Yüeh-chihs. From them it came to India, thence to South-East Asia, and in recent times from Malaysia to European languages as China. The very name of China is thus a tribute to the Yüeh-chihs. Sanskrit was the glory of the Yüeh-chihs. One of their monks Shih-li-fang brought a number of Sanskrit manuscripts to China during the reign of Ch'in Shih-huang-ti (221–208 BCE) who built the Great Wall of China. Unwilling to accept the new doctrine he imprisoned the monks. These manuscripts were buried to save them from burning. Later on sixty scrolls were discovered by Liu Hsiang.

The king of the Yüeh-chih ordered the Crown Prince to teach Sanskrit to Ching Lu of the Imperial Academy of China who had gone to them on a mission.

Mātaṅga Kāśyapa and Dharmaratna came to China in CE 67 on imperial invitation from the court of the Yüeh-chih. They wrote the first Buddhist work in Chinese. Thus the very first steps of Chinese Buddhism are rooted in a kingdom of the Silk Route which had rich traditions of Sanskrit learning.

The second translator of Sanskrit texts into Chinese was the Yüeh-chih Laugākṣin who worked at Loyang from 167 to 186 and introduced Mahāyāna. He translated twenty-three works of which twelve are preserved in the Chinese *Tripiṭaka*. The texts translated by him are an indication of the Sanskrit literature studied in the monastic universities of the Silk Route. Some of the works translated by him are: *Aṣṭasāhasrikā-Prajñāpāramitā* (T 224, Nj 5), **Tathāgata-Viśeṣana-Sūtra* (T 280, Nj 102), *Akṣobhya-Vyūha* (T 313, Nj 28), *Kāśyapa-Parivarta* (T 350, Nj 57), *Sukhāvatī-Vyūha* (T 361, Nj 25), *Bhadrapāla-Sūtra* (T 417, Nj X, T 418, Nj 67), **Mañjuśrī-Paripṛcchā* (T 458, Nj 112), *Druma-Kinnararāja-Paripṛcchā* (T 624, Nj 161), *Ajātaśatru-Kaukṛtya-Vinodana* (T 626, Nj 179) and *Lokānuvartana-Sūtra* (T 807, Nj 386). These texts pertain to five different genres: Prajñāpāramitā, Avataṁsaka, Ratnakūṭa, Mahāsannipāta and Sūtras. The Central Asian monasteries were centres of advanced learning and held rich collections of Sanskrit works. He translated *Avataṁsaka "Sūtra on the Tuṣita Heaven"* (T'u-sha ching, T 280, K 90, Cleary 1983: 181).

The Laukākṣāḥ (plural) is the name of a school of the Chandogas in *Divyāvadāna* 632.23, 25. It is a *gotra* of the brāhmaṇas (*Divyāvadāna* 635.16). The Sanskrit *Laugākṣi-Gṛhyasūtra* for family rites is extant.

The greatest of Yüeh-chih masters was Dharmarakṣa who came to Loyang in 266 and ninety translations of Sanskrit Sūtras by him survive in the Chinese *Tripiṭaka.* He integrated Buddhism in the spiritual life of China. A Khotanese, a Yüeh-chih, two Kucheans, a Sogdian and Indians were his collaborators. He translated *Mātaṅgī-Sūtra* during the years 307-13. It had been written in Sanskrit in Samarkand. It had been translated (K 759) earlier by An Shih-kao (148-70), by Chu Lü-yen and Chih-ch'ien in CE 230 (K 766) and a fourth time by an unknown translator in CE 317-420 (K 762). Mātaṅgī is the presiding deity of music, the pure innate spirit of woman. There is a large modern temple to her in the suburbs of Delhi at Chhatarpur.

In 284 Dharmarakṣa got a manuscript of *Avaivartika-Cakra-Sūtra* from the Kuchean envoy, and in 286 he obtained *Pañcaviṁśati-Sāhasrikā* from the Khotanese monk Gītamitra.

Parthians

The first translator of Sanskrit texts An Shih-kao was a Parthian prince who ceded the throne to his uncle to enter the Saṅgha. He came to Loyang in 148 (variants 147, 149) and worked till his *nirvāṇa* in 170. He translated 176 Sanskrit works into Chinese. Out of them fifty-four exist in the *Taishō Tripiṭaka.* They represent Āgamas, Avadāna, Ratnakūṭa, Sūtras, Vinaya, Abhidharma and historic traditions. I shall enumerate his extant works to show the extensive Sanskrit holdings of the monastic libraries of the Silk Route.

T 13, Nj 548	*Dīrghāgama Law of Ten Rewards*
T 14, Nj 553	*Mahānidāna-Sūtra*
T 16, Nj 555	*Sṛgāla-Vāda-Sūtra*

T 31, Nj 559	Sūtra on the cause of sins
T 32, Nj 598	*Catuḥ-Satya-Sūtra*?
T 36, Nj 601	Sūtra on fundamental relationship
T 48, Nj 565	Sūtra on the true and false law
T 57, Nj 567	Sūtra explaining āśrava?
T 91, Nj 582	Sūtra addressed to a brāhmaṇa
T 92, Nj 583	Sūtra addressed to a gṛhapati
T 98, Nj 586	*Artha-Vistāra*
T 105, Nj 743	Sutra on the five elements not returning again
T 109, Nj 741	*Dharmacakra-Pravartana-Sūtra*
T 112, Nj 659	**Aṣṭāṅga-Samyaṅ-Mārga-Sūtra*
T 131, Nj 617	Sūtra on a brāhmaṇa who wished to avoid death
T 140, Nj 649	Sūtra on the conversion of Anāthapiṇḍada's seven sons
T 149, Nj 633	Sūtra on Ānanda's fellow-student
T 150a, b Nj 648	**Saptāyatana-Tridhyāna-Sūtra*
T 151, Nj 687	**Āgama-Samyak-Caryā-Sūtra*
T 167, Nj 220	*Mūka-jātaka*? (Avadāna)
T 348, Nj 54	*Maitreya-Paripṛcchā-Dharmāṣṭaka* (Ratnakūṭa)
T 356, Nj 251	*Ratnakūṭa-Sūtra*
T 492, Nj 635	Ānanda's question (Sūtras)
T 506, Nj 695	**Gandhāra-Deśa-Rāja-Sūtra*
T 525, Nj 694	Sūtra on a *śreṣṭhiputra*'s causing three places to be harassed

T 526, Nj 227	**Śreṣṭhiputra-Jeta-Sūtra*
T 551, Nj 643	*Mātaṅgī-Sūtra*
T 553, Nj 667	**Āmrapālī-Jīva-Nidāna*
T 554, Nj 668	*Āmrapālī-Jīva-Nidāna*
T 602, Nj 681	**Ānāpāna-Dhyāna-Sūtra*
T 603, Nj 780	**Skandha-Dhātv-Āyatana-Sūtra*
T 604, Nj 724	**Dhyāna-Caryā-Saptatriṁśad-Varga*
T 605, Nj 683	**Dhyāna-Caryā-Dharma-Sañjñāna-Sūtra*
T 607, Nj 1326	*Yogācāra-Bhūmi*
T 621, Nj 451	**Buddha-Mudrā-Samādhi-Sūtra*
T 622, Nj 282	Sūtra on the *samādhi* called vow
T 684, Nj 762	Sūtra on the kindness of parents which is difficult to be returned
T 701, Nj 387	Sūtra on inviting monks to a bath-house
T 724, Nj 706	Sūtra on the teaching of hells as the recompense of sinful actions
T 729, Nj 685	Sūtra on the origin of goodness and evil
T 730, Nj 684	Sūtra on several objects
T 731, Nj 688	**Aṣṭādaśa-Naraka-Sūtra*
T 732, Nj 682	Sūtra on the mind of reproaching
T 733, Nj 731	**Sthiramati-Sūtra*
T 734, Nj 675	Question addressed by *preta*s to Maudgalyāyana
T 779, Nj 512	Sūtra on the eight understandings of great men

T 791, Nj 686	**Abhiniṣkramaṇa-Nidāna*
T 792, Nj 689	**Dharma-Sañjñāna-Rajas-Sūtra*
T 1467, Nj 1112	Sūtra on the lightness and heaviness of the sin of transgressing precepts (*śīla*) (Vinaya)
T 1470, Nj 1126	**Mahābhikṣu-Trisahasra-Karma*
T 1492, Nj. 1106	*Triskandhaka*?
T 1552, Nj 1287	*Abhidharma-Sāra-Pratikīrṇaka-(Śāstra)*? (Abhidharma)
T 2027, Nj 1363	Sūtra on Kāśyapa's collection of the *Tripiṭaka* (historic tradition)

The lack of Sanskrit titles is due to the loss of immense Sanskrit literature during the political upheavals in Central Asia. Treatises on logic or philosophy do not seem to have been popular.

The Parthian An Hsüan translated two Sūtras in 181 and at the same time he was a commander of the cavalry. The Parthian shot is well known.

Khotan

Chinese undertook arduous trek to obtain Sanskrit originals from Khotan. Chu Shih-hsing went to Khotan in CE 260 to get *Pañcaviṁśati-Sāhasrikā Prajñāpāramitā* copied on birch bark. The Sanskrit manuscript was preserved in a Chinese monastery till the sixth century.

In CE 422 Buddhabhadra of Khotan translated the *Avataṁsaka-Sūtras*. Among them is *Gaṇḍavyūha* (*Gv.*) which has survived in original Sanskrit. Its main Tathāgata is Rocana or *abhyuccadeva* as a colossus. *Gv.* has inspired the Borobudur and the Daibutsu of Nara. In the seventh century Empress Wu Tsö-ts'ien (r. 684–705) wanted to legitimate her reign and she sent a special envoy to Khotan for the Sanskrit text as well as the Khotanese master Śikṣānanda to translate the text into Chinese. Khotan was an important source for Sanskrit manuscripts throughout the centuries. A Khotanese–Sanskrit conversation scroll from Tun-huang, the only one of its kind, indicates that the transmission of Sanskrit Sūtras to China from Khotan was an ongoing process. The conversation centres around the books the Khotanese monk was carrying on his pilgrimage to Wu-t'ai-shan:

> Have you equipment for the road or not?
>
> I do not like equipment for the road. A horse or two and I shall go.
>
> Have you books or not?
>
> I have some.
>
> What is the book?
> Sūtra, Abhidharma, Vinaya, Vajrayāna.
> Among these what book (i.e. title) is there?

Bhagavaddharma translated the hymn to Thousand-armed Avalokiteśvara at Khotan, in CE 650-61 (K 294), as per the colophon of the Stein scroll 3793 from Tun-huang. It is a garbled version of a *Nīlakaṇṭha-Stotra*, and has been popular in China ever since the T'ang dynasty. Bhagavaddharma's transliteration of the Sanskrit text is recited to this day every morning, noon and evening in the Buddhist monasteries of East Asia. The inauguration of the World Olympics at Shanghai began with 1,000 young girls dancing with the Sanskrit hymn set to powerful modern music.

A Kharoṣṭhi inscription has been found in China (Brough 1961: 24.517-30).

The Avataṁsaka collection has 39 Sūtras in the translation of Śikṣānanda (652–710). The very first text to be translated into Chinese in 167-87 by the Yüeh-chih Laukākṣin was *Tuṣita-Sūtra* (no. 7 in Śikṣānanda). A partial translation of *Gaṇḍavyūha* was done by *Āryasthira under the title *Ramyaka-Sūtra* (Chin. Lo-mo-chia ching, T 294, K 102) between 388–407. The place name Rammaka occurs in *Jātaka* 1.11, 13, 29 and Dhammapada Commentary 1.83. Ramyaka is the original Sanskrit name of Lamqan or Lamghan. *Ramya* means "beautiful" and it is no wonder that Babur expatiates on the beauty of its forested hillsides. The two colossi of Bamiyan represent the first and the 1000th of the Thousand Buddhas namely from Maitreya to Rocana. The 32nd book of *Avataṁsaka-Sūtra*, available only in Chinese and Tibetan translations, says:

> In Afghanistan there is a dwelling place called "Producing Compassion" where enlightening beings have lived since ancient times. Cleary's translation 2.219

The various partial and complete translations of the Avataṁsaka corpus into Chinese are shown below in chronological order (Table 10.1).

Sanskrit fragments from the Khotan region on the southern route in the British Library in the Hoernle and Stein collections consist of about 10,000 items. Seishi Karashima started the Brahmi Club at the Soka University which convenes every two weeks to read Sanskrit fragments from the Silk Route (Karashima and Wille 2006: 273). These items have been edited and compared with Chinese and Tibetan versions in vols. I, II.1, II.2 of *The British Library Sanskrit Fragments* (Tokyo, Soka University). The crystal-clear photographs of the fragments and the excellent and painstaking scholarship of the distinguished editors make these literary treasures of the Silk Route part of the literary heritage of India and other countries. The identified titles are listed in vol. II/1.31-33. The dedication

Table 10.1: Translation of the Avataṁsaka Corpus into Chinese

CE	*Book no. in Śikṣānanda*	*Cleary p.*	*Translator*
167-87	7	181	Yüeh-chih Laukākṣin
3rd century	15	185	Gītamitra
3rd century	37	202	Pai Fa Tsu
3rd century	37	202	Unknown
3rd century	38	203	Unknown
220-65	11	183	Chih-ch'ien
265-89	15	185	Dharmarakṣa
265-89	26	192	Dharmarakṣa
265-89	27	197	Dharmarakṣa
265-89	37	202	Dharmarakṣa
265-89	38	203	Dharmarakṣa
265–316	11	183	Nieh Tao Chen
385–431	39	205	Partial translation by Āryasthira
401-13	26	192	Kumārajīva and Buddhayaśas
422	Corpus in 60 fasc.	171	Buddhabhadra of Khotan
—	36	201	Buddhabhadra of Khotan (alternate translation)
602-64	31	199	Hsüan-tsang
699	Corpus in 80 fasc.	171	Śikṣānanda (MS from Khotan)
704-74	36	201	Amoghavajra
785–805	26	192	Śīladharma
798	39	205	Prājña (MS from South India)
—	36	201	Prājña (alternate translation)
985	31	199	Dharmabhadra

Source: Cleary, 1983.

of young Japanese scholars like Tatsushi Tamai "transcribing joyfully (!) and enthusiastically . . . everyday from eight in the morning until seven in the evening" evokes our admiration. Karashima's enthusiasm for the boxes with Sanskrit fragments reflects in his words: "For me, these boxes truly contained a Ratnakūṭa 'a heap of jewels'". The Japanese discovered a fragment of *Sukhāvatī-Vyūha* on the Silk Route, the very first outside Japan. On 23 December 1900 Sir Aurel Stein dug a manuscript of *Vajracchedikā* from the ruins of a small dwelling place in Dandan Uiliq. F.E. Pargiter dated it to the fifth century on palaeographic grounds (Hoernle 1916: 176f). It reminds me of a Japanese in Koyasan reading *Vajracchedikā* everyday. The Dandan Uiliq manuscript is a hallowed Sūtra of a devoted Buddhist.

Discovery of the Earliest Sanskrit Manuscripts

The so-called Silk Route was really the Path of Sūtras over the centuries. This is clear from the decline of this international highway when śramaṇas, Sūtras and sancta were annihilated by fundamentalist terrorism, the route lost its glorious heritage as well as its flourishing economy. Takayasu Higuchi says that the desert and oasis became an embodiment of Buddhist teaching. The desert symbolized hell and the oasis paradise.

The discovery of Sanskrit and its close nexus with European languages at the end of the nineteenth century was a major sensation of an emerging new world of Europe of fundamental discoveries that raised human thought and life to unprecedented heights. Sanskrit came to be taught in all the major universities of Europe and Russia. Oxford came to be a famous seat of Sanskrit learning due to F. Max Müller. At the same time Japan was emerging as a modern nation after the Meiji restoration in 1868. In 1879 the most influential and liberal Jodo Shinshu sect sent two monks, Bunyiu Nanjio and

Kasawara to learn Sanskrit at Oxford. Max Müller edited the palm-leaf manuscript preserved at the Hōryūji monastery that had come to Japan in 609. It was then the oldest known Sanskrit manuscript in the world. Lt. H. Bower had gone to Kucha in 1890 in quest of a murderer on a confidential mission from the Government of India. A Kucha man took him to a subterranean town to dig treasures but found only a book. Some merchants excavated a house to find treasure, "but found only the bodies of some cows, which on the first touch, crumbled into dust. On that occasion they found also the above-mentioned book" (Hoernle 1893: vi). The Bower manuscripts contain an Ayurvedic text *Nāvanītaka*, and *Pāśaka-Kevalī* and *Mahāmāyūrī*. The manuscripts must have belonged to a medical practitioner who looked into the astrology of his patients to administer the correct medicine. His books must have been placed in a cow so that he could carry on his medical profession in heaven. The cow was the Vaitaraṇī that transports a deceased person over the Vaitaraṇī River (Greek Styx) that flows between the earth and the abode of departed spirits presided over by Yama. Within two years, Dutreuil de Rhins and Grenard discovered in 1892 a birch-bark manuscript of *Dharmapada* in Gāndhārī Prākr̥t from Kohmārī Mazar, 21 km from Khotan, identified with ancient Gośr̥ṅga-vihāra. The remaining pieces of the manuscript were acquired by the Russian Consul-General in Kashgar N. Th. Petrovskii that reached S.F. Oldenburg in 1897. John Brough dates it to the first or second century CE. These discoveries led to the whole movement of the exploration of Central Asia.

Kambuja (Chin. K'ang), Sogdiana

K'ang Seng-hui from K'ang or Kambuja (Sogdiana) gives a brief version of *Rāmāyaṇa* in his *Ṣaṭ-Pāramitā-Sūtra* (CE 251). Kumārajīva studied the Vedas, along with their six ancillary sciences, at Kashgar.

Kucha

In 307-12 Śrīmitra the Crown Prince of Kucha gave up the kingdom and became a monk. He translated three Sūtras including *Mahāmāyūrī*.

In 402 Kumarajīva arrived in China from Kucha. He was the son of a Kuchean princess and Kumārāyaṇa of Kashmir and became "the greatest translator of all time" in the words of Wright (1959: 62). He transcreated a new literary style that continues to illumine the spiritual consciousness of East Asia. His unusual knowledge of Sanskrit, Tocharian and Chinese became the vocabulary of wonder. Kucha had a Hindu temple. Kumārajīva studied the Vedas and their six auxiliary disciplines in Kashgar. A chart of the recensions of *Yajurveda* mentions the recensions prevalent in Śvetadvīpa which is Kucha. In Chinese Po (white) is the ethnicon for the people of Kucha. Varāhamihira mentions Kucika (var. Kuśika) along with Cīna.

Indian music was in vogue in Kucha. Prince Sujīva of Kucha introduced the seven notes of Indian music to China in CE 568.

The Russian botanist Albert Regel reported "numerous idols". He was the first European to see the ruins of Khocho near Karakhoja. From 1902 to 1914 German expeditions (fig. 10.1) to sites on the northern Silk Route discovered folios and fragments of Sanskrit texts. In the Cave of the Red Dome at Kizil Grünwedel found "the remains of a library of very old manuscripts on palm leaf, birch bark and paper, together with inscribed wooden tablets. This cave was also the source of leaves from the oldest Sanskrit manuscript, which at the same time is one of the oldest Indian manuscripts ever found" (Härtel et al. 1982: 41). One thousand and fourteen items of Sanskrit manuscripts have been catalogued in the four volumes of the *Sanskrithandschriften aus den Turfanfunden* under the

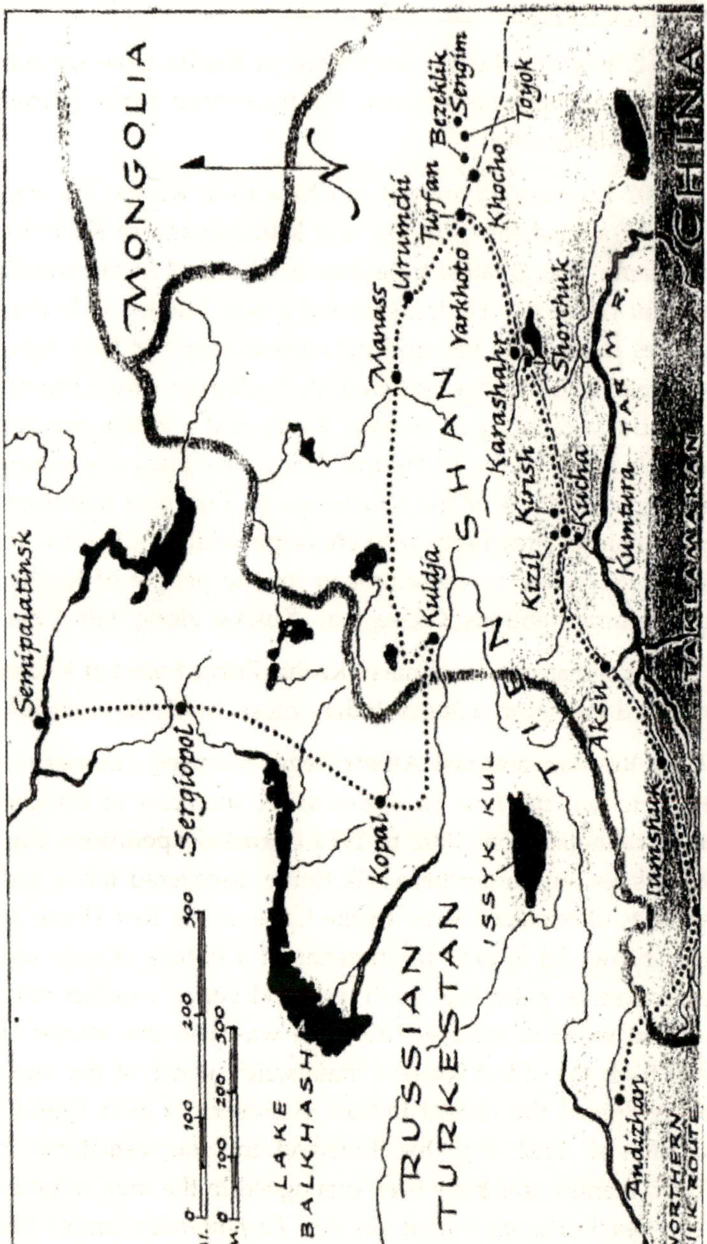

fig. 10.1: Itinerary of the German Expeditions

editorship of Ernst Waldschmidt. These manuscripts come from four areas:

(a) Tumshuk

(b) Kucha region (Kizil, Kumtura, Kirish, Achik-ilek)

(c) Shorchuk, and

(d) Turfan oasis (Khocho, Yarkhoto, Murtuk, Sengim, Toyok).

The Kucha region has yielded the largest number of manuscripts (nos. 15-375) of Buddhist texts. The most interesting are the fragments of three dramas of Aśvaghoṣa from Kizil, written on palm leaves in the Kuṣāṇa script (no. 16). The first drama is a dialogue between Buddhi, Dhṛti and Kīrti. The second is Śāriputra-Prakaraṇa and the third pertains to a hetaera. Another fragment of the Śāriputra-Prakaraṇa written on palm leaves in Turkistan Brāhmī from the Cave of the Red Dome of the Ming-öi of Kizil has the colophon of the last and ninth act. It reads:

śāriputraprakaraṇe navamo=ṅkaḥ 9 āryyasuvarṇṇākṣiputrasy = āryy =
āśvaghoṣasya kṛtiś=śāradvatīputrapprakaraṇaṁ samāptaṁ [sa] māptāni
c=āṅkāni nava . . . gyam=anu(ṣṭubhe)ccha.

The name of the mother of Aśvaghoṣa is given as Suvarṇākṣī, but his father's name is conspicuously absent.

Manuscripts (nos. 376-531) from the Manuscripts Cave of Shorchuk include *Buddhacarita* of Aśvaghoṣa (no. 432) written in North Turkistan Brāhmī. Fragments of *Saundarananda-Kāvya* written in North Turkistan-Brāhmī on paper (no. 515) were also found.

Why did Aśvaghoṣa become popular in this region? Did his father come from Central Asia as a trader or pilgrim and gave birth to him as the son of Suvarṇākṣī while he remained unknown. Japanese iconographic treatise Besson-zakki (*fig*. 10.2) by Shinkaku (CE 1117-80, TZ 87.148) shows him six-armed, sitting on a horse and with a retinue of six. The second part of his name *ghoṣa* can be a Sanskritization of *kuṣa* in Kuṣāṇa and Kuśadvīpa "Kushanshahr".

A work of eighty stories and ten parables by Kumāralāta found at Kizil, written on palm leaves in the Kuṣāṇa–Gupta script is *Kalpanā-Maṇḍitīka Dṛṣṭānta-Paṅkti*. It is the only Sanskrit work that shows the travel of Indian merchants to China. The third German expedition found fragments of Kumāralāta's grammar with a commentary, written in the Kuṣāṇa–Gupta script on palm leaves, from the Cave of the Red Dome of the Ming-öi of Kizil. It pertains to the *sandhi* chapter (no. 22).

fig. 10.2: Aśvaghoṣa in the Besson-zakki

Turfan Oasis (Khocho, Yarkhoto, Murtuk, Sengim, Toyok)

Among those who opened Abhidharma literature to the Chinese were Dharmanandin from Tukhāra, and Kumārabodhi the *ābhidhārmika* who was the *purohita* of King Mi-ti of Turfan. The latter had been a member of the tribute mission to the Chinese Emperor in 382. They brought Abhidharma texts which were translated into Chinese.

Manuscripts from the Turfan Oasis come from Turfan, Khocho, Yarkhoto, Murtuk, Sengim and Toyok (nos. 532-648). Fragments of *Kātantra* grammar from the *stūpa* on the right side of the river flowing by the Nakṣatra Temple at Sengim Agiz contain the chapters on *taddhita, strī-pratyaya* and *ākhyāta* (no. 633). From the Toyok monastic ruins the second German Turfan expedition found the fragments of Āryaśūra's *Jātakamālā* and Kumāralāta's *Kalpanā-maṇḍitīkā Dṛṣṭānta-paṅkti* (no. 638). Toyok yielded fragments of *Bheḍa-Saṁhitā*, written on paper in the Gilgit script (nos. 641, 642). The metrical text *Chando-Viciti* (no. 654) written on birch bark in Turkistan–Gupta script comes from an unknown site.

All the manuscripts are Buddhist texts of Vinaya, Sūtra, Gāthās, Avadānas, Abhidharma, Yoga, Commentaries, Dhāraṇī, Mantra, Nāmāvalī, Stotra and other genres.

The mural of a brāhmaṇa was found in temple 9 of Bezeklik. It has been dated to seventh-eighth century, but could not be identified (Härtel et al. 1982: 146). The third eye on the forehead identifies him as Nīlakaṇṭha, the great *siddha*. The hymn to Thousand-armed Avalokiteśvara translated by Bhagavaddharma has *siddhāya svāhā/mahāsiddhāya svāhā/siddha-yogeśvarāya svāhā/nīlakaṇṭhāya svāhā/* (Lokesh Chandra 1988: 268). The two opening verses show that it was originally a hymn to Nīlakaṇṭha recited by Avalokiteśvara and not a hymn addressed to Avalokiteśvara:

sarva-bhaya-trāṇakarāya tasmai namaskṛtvā imaṁ।
āry-āvalokiteśvara-stavanaṁ nīlakaṇṭhānāṁ॥

hṛdayaṁ vartayiṣyāmi sarvārtha-sādhanaṁ śubham।
ajeyaṁ sarva-bhūtānāṁ bhava-mārga-viśodhakam॥

Bhagavaddharma translated the work at Khotan which means that Nīlakaṇṭha was popular in the Silk Route monasteries.

The most important site in the Turfan region is of temples of Bezeklik ("place with paintings" in eastern Turkish). These paintings have Sanskrit captions. For example, the *praṇidhi* scene in temple 9 is captioned in Sanskrit, evidently written by an Uigur master:

upasthito brāhmaṇena mahendro lokanāyakaḥ
jyentākakarmaṇā gandhai kālenaguruṇā tathā

vihāraṁ kṛtvā sarvai ca upasthanai nimantrita
— Albert von le Coq, *Chotscho*, repr. 1979, Tafel 17

The Sanskrit tradition can also be seen in the ruins of free-standing Stūpa Y in Khocho, the ancient Karakhoja. It is a three-storeyed structure with niches for statues on all sides. It rests on a square base with stepped tiers for circumambulation. On every tier there are twenty-four niches (six niches in each direction), totalling to seventy-two on the three tiers. It is a *śata-dvāra* or Tib. *sgo.maṅ* (many doors). It must have enshrined seventy-two images of a Buddhist Sūtra, for paying homage. A similar structure exists in Hauz Khas, New Delhi known as Chor Minar. It has eleven niches on the base and one large niche on the first tier. It reflects an earlier sacred structure whose twelve niches could have held the statues of the Twelve Light Buddhas of the Amitābha cycle. The present structure is Islamic derived from an earlier type prevalent in Central Asia.

References

Brough, John, 1961, "A Khoroṣṭhī inscription from China", *BSOAS* 1961: 24.517-30.

———, 1962, *The Gāndhārī Dharmapada,* London: Oxford University Press.

Chandra, Lokesh, 1988, *Thousand-armed Avalokiteśvara,* New Delhi: Indira Gandhi National Centre for the Arts.

Cleary, Thomas, 1983, *Entry into the Inconceivable,* Honolulu: University of Hawaii.

Foucher, Alfred, *L' Art gréco-fouddhique du Gandhara,* Paris: Imprimérie Nationale.

Härtel et al., 1982, *Along the Ancient Silk Route: Central Asian Art from the West Berlin State Museums,* New York: The Metropolitan Museum of Art.

Hinüber von, Oskar, Haiyan Au, 2010, in the *Annual Report of the International Research Institute for Advanced Buddhology* at Soka University, for the academic year 2010.

Hoernle, A.F. Rudolph, 1893, *The Bower Manuscript,* Calcutta, 1893–1912.

———, 1916, *Manuscript Remains of Buddhist Literature Found in East Turkestan,* vol. 1, Oxford: Clarendon Press.

Karashima, Seishi and Klaus Wille, 2006, *The British Library Sanskrit Fragments,* Tokyo: Soka University.

Mayrhofer, Manfred, 1956, *Kurzgefasstes Etymologisches Wörterbuch des Altindischen.*

Waldschmidt, Ernst, Walter Clawiter and Lore Holzmann, 1965, *Sanskrithandschriften aus den Turfanfunden,* Wiesbaden: Franz Steiner Verlag.

Watters, Thomas, 1904-05, *On Yuan Chwang's Travels in India, 629-645* AD, vols. I-II, London: Royal Asiatic Society.

Wright, Arthur F., 1959, *Buddhism in Chinese History,* Stanford: Stanford University Press.

Zürcher, E., 1972, *The Buddhist Conquest of China,* Leiden: E.J. Brill.

11

Fascinating Sanskrit Manuscripts in the Asiatic Society, Calcutta

Manabendu Banerjee

THE manuscript collection of the Museum of the Asiatic Society, Calcutta, is very rich and varied in textual contents. The collection includes records of India's achievements in diverse spheres of learning. Almost all the Indian languages and scripts have been used for the preparation of the manuscripts. It has in its collection manuscripts in all prominent Asian languages such as Sanskrit, Simhalese, Arabic, Persian, Armenian, Burmese, Chinese and Tibetan. But manuscripts in Sanskrit far outnumber the others. The materials used for the manuscripts are palm and palmyra leaves, birch barks and papers of various grades, i.e. country-made, machine-made, foreign and Nepalese paper. The copying of these manuscripts covers the period from the seventh century CE down to the nineteenth century. Regular search of Sanskrit manuscripts for the Asiatic Society began in the year 1868 under the government instruction, and through the active efforts of R.L. Mitra, H.P. Sastri, Cintaharan Chakraborty and many other ebullient scholars. The Asiatic Society has once in its possession about 50,000 (fifty thousand) Sanskrit manuscripts. Of these only 12,000 (twelve thousand) manuscripts are so far been included in the printed Descriptive Catalogues, published from the Asiatic Society nearly hundred years back. About three-fourth of this collection have not yet been sorted out and catalogued. On the other hand, hundreds of new manuscripts have been accumulated in the Society's Museum from different sources.

A manuscript on Tantra with the title *Kubjikāmatam,* written in later Gupta character on palm leaves, dated seventh century CE, is so far the oldest manuscript in the Asiatic Society. Mention may be made to an illustrated palm-leaf manuscript of *Aṣṭasāhasrikā-Prajñāpāramitā,* dated tenth century CE, which contains beautifully illustrated representations of the Buddha in meditative postures. A birch-bark manuscript of the Sanskrit poem, *Naiṣadhīyacarita* (4067/5132) and another of *Rāmāyaṇa-mañjarī,* both belonging to tenth-eleventh century CE, are preserved in the Asiatic Society. A manuscript of *R̥gveda,* copied in the thirteenth century and available in fragments, is probably the oldest paper-manuscript of the work known so far.

There are a good number of manuscripts which do not come under the purview of the well-known branches of Sanskrit languages and literature so far as the subject matter is concerned and they sufficiently establish that ancient Indian literature does not include only a number of stereotyped subjects, but touches a wide range of topics — some of which are very interesting and thought-provoking. The present paper deals with a few of the manuscripts, having uncommon but interesting themes, that are preserved in the Asiatic Society Museum. Most of these manuscripts are yet to be properly edited and published.

In the collection of manuscripts of the Kāvya literature, we find that besides the works of the popular poets like Kālidāsa, Bhavabhūti and others, there are more than a dozen

Śatakas and about eight Dūtakāvyas. Though these are unsuccessful imitations of the works of previous poets of distinction, they bear some signs of uniqueness. In this collection we find a complete manuscript of a work, named *Vāgmaṇḍana-Guṇa-Dūtam* (8305/5174), composed by one Vīreśvara. It is a poem consisting of 100 verses eulogizing King Bhīmasena *alias* Kāmarūpa and his associates. The poem itself is depicted as the messenger here and is sent from Vardhanapura to Bhīmasena (or Kāmarūpa) stationed at Māyāpura. The second half of the 1st verse runs thus:

dūtye sūktaguṇaṁ niyoktumanasas taṁ kāmarūpaṁ prati ।
proddāmāṁ mudaṁ ātanotu bhavatāṁ vāgdevateyaṁ mama ॥

Like *Meghadūta* of Kālidāsa and almost with the same expression, the present work also points to its two parts, i.e. the journey route and the message. Thus the poet says:

yānaṁ te vinivedayāmi purataḥ paścāt-prayāṇocitam ।
mārgaṁ śrośyasi sūkta-nāyaka tataḥ sandeśavāco mama ॥

— Verse 7

This manuscript was copied sometime in the eighteenth century, and the poet seems to have appeared after twelfth century CE, as the poets like Bhavabhūti, Bāṇa and others, referred to in verse 6, flourished before the twelfth century.

Rāmaliṅga-Varṇanam or *Takra-Rāmāyaṇam* (533/5214) was composed by Advaita Bhaṭṭa, a Vaidika brāhmaṇa who was the son of Bhāya Bhaṭṭa and grandson of Kṛṣṇa Bhaṭṭa. The author was a native of Mārjāratīrtha at the confluence of Phenā and Godāvarī (Folio 57A). The work was composed in the Śaka year 1550 (CE 1628) at Varanasi. The present manuscript was copied in Saṁvat 1877. The work is a poem in 9 cantos and is unique in respect of its contents. It is in the form of a conversation between a milkmaid engaged in churning butter and a brāhmaṇa girl who arrived at that place for buying sour milk (*takra*). On being enquired by the milkmaid, the brāhamaṇa girl satisfied her queries by narrating the events related with Rāmacandra of Vālmīki's *Rāmāyaṇa.* In the beginning the poet calls the poem a *surasa-sugama-kāvya;* then he praises the god *Hayagrīva,* also called Ramānātha. As the milkmaid was an illiterate lady, she asked about the incidents of Rāmacandra somehow unconnectedly. Thus, she addresses the brāhmaṇa girl:

> *bho mātaḥ kathaṁ rāghavaḥ sītāyug vipinam gato vanacaraiḥ sākaṁ kathaṁ saṁgataḥ setur yena kathaṁ kṛto daśamukho yuddhe kathaṁ nāśitaḥ* ।

Thereafter she asked: *rāmaḥ kasya suto kayā sujaṭhare saṁsthāpitaḥ?* and so on. The brāhmaṇa girl became much pleased and stated that she would narrate the story of Rāmacandra in the way Mahādeva described it before Pārvatī (*dhanyā 'haṁ sakhi varṇayāmi girijāṁ yām avravīc chaṅkaraḥ*).

Though a poem of *śataka* type, *Mahīṣa-Śatakam* (9296/5252) attracts attention for novelty of its treatment. Out of 100 verses, only 58 are available in this manuscript. But the story can however be framed from these verses. A brāhmaṇa, residing in the Tanjore region where the rulers were the Bhoṅslā kings, was disappointed being unable to earn money by his learning; he decided to earn his livelihood through agriculture and for that purpose he purchased a buffalo. But the royal officers of the district to which he belonged expropriated from him much of the produce of the agriculture; so he composed this poem with 100 verses in praise of his buffalo, and this is in fact a lampoon wherein the brāhmaṇa had attacked and ridiculed the king who being a Bhoṅslā is supposed to derive his patronymic from Bhohiṣa (Mahiṣa) or a buffalo.

While the brāhmaṇa has praised some of the previous kings, he has described the ruling king as a simpleton and the ministers as worse than ordinary halfwits; on the other hand the royal ministers are stated to have been cheated by notorious people who also robbed the peasantry. In verse 5 he maintained that the country of the Coḷa where the Bhoñslās used to rule had no hope for prosperous agriculture.

In verse 6, the poet laments for the death of Nānājī, Prabhucandra, Bhānusāhajī, Indrananda Ray and other noble persons of the territory.

The manuscript of *Prema-Rāmāyaṇa* (10391/5254), composed by Ramu Dviveda of Varanasi, is a partly retained Sanskrit version of Tulsīdāsa's Hindi *Rāmāyaṇa*, famous by the name of *Rāmacaritamānasa*. It is however called a versified but easy Sanskrit commentary of Tulsīdāsa's work, meant for minor students:

tasyeyaṁ racitā ṭīkā ślokavaddhā yathāmati ।
kāśyāṁ rāmudvivedena saralā taralātmanām ॥

The script of this manuscript is *Nāgara* of the seventeenth century CE.

An anonymous and incomplete manuscript of a work, attributed to Brahmā (9957/5474), denounces smoking of tobacco, for, this harmful habit of Kali age is said to be the destroyer of the merits which a man gains in various ways; this habit degrades a man to a position lower than a *cāṇḍāla*. Thus the manuscript begins with a statement made by Brahmā to Nārada:

ghore kaliyuge prāpte sarve varṇāśramā narāḥ ।
nirayeṣu patiṣyanti tāmākukali-rūpataḥ ॥
upāsate tamākuṁ vai kalau nārada ye narāḥ ।
kṣīṇapuṇyāḥ patiṣyanti mahāraurava-saṁjñite ॥

abhakṣya-bhokṣaṇāt pāpam agamya-gamanācca yat ı
madya-pānācca yat pāpaṁ tamākupāna-mātrataḥ ıı

Again in verse 11, it is said:

brāhmaṇaḥ kṣatriyo vaiśyaḥ śūdraś ca munisattama ı
svapacaiḥ sadṛśā jñeyās tāmākupāna-mātrataḥ ıı

The word *tāmāku* has been written in the margin of every leaf. The manuscript is not dated, but it is not very old.

A complete manuscript of a work named *Tāmbūla-Kalpa* (8238/5506), composed by Nṛsiṁhha Bhaṭṭa, narrates the importance of chewing betel-leaves, and in support it quotes verses from Smṛtis and Purāṇas. It prescribes some special occasions when taking of betels should be a must. Thus in the beginning it states that at dawn, after lunch or dinner, while in unison with a fair sex, at the time of leisure, and while sitting amongst elites at the royal court, a man should chew betels; otherwise he should be treated as a beast:

pratyuṣasi bhukti-samaye vara-yuvati-saṁgame virāme ca ı
rājasabhā-vidvanmadhye yas-tāmbūlaṁ na kuryāt sa paśuḥ ıı

At the end of this manuscript there are some general discussions on the household duties (*ācāra*). It was composed, according to the *New Catalogus Catalogoram*, in CE 1350.

A manuscript of a very interesting and at the same time a voluminous work, entitled *Jayamādhava-Mānasollāsa* (1274/2837), has been preserved in the Society's Smṛti Collection. But along with Smṛti materials, some historical events have been treated here with equal importance. The work is attributed to King Jayasiṁhadeva of Gorakṣapura, now in Uttar Pradesh. Jayasiṁhha, the independent sovereign of Gorakṣapura, has been presented in this work as the 14th king of the *Brahma-kṣatriya* family; the names of thirteen ancestors of Jayasiṁhha are mentioned, of which the thirteenth king,

Śaktisiṁha appears to be the father of Jayasiṁha. In the work, Jayasiṁha's involvement in the battle with the sultans have also been stated. Under these kings of the Brahma-kṣatriya family, the tract of land to the north of the Sarayū River tried its best to maintain its independence with Gorakṣapura as its principal city. Jayasiṁha is stated to have renamed Gorakṣapura as Nārāyaṇapura because of the reason that the king became a devotee of Nārāyaṇa or Viṣṇu (verse 31). With the help of some reputed scholars and after consulting some Purāṇic works, Jayasiṁha wrote this work:

> *nānā-purāṇa-smṛti-vākyajātaṁ* । *sārodayaṁ sāratarāṁ mahīśaḥ* ।
> *budhaiḥ samāhṛtya samāhitātmā vyarīracat sādhu nibandham etat* ॥
>
> — verse 36

In the last few pages a table of contents is added by a different hand and it shows that the present work is on Vaiṣṇava ritual, both compulsory and optical. Viṣṇu is often called here as Jayamādhava. The present manuscript was copied in Saṁvat 1526 (i.e. CE 1470) and therefore the composition of the work was made a few years back.

The manuscripts of Smṛti works in the Asiatic Society Museum include a variety of subjects — the special stress being on the codification of the laws prevalent in ancient India. In this collection, however, we come across a very interesting manuscript which does not follow the familiar path taken by the well-known Smṛtis. It is *Dampatī-Pūjana-Vidhi* (1956/2926). In this work suggestion has been made to the fact that when a husband and wife cannot stand each other and are in quarrelling mood, anyone of them may invite a brāhmaṇa couple and worship them with ornaments, clothes and *madhuparka:*

> *āhūya dampatī rājan sālaṁkārau savastrakau* ।
> *madhuparkenārcayitvā pratimāṁ ca prayacchati* ॥

It is stated here that golden images of the divine couple, Lakṣmī and Nārāyaṇa, are to be made and presented to the invited brāhmaṇa couple. The object of this worship and that of the gift are believed to be that the quarrelling couple would be able to enjoy a peaceful life in their present and future birth. The present manuscript warns us that if any couple causes separation from each other, the man, in the next birth, becomes a spiteful woman and the woman becomes a female jackal or a bitch:

> *pūrvajanmani strī-puruṣayoḥ parasparaṁ duṣṭabuddhyā viyogaṁ karoti sa pumān strī bhavati* । *sā strī śṛgālī śunī vā bhavati* ।

While condemning a separation between a husband and a wife, the work quotes the sayings of Vṛddha-Viṣṇu. Of the two manuscripts of this work, one is complete and is said to have been composed in Śaka year, 1753, i.e. CE 1831.

A good number of manuscripts are of the works on the worship of various gods including Rāma, Gaṅgā, Śiva and others. In this section there is a manuscript of a work entitled *Jānakī-Pūjā-Paddhati* (10406/2888) consisting 72 *śloka*s on the worship of Sītā. Sītā as the consort of Rāmacandra is certainly a highly revered lady, but to worship her as an independent deity is not very common. Rāma and Sītā are however jointly worshipped in many places. The present manuscript acquaints us with the fact that Sītā alone was also worshipped in some parts of our country.

There was a time when a tendency grew among many wealthy persons to direct *paṇḍit*s to compose new grammars which were to be taught to their children. As a result, a considerable number of short books on grammar came into existence. About the end of the sixteenth century, Vajjala or Vaijala, belonging to the Cauhāna family (*cauhāna-vaṁśa-tilaka*) of Rājpūts, held four *pargaṇā*s as his *jāgīra* and Paṭanā was his principal residence (*paṭanādhināṭha*). For the benefit of his son Hīrādhara, he ordered one Viśvaśarman to compose a grammar and the latter composed the *Prabodha-Candrikā*, four manuscripts of which (8191/4570; 9865/4571; 6707/4572; 1664/4572A) are preserved in the Asiatic Society. The verses in these manuscripts vary from 450 to 500. The peculiarity of this work is that the king makes his son aware of the fact that everything is achieved by education which again rests on the true knowledge of the science of Grammar. In the beginning it is stated:

> *bālakānāṁ prabodhāya toṣāya viduṣāmapi* ।
> *ākalpam api saṁsāre kīrty avasthāpanāya ca* ॥
> *cintayanniti niryātaḥ krīḍantaṁ śrīhīrādharam* ।
> *śrīmān vaijalabhūpālo vilokyetad avravīt sutam* ॥
> *vidyayā dyotate rājyaṁ vidyayā jayate ripuḥ* ।
> *vidyayā jayate kṛtyaṁ vidyayā labhate yaśaḥ* ॥
> *vidyayā jāyate dharmo dharmenārthaḥ prajāyate* ।
> *arthena jāyate rājyaṁ sukhaṁ rājyena jāyate* ॥
> *vidyā piteva hitakṛd vidyā māteva rakṣikā* ।
> *vidyā priyeva sukhadā vidyā kalpalatopamā* ॥

And after a few lines it is stated — *vinā vyākaraṇaṁ vāṇī ramaṇī ramaṇaṁ vinā.*

In this work brief lessons are given regarding the leading topics of Sanskrit grammar. The other specificity of this work is that Vijjala-Bhūpati being a devoted worshipper of Rāma, the examples of this book are cited mainly from *Rāmāyaṇa*. Vaijala employed a scholar, named Jagamohana, to prepare a topography of eighteen different countries of eastern India and Indo-Chinese peninsula, and Jagamohana subsequently wrote *Deśāvalī-Vivṛtti*, fragments of which are preserved in the Asiatic Society. A complete manuscript of this work is deposited in the Government Sanskrit College Library, Calcutta.

Two interesting works are found in the group of Alaṁkāra section, namely, *Varṇa-Ratnākara* (4834/4857A) of Jyotirīśvara Kaviśekhara who lived in Mithilā at the beginning of the fourteenth century CE. The other work is *Kāma-Samūha* (8157/4859A) of Ananta, the son of Trimaṇḍana, bearing the title of *Bhiṣag-Mukuṭālaṁkāra-Hāraḥ*. According to Aufrecht, this work was composed in Saṁvat 1457. *Varṇa-Ratnākara* is not in Sanskrit, but in old Maithilī. It is written in Bengali script of the fourteenth century CE. This is a palm-leaf manuscript and the work is available in incomplete form. *Varṇa-Ratnākara* and *Kāma-Samūha* were written for the purpose of giving instructions to the poets as to how a heroine, a city, a season and such other requisites for a poem are to be described. Towards the close of *Varṇa-Ratnākara* it is stated to be an ideal treatise (*ādarśa-pustakam etat samāptam*); the chapters of this work are named *kallola*. Besides the topics on city, heroine, etc. it deals with *siddha*s such as Mīnanātha, Gorakṣanātha, and others, as well as with various aboriginal tribes, such as Jaga and Yogī who are called by the author *mandajāti*. *Kāma-Samūha* is available in complete form. Another manuscript of this work is preserved in the India Office Library. The manuscript in the Asiatic Society was copied sometime in eighteenth century CE. This work stresses on the situations in love to be described by a poet in his poem and on peerless beauty of a young lady, and also on her hair, her eyes, her breasts and such other physical parts. The author has often called this work by the name of *mahākāvya-prabandha* or *kāvya-prabandha*.

That the method of writing letters by and to persons of various fields was in practice in ancient India has already been established by some prominent poems and dramas. We have in the Asiatic Society some manuscripts of a work, named *Patra-Kaumudī* (3755/4938; 5171/4939) of Vararuci who is believed to be the reputed author of *Prākṛta-Prakāśa.* This work devotes fully on diverse methods of letter-writing. One manuscript of *Patra-Kaumudī,* in the Asiatic Society, is in Bengali character of eighteenth-nineteenth century and this fact goes to prove that this work was popular in the Bengal region. R.L. Mitra in his *Notices of Sanskrit Manuscripts* (vol. I) has written about *Patra-Kaumudī* (no. 347) that it is the universal method of letter-writers, containing rules for determining the size, shape and decorations of letters, different ranks of the parties to whom these are to be addressed, qualifications of letter-writers, forms of addresses, etc. *Patra-Kaumudī* contains the processes of writing different types of letters, such as a letter from the Royal Court, letter from or to a minister, letter to a scholar, letter from a husband to his beloved wife and vice versa. Information is also supplied in this work as to the method of writing a letter even to an enemy and also to a saint. The colour of a letter and qualities of a letter-writer who is to be appointed by a king in his court are some other topics dealt within this text. About the qualifications of a letter-writer to be appointed by the king, the work states:

> *brāhmaṇo mantraṇābhijño rājanīti-viśāradaḥ* ।
> *nānālipijño medhāvī nānābhāṣā-samanvitaḥ* ॥
>
> *mantraṇācaturo dhīmān nītiśāstrārtha-kovidaḥ* ।
> *sandhi-vigraha-bhedajño rājakārye vicakṣaṇaḥ* ॥

Here we find an echo of a similar expression of Kauṭilya's *Arthaśāstra* (2.10.3) where the merits required for a scribe of a royal edict are enumerated. Thus Kauṭilya says:

> *tasmād amātya-sampadopetaḥ sarva-samayavid āśu-granthaḥ cārvakṣaro lekha-vācana-samartho lekhakaḥ syāt,* etc.
>
> The scribe should be endowed with the excellences of a minister, conversant with all conventions, quick in

composing, with a beautiful hand and capable of reading a document. — tr. R.P. Kangle

Besides *Patra-Kaumudī,* some other manuscripts of works on letter-writing are also preserved in the Asiatic Society. These are — *Praśasti-Kāśikā* (3026/4940) of Śambhu-deva, *Praśastikā-Prakaraṇam* (2870/4942), *Praśasti-Prakāśikā* (2365/4943) and *Praśastiḥ sa-ṭīkā* (8750/4944) — the last one being a work on letter-writing with a commentary; in this work some authorities on letter-writing are named, such as, Viśveśvara Chakravarti, *Prastāva-Cintāmaṇi,* Parāśara, Bhāskara, Pradhāna, Sārvabhauma and Kālidāsa. The last three works mentioned above are anonymous and were copied during seventeenth-eighteenth century. R.L. Mitra, in his *Notices* (vol. 3), says about *Praśati-Prakāśikā* that it was written in the reign of Bhoja Rāja of Dhārā. It is a work on letter-writing and in it detailed directions are given for folding the material on which a letter is to be written, for leaving a considerable space on the right side of such letters as margin, for cutting a portion of the left lower corner, for decorating the front with gold-leaf, for writing the word *śrī* a number of times on the back, etc., etc. In this context we may mention the manuscript of a work, namely, *Vīra-Virudāvali* (10739/4941) composed by Raghudeva Miśra of Mithilā. It is written on Nepalese paper, consisting of 500 verses and gives several epithets that are applicable to a heroic king.

It is known to all that the popular epic, *Mahābhārata,* is full of anecdotes of varied nature which sometimes may disturb the smooth running of the principal story. Some poets made occasional attempts to bring out abstracts from the principal theme of the *Mahābhārata* so that readers could find it easy to grasp the main story of the great epic. The manuscripts of two such works are *Bhārata-Sāra* or *Bhārata-Samuccaya* (1649/3436) and *Bhārata-Sāvitrī* (10672/3449). *Mahābhārata-Kathā-*

Saṁgraha (3788/3437) is another work of this category. All these works attempt at presenting only the historical portion of the great epic to which easy access would be possible for the interested readers. Among these, *Bhārata-Sāra* was composed in Saṁvat 1680. *Bhārata-Sāvitrī* has nothing to do with the episode of Sāvitrī and Satyavān, but it gives the essence of the *Mahābhārata*. We have a good number of manuscripts of the work named *Itihāsa-Samuccaya* of which one copy (4719/3442) is dated CE 945. *Itihāsa-Samuccaya* is a collection of the minor episodes of the *Mahābhārata*. One of the manuscripts of this work (2925/3445) contains forty-two stories some of which, such as Gajendra-Mokṣaṇam and Bahulopākhyānam, are not found in the now available editions of the *Mahābhārata*. Several manuscripts of this work are preserved in some of the libraries of India as well as in India Office Library in Oxford. An *Itihāsa-Samuccaya* with thirty-two legends was published in 1916 from Venkatesvara Press, Bombay.

The manuscripts of two works, namely *Caturaṅga-Dīpikā* and *Caturaṅga-Taraṅgiṇī*, have become popular after the publication of the first one (published in 1936, Calcutta Sanskrit Series, no. XXI). These texts deal with the earlier form of *caturaṅga* (four-handed chess). The former is believed to have been composed by Śūlapāṇi who is supposed to be identical with the famous Smṛti-writer of that name and who flourished in Bengal in the fifteenth century. Two manuscripts of *Śatarañja-Kutuhalam* (8222/83), otherwise known as *Buddhibala* — a small work on the game of chess, are preserved in the Asiatic Society. This anonymous work is in the form of a discourse between Kṛṣṇa and Rādhā; it is complete in ten verses and on the basis of the manuscripts of the Society, it has been published from Sanskrit Sahitya Parishat, Calcutta, in 1946.

A similar work called *Śatarañjinī* has been noted and described by R.L. Mitra in *Descriptive Catalogue of Sanskrit Manuscripts in the Library of His Highness the Mahārāja of Bikaner* (no. 1546). It is composed by Kr̥ṣṇarāma. It is a bigger one and a small portion of it is preserved in the Asiatic Society where the names of the work and of the author are respectively given as *Caturaṅga-Racanā* (10326/81) and Giridhara, son of Śaṅkara and grandson of Śiva, the astronomer (*jyotirvid*). The Society possesses a manuscript of the commentary on *Satarañja-Kutuhala* (8223/85). Interestingly in its post-colophon statement the copyist claims that the manuscript was copied for the benefit of the students of a primary school (*likhitam idaṁ śrīmadakṣara-pīṭhaśālā-vidyārthinām upkr̥taye*). That the game of chess was actively taught to the school students is further corroborated in a folio of the above-mentioned manuscript of *Caturaṅga-Racanā* which states — *krameṇa vakṣye śiśu-kutukārthaṁ santo 'pi santoṣavahā vimr̥śya*, etc. An incomplete manuscript of the *Vilāsa-maṇi-mañjarī* (8322/82), a work on the problems of the game of chess, by one Trivengaḍācārya, is preserved in the Asiatic Society. The work, complete in four chapters, was published with a Mārāṭhī translation from Kolhapur in 1937.

The Asiatic Society possesses some manuscripts of works of more or less technical nature. *Kādamvarī-Svīkaraṇa-Sūtra* (10348/4) is a small work of only six folios and it consists of thirty-one *sūtras*, accompanied by a commentary. It speaks of the utility of drinking wine from aphrodisiac standpoint. In the colophon the name of the author is given as the great king, Purūravā and the purpose of writing this work is also referred to there:

> *iti śrī-mahā-rājarṣivaryeṇa purūravasā viracitaṁ kāmijanānāṁ vinodāya ratīvilāsāṅgabhūtaṁ kādambarasvīkaranasūtraṁ savyākhyānaṁ samāptim agamat* ।

It is interesting to note here that after the completion of the text, the author pays homage to Lord Dvārakādhīśa Kṛṣṇa and the commentary ends with a line from *Bhagavad-Gītā* (9.27) — *yatkaroṣi yad aśnāśi yajjuhośi dadāsi yat.*

Among the works on the science of music, *Saṁgīta-Śiromaṇi* (1713/59) is a very interesting one. It was written jointly by various experts on music, belonging to different localities, at the instance of Malik Sarak Suluta Sahi who used to reside at the city, Kaḍā, near Veni. From a lengthy account given in the beginning, it appears that the Muslim king was a great patron of Indian music and musical literature. At his initiative, various Sanskrit works on music were collected from various sources and scholars were invited from different parts of the country with the assurance of making to them grants of lands and gifts of gold, cloth, etc.:

padavākya-pramāṇajñān saṁgītārtha-viśāradān ।
ānāyya paṇḍitān uccaiḥ grāma-hemāmbarādibhiḥ ॥

With the assistance of these scholars, Suluta Sahi composed this work in CE 1428.

Another work on the science of music is *Pañcama-Saṁhitā,* also called, *Pañcama-Sāra-Saṁhitā* (5040/54), composed by one Nārada. It is a short but important treatise which enumerates the *rāga*s and their consorts, *rāgiṇī*s; it refers to the proper time of their practice and gives their anthropomorphic description. It is an incomplete manuscript and was composed in Śaka 1632 = CE 1710. *Saṁgīta-Nārāyaṇa* (2513/60) by Puruṣottama Miśra is composed in four chapters and consists of 2,000 verses. It may be pointed out here that though at the end, Puruṣottama Miśra is said to be the author, the colophons of the chapters attribute the work to the Gajapati hero Nārāyaṇa Deva. It appears that Puruṣottama Miśra composed this work under the patronage of Nārāyaṇa Deva of

Parlakhimedi of the southern Gajapati dynasty about the years CE 1730-50. *Saṁgāna-Sāgara* (4852/61), composed by Śubhaṁkara-kavi belonging to the fourteenth century CE, and *Rāgamālā* (1195/62) of Kṣemakarṇa are two very important works on music. The first one is written on palm leaf in Newārī character. A good number of its folios are missing. The remaining folios show that these may be placed into two sets — one containing discussions on vocal music and the other portion on instrumental music and dancing. The above-mentioned unpublished manuscripts on the science of music have attracted the attention of an expert like O.C. Ganguly who has coined some of his artistic ideas on the basis of these works, in his valuable book *Rāgas and Rāgiṇī*s (repr. edn., 1989).

We have in the Asiatic Society a considerable number of manuscripts of historical or biographical works some of which are already published. But many of those manuscripts are yet to be properly edited and published. A very important and interesting manuscript is of the *Kavīndra-Candrodaya* (2858/3110) which contains about 100 addresses presented to Vidyānidhi Kavīndra of Varanasi about the middle of the seventeenth century CE. During this time, the Mughal emperors used to levy taxes on pilgrims visiting Varanasi and Prayāga. Vidyānidhi went with a band of scholars to Agra and pleaded the cause of the pilgrims at the *ām darbār*. Being pleased at the eloquent speech of Vidyānidhi, Shāh Jahān abolished the tax and at the same time conferred the title of *Sarva-Vidyānidhāna* on him. After his return to Varanasi, praises by scholars from all over India poured upon Vidyānidhi, and of the addresses presented to him, 100 were collected and edited by Śrīkṛṣṇācārya. It may be pointed out here that the addresses were signed by the sender-*paṇḍit*s and the most remarkable of them was of Rāmadeva, the son of Viśvanātha Tarkapañcānana of Navadvīpa, the author of *Bhāṣāparichheda*.

Vidyānidhi Kavīndra wrote a commentary on the *Ṛgveda*; a fragment of this commentary in the name of *Sarva-Vidyānidhāna Kavīndra*, has been preserved in the Asiatic Society.

Among some other unique manuscripts, we may mention *Ṣaṇmukha-Kalpa*, by an anonymous writer, which deals with incantations and descriptions of magic rites connected with the science of theft. It is a complete palm-leaf manuscript written in Newārī script. References have been made in it to various techniques to be adopted by an expert thief, such as, *antardhāna* (concealing), *pāda-praticāraṇa* (silent stepping of feet), *bhelki* (jugglery) and *kapāṭodghāṭana* (opening of doors).

The manuscripts, referred to above, are only a handful and there are a large number of more remarkable manuscripts preserved in the Asiatic Society. These are lying in several hundred bundles and many of them have not yet been untied. When these will be sorted out and be displayed, there is every chance of getting therein more valuable manuscripts on uncommon topics. If these are properly edited, the horizon of the Sanskrit studies and the cultural history that rests in many aspects on the study of manuscripts would certainly extend further. But at the same time, I am afraid that this would not come up to expectations, as, Sanskrit learning is swiftly going lame in our country due to the indifference of the authorities to the study of classical languages and after ten or fifteen years there will remain microscopic Sanskrit scholars who would be capable of deciphering the scripts and finding out the meanings of old Sanskrit manuscripts.